To: Stephanie,

Wishing you a
great, wonderful
friendships!

Joy

Canvas and Cuisine

The Art of the Fresh Market

Stephanie

Enjoy!

W0008729

Maiden Resilience

FOR MARTI

If you're very lucky, once in your lifetime, you'll meet a person that molds you into the somebody you want to be. That person will have such a positive impact on your life, that you will be forever changed.

Sue and I are lucky to have known and loved our great influencer, Marti Huizenga. Together with her husband, Wayne, she hugged us into their circle, bringing us along on their adventures. All the way, they demonstrated their sincerity, civility, thoughtfulness, and compassion. Their legendary monetary generosity is well documented. But not everyone was privy to Marti's generosity of spirit, her compassion for critters big and small and most importantly, her generosity of friendship.

It is because of Marti's inspiration, that Sue and I proudly donate the profits from this book to our charities, the Boys and Girls Club of Hendersonville, and Hospitality House of the Boone Area, both in North Carolina.

Marti and Wayne are no longer with us. They are basking in the love and light that keeps them together eternally.

We dedicate *Canvas and Cuisine* to Marti, with love and wonderful memories of a life well-lived. Your voice is forever in our hearts.

Contagious Enthusiasm

TABLE OF CONTENTS

Roasted Pork Tenderloin with Cilantro Vinaigrette, Smothered Onions and Board Sauce

Fried Pork Chops with Sautéed Dandelion Greens and Dijon Cream Gravy

Stuffed Cousa Squash with Chorizo, White Beans and Cheddar

Grilled Strip Steaks with Herbaceous Chimichurri Board Sauce

Company's Comin' Gumbo

Meatballs 'n Peppers over Creamy Polenta

Moussaka Stuffed Eggplant

Croquetas de Jamón

Butternut Squash Choriqueso (Spicy Cheese Dip)

Baked Brie with Cherries Poached in Wine

CHAPTER VII. FISH AND FOWL 249

Sea Bass with Pickled Pantry Sauce

Cajun-Style Shrimp in Spaghetti Squash Boats

Shrimp Étouffée with a Scoopful of Cauliflower Rice

Coconut Crusted Tilapia with Grilled Pineapple and Black Bean Salsa

Fresh Fish of the Day in Puttanesca Sauce

Pan Seared Snapper over Ratatouille with Lemon Caper Sauce

Cod and Chili-Infused Sweet Potato in a Coconut-Leek Milk Broth

Swordfish Kabobs with Kale-Mint Pesto

Chicken Milanese with Zucchini, Arugula and Fennel Salad

Chicken Marsala Bowl with Orzo, Sautéed Kale, Curried Eggplant and Roasted Carrots

Lemony Chicken Fingers with a Side of Spaghetti Squash in Peanut Sauce

Chicken and Mushroom Paprikash

Indian Butter Chicken with Ginger-Lemon Rice

Stir Fry Orange Chicken with Cauliflower

Grilled Lime-Chili Chicken over Black Bean and Toasted Corn Salsa

Sautéed Chicken Breasts with Veggie Butter Sauce

CHAPTER VIII. BREADS, PASTRIES AND SWEETS . . 295

A Tale of Two Loaves

Seeded Whole Grain Bread

Focaccia Bread

Really Cheesy Garlic Bread

Breakfast Flatbreads

Blueberry-Lime Breakfast Rolls

Orange Poppy Seed Scones

Maple Frosted Hazelnut Scones

Strawberry-Ricotta Topped French Toast

Cobbler Bars with Jam Filling

Chocolate Swirl Sour Cream Banana Bread

Ricotta-Almond Pancakes with Berry-Maple Syrup

Peanut Butter and Mocha Cake in Mini-Mason Jars

Blueberry Crumble Parfaits

Southern-Style Strawberry Shortcake

Layered Banana Split Brownies

Caramel Apple Cake Desserts

Apple Butter Cake with Cream Cheese Frosting

Favorite Fruit Crumble

Meyer Lemon Olive Oil Cake

Iced Thyme-Lemon Pecan Sandies

Chocolate Chunk, Cranberry and Pistachio Cookies

Roasted Peach and Caramel Ice Cream

Frozen Strawberry and Avocado Cream with Coconut

Handy Fried Peach Pies

Churros with Cinnamon Sugar and Chocolate Dipping Sauce

Apple Cider Donut Holes with Cinnamon Sugar and Caramel Sauce

Baklavah!

A COOK'S NOTE ABOUT STUFF

Every cook has their favorite ingredients, brands, and particularities. After forty some years, I've tried a lot of foods and food varieties. Whole milk, skim milk, low fat milk, 2% milk, half and half, heavy cream, whipping cream . . . well, you get the picture. For this book, I tested the recipes with what I call specific staples. Specific every day ingredients that you use . . . every day. These are a few things for you to consider.

When I put milk in an ingredient list, I use whole milk. I just like it better than the rest. You can feel safe if you use reduced fat milk. The dish will come out just fine. You probably like the taste of reduced fat milk more than I do. The same goes for sour cream, yogurt, and cream cheese. I use the full fat versions of these dairy products.

I use unsalted butter and then add salt. I'm a bit of a control freak. You can certainly use salted butter, just taste before you add more salt to the dish.

I use kosher salt and suggest an amount in the recipes that should bring out all the other flavors of the dish. Usually, that is about 1 teaspoon of salt and ½ teaspoon of pepper. You can certainly increase or decrease the amount of salt. For this reason, I use the terminology, "taste and season with salt and pepper." My hubby salts food before he tastes it, so I probably err on the side of under-salting. Salting and peppering is all up to you.

My portions are based on my experience of raising three boys, who I found were much more pleasant with their tummies full than not! The portions you derive from the recipe may not be the same! Therefore, in most cases, I give you a range of portions.

I use gas stovetops. I believe the heat gets hotter, faster than with electric cooktops. I don't use an induction cooktop, so you have me on this one. You may find that you adjust the heat levels to accomplish simmering and boiling. My recommendation is to look for the bubbles, not the dial!

Summer Symphony

TWO PEAS IN THE SAME POD

Sue and I met over a decade ago on the trip of a lifetime, with about ten other couples. The trip began on a jet bound for Moscow. We left our hotel that evening in search of authentic Russian cuisine and dined on Borscht and dark bread. The food was better than it sounds, even if we were the only people in the restaurant after dark. We left Moscow the next day, continuing onto Stockholm where the food highlight was a multi-course dinner at the U.S. Ambassador's residence. It just got better and better from there; a cruise around the Baltic, lunches in quaint Scandinavian bistros, tours of museums in St. Petersburgh and then a stop on the way home in Cork, Ireland. Although Sue and I had already bonded over the delicious foie gras and abundant caviar served aboard the ship, our instant friendship was sealed when I found myself panicking on the way up the narrow circular stairway in Blarney Castle. Our group was on a mission to kiss that famous stone. As claustrophobia took hold, Sue pushed my backside while a true Irishwoman in front of me pulled my arms to keep us moving. After we spilled out on the top of the castle and took a great number of deep breaths, I passed that stone right by and ran all the way down the back stairs to the nearest pub. I promptly ordered the biggest ale they had on tap and a couple of meat pies to calm my tummy!

After that, we were girlfriends, BFFs, forever. We have so much in common. She's the mom of six kids, who are still adding to her growing number of grandchildren (seventeen at last count). I'm the mom of three boys with four grandchildren and more a possibility. She lives in Cashiers, North Carolina, in the summer and my hubby and I live in the mountains near Boone only a couple of hours away. We both live in Jupiter, Florida, in the winter. We have a mutual love of golf and a built-in expert in Sue's husband, famous golf course designer, Tom Fazio. She's manically creative with her artistic style, constantly testing out different mediums. She teaches workshops, has her paintings in galleries and gives back every penny she earns to the Boys and Girls Club of Hendersonville. I'm also blessed with creative ability and live to share new recipes, food trends, cooking tools and all things foodie with everyone I meet. I, too, teach classes: from cooking, to wellness and lifestyle enhancement. I work closely with local charities to raise awareness of the importance of healthy food and family meals. I guess we're two peas in the same pod!

So, when Sue invited me upstairs to her studio one morning to show me her new project, an idea was born. Sue had collected photographs from a farmer's market that she visited in Italy. The produce was jumping off the photo paper. I glanced at her painting of the photo. If you can photograph food that looks so good you want to grab it off the page and eat it . . .

then just think what you want to do with a bold, dazzling, oversized painting of that same food. It was a dizzying experience for a foodie like me.

It was then and there, we decided to collaborate professionally on this book. Our goal is to pair Sue's vision of the foods found in fresh markets around the world, with my scrumptious, fresh cuisine. United in a coffee table book, our combined vision is both beautiful and functional.

Sue and I are fortunate to have traveled all over the country and the world, often times together! She's dined at the finest tables in South America, Ireland and her favorite, Italy. I've shopped in markets and taken cooking classes in Spain, France, Italy and even Vietnam. We've eaten in China, Russia, and London, always seeking out the freshest native cuisine we can find, mostly depending on the recommendations of the locals.

Together, in this book, we offer a tribute to the freshest ingredients found in their most natural state. We have a reverence for the food grown by rural farmers, the breads and pastries baked in artisan ovens, treasures gathered by craftsmen from the sea, aged meat hanging by ropes, and thinly sliced onto brown paper packaging. Sue and I not only love the food, but we love the travel and exploration that leads us to local cuisine.

But, most of all, we love sharing these flavorful experiences with friends and family. We love the joy of legacy as we bring our children and grandchildren to the table. We love the communal environment of shared meals with friends and friends of friends. We love the art of the meal and we hope that through this book, we can share our art with you.

BULBS AND FLOWERS

/bəlb/
noun
plural noun: bulbs

1. a rounded underground storage organ present in some plants, notably those of the lily family, consisting of a short stem surrounded by fleshy scale leaves or leaf bases and lying dormant over winter.
2. an object with a rounded or teardrop shape like a bulb, in particular.

flow·er
/flou(ə)r/
noun

1. the seed-bearing part of a plant, consisting of reproductive organs (stamens and carpels) that are typically surrounded by a brightly colored corolla (petals) and a green calyx (sepals).

   synonyms: bloom, blossom, floweret, floret.

"blue flowers"
verb

1. (of a plant) produce flowers; bloom.
   "these daisies can flower as late as October"

Tuscany Focused

When I study *Tuscany Focused*, I take one look at Sue's artistic rendition and I am immediately drawn back to my life-long relationship with lemons and artichokes.

I ate my first artichoke on my first date with my now husband of forty-plus years. I dipped those tender leaves into a rich, lemony sauce and pulled each one through my teeth. I fell in love . . . two times over!

My lemon-artichoke relationship deepened during a trip to Italy. We dined our way through Rome and drifted south towards Positano. While there, I took a most memorable cooking class. We began in Sorrento when at three in the afternoon we were picked up by our driver and careened across the fourteen miles of curvy, narrow roads to arrive forty-five minutes later at Quattro Passi, the ambitious restaurant/cooking school/bed and breakfast owned by the incredibly personable chef, Antonio Mellino.

I was ushered into the kitchen, hubby in tow. The chef asked me what I would like to learn to make, and my hubby promptly answered, "Teach her to make really good marinara sauce." Whaaaaat? I finally get to Italy, I meet an authentic Italian chef. I'm in a state of the art kitchen and he wants marinara sauce. Ugh! Let's just say that thankfully, my cooking experience far outweighed my husband's request. We started with a lesson on preparing the freshest ingredients available from Chef's surrounding gardens. I used a mandoline slicer to shave fennel and baby artichokes for a simple salad. The vinaigrette was an unpretentious combination of fresh lemon juice with the Chef's own home-pressed virgin olive oil.

Then things got dicey. Chef asked if I'd like to see the fish on the menu tonight. We agreed, and he walked us outside. Quattropassi translates to twenty steps in Italian. There are twenty steps up to the restaurant and twenty steps down to the beach. We walked down to an inlet where an itty bitty wooden boat was tied to an ittier bittier plank of a dock. The chef got into the boat and held out his hand. Nope, nada, no way I was not getting into that boat. How is this a cooking class? Uh-uh. And then with a push from behind, on my behind, hubby and I were off. We motored for a bit and then stopped at what looked like a buoy. The chef tugged at the rope on the float and pulled up a long cylinder. Attached to the cylinder were squid; silvery pale and glued to the sides of the metal container. It was amazing to see. He dropped the cylinder back into the water and we motored toward another point. Another tug and here was a net that held our dinner. Swimming around and flapping all about were several fish of various sizes. He called them red fish. I think they were mullet. He dropped the net with the fish back into the water as he had already harvested the fish he needed for his dinner menu that evening.

After we made it to land, we were escorted to his wine room, which was not a room but a cave built into the side of the hill. Dusty wine bottles were sorted into wooden shelves and boxes. The stone walls held bottle after bottle after bottle. He explained that he had to hide his wine deliveries in this cave lest his wife finds out he bought another cache! She didn't like the spiders that shared space with the wine, so she left the cave alone. Outside we were led to a sweet-smelling lemon orchard where we sat and enjoyed a lovely glass of wine. A glance around proved we were enjoying more than the heady fragrance of lemons; we breathed in, as well, olives ripening on their branches and, of course, row after row of artichokes.

Later that evening, we were treated to the Chef's *Sapere Aude* tasting menu featuring ten dishes based on the whim of the Chef and the bounty of the local fresh market. I remember the salad of fresh squid nestled between my thinly sliced fennel and artichoke, lightly dressed with lemony vinaigrette; the lemons picked fresh from the trees in Chef's orchard. Red fish served with stuffed zucchini flowers and spinach ravioli dressed with fresh rosemary and orange. Lobster dumplings accented with grilled banana and ginger and shrimp served with peaches. The combination of fresh ingredients was beyond delicious. We cleaned all ten plates (twenty if you count hubby's)!

We arrived back in Sorrento late that night and enjoyed a sip or two of limoncello at an outdoor café before we went back to our room. From that day on, I have embraced Chef Antonio's style of using the freshest ingredients to incorporate into a creative dish. His blend of herbs and fruits with freshly grown vegetables and seafood remains an inspiration for my cooking today.

TOMATO BRAISED ARTICHOKES WITH PESTO RUB

Serves 8 as an Appy, 4 as a Main Dish
90 Minute Cuisine

In Italy, everyone is family, and family dining is all about platters of delicious food passed around the table to loud kudos and sighs of delight. Foremost on these platters are fresh vegetables plucked from their roots. This is one of those dishes. Artichokes are an Italian staple. Trimming them takes some time, but after that, this dish is all about infusing flavors. These artichokes are covered in a salty, rich pesto and then simmered in a tomato-wine broth. They take on the flavors that they swim in. Serve these in a large, shallow bowl with the resulting juices spooned over the top. Everyone rolls up their sleeves and pulls the leaves through their teeth. When you get down to the artichoke heart . . . life is just a bowl of goodness!

FOR SAUCE:

1 (14-ounce) can diced tomatoes

1 cup dry white wine

2 cups homemade vegetable stock, or prepared low sodium vegetable broth

¼ cup olive oil

2 teaspoons kosher salt

½ teaspoon crushed red pepper flakes

FOR PESTO:

1 (7-ounce) tin flat fillets of anchovies, packed in oil

1 whole head garlic, cloves peeled

1 bunch fresh basil leaves

½ cup olive oil

FOR ARTICHOKES:

4 large artichokes

2 lemons, halved

Pour the tomatoes, wine, vegetable broth and ¼ cup olive oil into a large roasting pan. Season with some of the salt and crushed red pepper. Set the pan on the counter while you move on to make the pesto rub.

Place the anchovies, garlic, and basil into the bowl of a food processor. Pulse to combine. With the bowl running, slowly pour in ½ cup olive oil to make a thick paste.

Trim the first artichoke by first pulling off the thick, dark green outer leaves, leaving the tender green leaves in place. You'll lose about a fourth of the leaves. Use scissors to cut of the thorny tip of the remaining leaves. Cut off the top third of the remaining artichoke leaves and discard. Use a vegetable peeler to trim the stem removing the tough partial leaves from the bottom of the artichoke. Cut off the tough end of the stem, leaving about 1 to 2 inches of freshly peeled, tender stem. With every cut or peel that you make, rub lemon over the cut ends. Slice the artichokes in half. Use a spoon to remove the spiny choke from the center. Pull out the spiky inner leaves. You'll see these. They have, prickly little points on the end of the purple leaves. You don't want to eat these. Place the trimmed artichoke into a bowl of cold water with lemon slices. Repeat with the remaining artichokes.

Remove the artichokes from the lemony water one at a time. Brush anchovy pesto on both sides of the artichoke and place cut-side down into the pan with tomato-wine sauce. Place the pan on the stove top and bring the sauce to a boil over medium-high heat. Reduce the heat to medium-low and cover the pan with a lid (or with aluminum foil). Simmer the artichokes, low and slow (over low heat and for a long time). Turn the artichokes in the sauce several times to coat while they simmer. Continue cooking until a fork easily pierces the artichoke hearts and the sauce reduces and thickens, about 45 to 60 minutes. If the sauce evaporates too quickly, pour in more stock.

Come Saturday Morning

FARMER'S MARKET TIP

Here's a little traveling tidbit. Did you know that California is the largest producer of artichokes here in the states? Monterey County is so well-known for their artichoke production that they hold the country's only annual artichoke event, the Castroville Artichoke Festival in early summer. Along with their famous 17-mile drive next to the coast of the Pacific Ocean, Monterey County is also home to Pebble Beach Resorts which boasts several of the country's most famous golf courses. All manner of golfers book their tee times months and months in advance just to get a chance to play on these famous fairways. If you plan to visit Pebble Beach during the Castroville Artichoke Food and Wine Festival, then you just might get the best that Monterey has to offer, great weather, gorgeous golf, and all varieties of their famed artichokes.

ARTICHOKE AND FENNEL STRATA

serves 6 to 8

40 minute prep, at least 2 hours to chill, about an hour to bake

Dining al fresco in a Positano coastal town, your senses are overwhelmed with the fresh ambience of an ocean paradise. Picture it: lemons and olives ripen on tree branches, shading you from the Italian sun. Salads are so fresh, the fennel sliced so thin, you think it just might be a translucent noodle instead of a licoricey veg. Artichokes are trimmed and brined with so much labor and love, you are compelled to slowly consume each bite. It's all a foodie delight. This dish is my tribute to these flavors. You can prepare it in advance, making it an ideal brunch dish and perfect for your backyard luncheon. Serve the strata alongside a lightly dressed green salad and a hunk of crusty bread with earthy olive oil for dipping. Bueno!

1 tablespoon olive oil

8 ounces mild Italian sausage (if you buy these in links, remove the casings)

1 small fennel bulb, tops trimmed, cored, and chopped, about ¾ cup

1 (16-ounce) loaf brioche bread, cut into 1-inch cubes

1 (14-ounce) can marinated artichoke hearts, drained, squeezed dry and chopped

8 eggs, beaten

2 cups milk

4 ounces Gruyere cheese, grated, about 1 cup

2 ounces Parmigiano Reggiano cheese, grated, about ½ cup

4 to 5 green onions, thinly sliced, about ½ cup

1 tablespoon Dijon-style mustard

1 tablespoon chopped fresh parsley

1 teaspoon herbes de Provence

1 teaspoon kosher salt

½ teaspoon coarse black pepper

Heat 1 tablespoon olive oil in a large skillet over medium-high heat. Add the sausage and fennel. Cook until the sausage is browned and crumbly and the fennel is soft and fragrant, about 5 minutes. Remove the skillet from the heat. Place half of the bread cubes into a large baking dish that has been coated with vegetable oil spray. Cover the bread with sausage and fennel. Top with artichokes. Place the remaining bread cubes over the top.

Whisk together the eggs and milk in a large bowl. Stir in the cheeses, green onion, mustard, parsley and herbes de Provence. Season with salt and pepper. Pour this custard over the bread cubes. Push down the top bread cubes into the liquid so that all the ingredients are completely submerged. Cover the baking dish with plastic wrap and chill for at least 2 hours or as much as overnight. This will allow the bread to absorb all the liquid and the flavors to merge together.

When you are ready to serve, preheat the oven to 350°. Take the strata from the fridge and remove the plastic wrap. Cover the strata with aluminum foil. Bake until the strata begins to set around the edges, about 20 minutes. Remove the foil and continue baking until the strata is puffy and golden, about 20 to 30 minutes more. Let the strata rest for 10 minutes before serving.

COOK'S TIP

If you are watching your carbs or having a Hatfield and McCoy feud with all things white bread, don't shy away from the ingredient combo in this recipe for a terrific brunch dish. These same items can combine into a delicious frittata or even better into a delish potato torte.

For a frittata, preheat the oven to 375°. Cook the fennel and sausage as described. Add the chopped artichokes to the pan. Whisk the eggs with half of the milk and all the cheese. Stir in the rest of the ingredients. Pour the eggy, cheesy liquid into the pan with the meat and veggies. Cook over medium-low heat until the edges begin to set and turn golden. Place the pan into the oven and cook until the center is set, about 20 to 30 minutes, depending on the size of your skillet. CAREFULLY, using pot holders, remove the skillet from the oven. The handle will be hot—it's been in the oven! Cool the frittata until you can touch the pan. Serve right from the skillet, or you can test your culinary skills by carefully inverting it onto a platter. You will be successful if you choose a platter that is larger than the skillet. Place the platter over the top of the pan. When you are ready, hold the platter and quickly turn the pan over letting the platter catch the frittata.

For a variation on a potato torte, check out my recipe on page 206. Cook the sausage and fennel as described above. Add the artichokes to the pan. Cool and finely dice these ingredients into small pieces. Add these to the beaten eggs noted in the potato torte recipe. Follow along with the rest of the directions in that recipe. The end result will not be authentically Spanish, but it sure will be yummy!

WARM BRUSSELS SPROUT CAESAR SALAD

serves 6 to 8

30 minute cuisine

Sue and I have enjoyed Caesar salad all over the world finding that it differs widely. My favorite is still the version that is served table side where the Maître D' starts the dressing with a coddled egg mushed into fillets of anchovies. There's a great restaurant in Las Vegas, Michael's Gourmet Room in a small casino off the Strip, that still does this salad the old-fashioned way and I cannot get enough! But, it took the inspiration of Sue's painting of fresh produce, a stem full of fresh Brussels sprouts found at the farmer's market and a local chef in a trendy Palm Beach restaurant to inspire me to create this version of the dish. I find the secret to cooking Brussels sprouts in all recipes is to pre-cook them to their most tender (not mushy) state using a steamer or microwave oven. It's only after they become tender that Brussels become the canvas for the rest of the flavors in this dish. Present the dish at the table and garnish as you serve to get the true Caesar experience.

24 Brussels sprouts, outer leaves removed, stemmed, and shaved, about 4 cups (you can shave the sprouts using a mandolin, food processor or just buy them already shaved in a bag!)

FOR DRESSING:

3 to 4 anchovies packed in oil (plus more for garnish)

1 tablespoon Worcestershire sauce

1 tablespoon Dijon-style mustard

4 large garlic cloves, peeled and minced, about 1 tablespoon

Juice of 1 lemon, about 3 tablespoons

3 tablespoons white balsamic vinegar

½ cup olive oil

1 teaspoon kosher salt

½ teaspoon coarse black pepper

FOR BREADCRUMBS:

1 tablespoon butter

3 slices bread, processed into crumbs

FOR SALAD:

2 tablespoons olive oil

4 ounces Parmesan cheese, grated, about 1 cup

Blanch or steam the shaved Brussels sprouts until they are softened.

In a small bowl, whisk together the anchovies, Worcestershire sauce, mustard, and garlic to make a paste. You can do this using a mortar and pestle or in a blender or mini food processor if you prefer a very smooth dressing. Stir in the lemon juice and vinegar. Slowly whisk (or blend) in the olive oil. Taste and season with some of the salt and pepper. Set the dressing aside.

Heat 1 tablespoon butter in a large skillet over medium heat. Spread the bread crumbs into the skillet. Toast the crumbs until they are golden, stirring them around to make sure they don't burn, for about 3 to 5 minutes. Scrape the toasted breadcrumbs into a bowl and set aside.

In the same skillet, heat 2 tablespoons olive oil over medium-high heat. Add the shaved Brussels sprouts to the pan and toss several times to warm through. Taste and season with salt and pepper. Pour enough dressing over the sprouts to just wet the leaves. Sprinkle the toasted bread crumbs and Parmesan cheese into the pan. Toss all the ingredients together. If the salad is too dry, add additional dressing.

Mound a handful of the salad onto a small plate. Sprinkle with coarse black pepper. Lay an anchovy or two atop the salad for garnish.

COOK'S TIP

You can blanch Brussels sprouts (and any hard veggie) in a microwave oven or in boiling water. After you cook them to the crisp-tender stage, place the sprouts into cold water to stop the cooking process. Drain and thoroughly dry the tender leaves using either a salad spinner or by using clean dry dish towels or paper toweling. You can do this hours in advance of preparing the salad. Place dry leaves in the refrigerator to store and bring to room temperature when ready to use.

ROASTED FENNEL, LEMON AND VEGGIE SALAD WITH AVOCADO DRESSING

serves 4

30 minute cuisine

Positano is one of many small towns on the beautiful Amalfi Coast. Sue and I travel there often. During a morning stroll down the narrow stone streets toward the beach, we pass stand after stand chock full of wares of local merchants. Sometimes it's food; sometimes touristy hats and bags. Sometimes it's portrait art or mosaic ceramics. Whatever the product, the experience is heady. The sun is intense, the ocean breeze is scented with salt and brine. The produce is alluring. While I was there, I fell in love with fresh fennel. Just one crunch of this aromatic veggie and your palate is refreshed and waiting for more. I love it shaved on a mandoline slicer, into paper thin strands. And, I love it just as much when it's roasted to a caramelly-sweet flavor profile. From fresh to roasted, this veg just gets better and better. I use roasted fennel as the star of this salad. I've surrounded it with similar veggies and top with a rich farmer's market fresh dressing. It's so easy to make, you can include this dish in your weekly repertoire to get a genuine feel of a sweet little town on the Amalfi Coast.

FOR ROASTED VEGGIES:

2 large fennel bulbs, tops trimmed, cored, and cut into thin wedges, about 2 cups

2 pints grape tomatoes, halved, about 2 cups

½ pound medium fresh asparagus spears, about 16, sliced into 1-inch pieces, about 2 cups

2 medium yellow bell peppers, seeded, veins removed, cut into 1-inch pieces, about 2 cups

1 medium lemon, very thinly sliced (use a mandoline slicer if you have one), about 1 cup

2 teaspoons herbes de Provence

2 teaspoons kosher salt

1 teaspoon coarse black pepper

2 tablespoons olive oil

FOR AVOCADO DRESSING:

1 medium ripe avocado, seed removed

2 cloves garlic peeled

Juice of 1 large lemon, about 3 tablespoons

2 tablespoons white balsamic vinegar

¼ cup olive oil

FOR SALAD:

4 small heads Bibb lettuces dried,

2 ounces Gorgonzola cheese, crumbled, about ½ cup

Preheat the oven to 400°. Place the fennel, tomatoes, asparagus, bell pepper and lemon slices onto a baking sheet. Sprinkle with herbes de Provence, and some of the salt and pepper. Drizzle with 2 tablespoons olive oil. Toss to coat all the pieces. Roast until tender and just beginning to brown, about 20 to 30 minutes.

Place the avocado, garlic, lemon juice and balsamic vinegar into a blender (or food processor). Pulse until smooth. With the machine running, drizzle in ¼ cup olive oil. Taste and season with salt and pepper.

Cut the lettuce into halves and place onto a chilled platter. Top the lettuce with roasted veggies and lemon slices (yes, you can eat these!!). Drizzle the salad with avocado dressing. Sprinkle with Gorgonzola cheese. Add an additional grind of coarse black pepper to garnish.

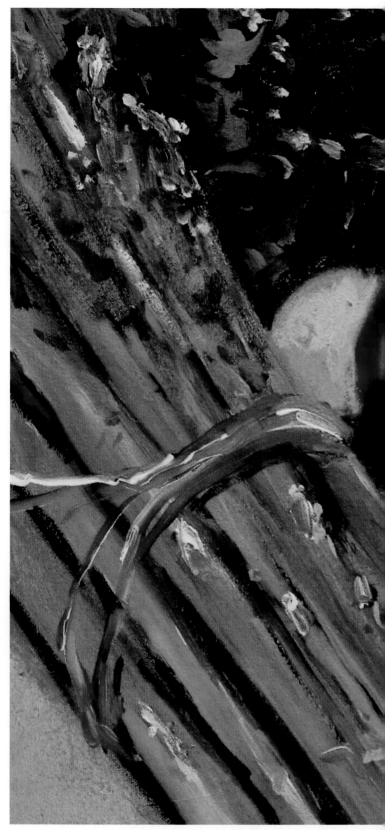

Gus and Tom

ORECCHIETTE CARBONARA WITH CHARRED BRUSSELS SPROUTS

serves 4

30 minute cuisine

It's hard to pass up pasta when you're anywhere in Italy. While the sauces may differ from heartier in the North, to lighter in the South, the pasta remains the same: simpler, airier, more delicate, and more varied. There are so many varieties of pasta, you need a dictionary to discern one from another! When I tasted my first dish of pasta in a little trattoria in Rome, I noticed the difference. The sauces are simply lighter and sassier than they are in the United States. Trying to be more veggie forward in my cooking, I wanted to recreate pasta carbonara, the dish eaten by chefs late at night, after meal service is finished. The ingredients are readily available, and the end result is deceptively light and fresh. I use this inspiration and add my favorite veggie to the dish. What goes better with the bacon in the traditional recipe than Brussels sprouts? If you blanch or steam Brussels sprouts before you roast them, the result will be a crisp, charred outside and a creamy, smooth inside. Add farm fresh eggs, cream, butter, and cheese to your basket when you are strolling down the aisles of the fresh market, and it all comes together to make a pasta dish that is just too good not to share with your many amici!

FOR SPROUTS:

½ pound fresh Brussels sprouts, trimmed, about 12

3 tablespoons olive oil

3 tablespoons grated Parmesan cheese

1 teaspoon kosher salt

½ teaspoon coarse black pepper

FOR PASTA:

1 pound orecchiette pasta

¼ pound bacon, diced, about 3 to 4 slices

½ medium red onion, peeled and diced, about ½ cup

½ teaspoon kosher salt

½ teaspoon coarse black pepper

2 eggs, room temperature

½ cup half-and-half

2 ounces grated Romano cheese, about ½ cup, plus more for garnish

1 tablespoon chopped fresh Italian parsley

Preheat the oven to 425°. Trim the stems and tough outer leaves from the Brussels sprouts. Steam or blanch the sprouts until they are just beginning to soften, about 3 to 5 minutes. Cool to room temperature and cut each sprout into slices. Place the sprouts onto a baking dish. Toss with olive oil, Parmesan cheese, salt, and pepper. Roast until the Brussels sprouts are soft, and the leaves are just beginning to char, about 10 to 15 minutes.

Cook the pasta in salted, boiling water until just al dente, about 10 to 12 minutes.

Cook the bacon in a large skillet over medium-high heat until beginning to crisp, about 4 minutes. Add the onion and cook until soft, about 5 minutes more. Add the Brussels sprouts to the pan. Season with salt and pepper. Reduce the heat to medium.

Whisk the eggs, half-and-half and cheese together in a small bowl. Drain the pasta (hold back a cup or two of the pasta water). Add the pasta to the skillet with the Brussels sprouts. Pour the cream sauce into the pasta and stir. Add 1 to 1 ½ cups of pasta water to the pan and toss the pasta in the sauce. If the sauce is too sticky, add additional pasta water until your reach your desired consistency. Garnish with additional cheese and fresh parsley.

COOK'S TIP

While in Rome, our guide told us many tales of the city, its rich history. The one story that I loved was how the dish carbonara came to be. It seems that after American soldiers liberated Rome from the oppression of the German Nazi army, they found themselves greeted as movie star heroes. Many of these American soldiers were of Italian descent. Trattoria owners opened their doors and fed the soldiers most abundantly, offering pasta with sauces that were either red (tomato) or white (with cream and cheese) with bits of meat, fish, and artichokes. After a while, the cooks noticed that the soldiers were homesick for their good-old American cuisine. Thus, they improvised, creating a pasta dish that incorporated bacon and eggs! Carbonara was born. Its name descends from the Italian word "carbone," which translates to coal, which is reminiscent of wood-burning fires and coal stoves found in both Italian and American family kitchens.

ROASTED GARLIC AND TOMATO SOUP WITH GRILLED ARTISANAL CHEESE CROUTONS

serves 4

45 minute cuisine

We have traveled to all sorts of beautiful destinations, and appreciated the beauty and luxury therein; however, lean years preceded those trips. Sue raised SIX kids and I raised three BOYS. And between us, that's a whole lotta meals! There were plenty of times when food rationing was smart budgeting. Many a leftover was reinvented into a comfort-filled soup. Today, when hubby and I are in for the night, I make a hearty soup. If you know me, then you know I just gotta mess with the dish—tweak it to unearth its specialness. For this play on good old-fashioned tomato soup, I find squeezing creamy, golden cloves of garlic from their roasted papery shells is a fun (or might I say, "yum") thing to do, and really enhances the flavor. Down-sizing grilled cheese sammies into croutons creates an extra crunchy dipping buddy. Using these little nuances to elevate an American staple, like comfort soup, makes cooking . . . well . . . so worth your efforts. I bet your kids will love it too!

FOR GARLIC:

3 medium heads garlic

1 tablespoon olive oil

1 teaspoon ground oregano

2 teaspoons kosher salt

1 teaspoon coarse black pepper

FOR TOMATOES:

3-pounds ripe plum tomatoes, about 12

2 tablespoons olive oil

FOR SOUP:

2 tablespoons olive oil

1 medium yellow onion, peeled and diced

2 tablespoons brown sugar

½ teaspoon crushed red pepper flakes

1 quart homemade chicken stock, or prepared low sodium chicken broth

½ cup heavy cream

FOR CROUTONS:

2 slices 1-inch thick bread

2 tablespoons butter, room temperature

2 ounces artisanal cheese, grated

2 tablespoons chopped fresh chives

Preheat the oven to 400°. Cut the top third from the garlic bulbs. Place the bulbs onto a sheet of aluminum foil. Drizzle the cut side of the garlic with 1 tablespoon olive oil and season with oregano and some of the salt and pepper. Close the foil to make a packet, leaving a small opening at the top. Place the packet onto a baking dish, and roast until the cloves are soft, caramelized and coming out of their skins, about 30 to 40 minutes. Remove from the packet and cool to room temperature.

Cut the tomatoes in half and squeeze the seeds from the centers. Place onto a rimmed baking sheet. Sprinkle with 2 tablespoons olive oil, and more of the salt and pepper. Roast until the tomatoes are beginning to char, about 30 to 40 minutes. You can roast the tomatoes and garlic at the same time.

Heat 2 tablespoons olive oil in a deep pot over medium-high heat. Add the onion and cook until soft. Sprinkle the onions with brown sugar and crushed red pepper flakes. Cook for 2 more minutes. Add the tomatoes and their juices to the pot. Squeeze the garlic cloves into the pot. Pour in the chicken broth. Taste and season with salt and pepper. Simmer for 5 minutes. Turn off the heat. Let the soup cool a bit. (If you put hot soup into a blender, it will blow the lid off when you pulse it!!) Use an immersion blender, food processor, or blender to puree the soup. Return the soup to the pot and stir in the cream.

Heat a skillet over medium-high heat. Spread one side of each slice of bread with butter. Place one slice of bread, butter-side-down into the skillet. Top the bread with cheese. Top the cheese with the second bread slice, butter side up. Flip the sandwich and cook for 2 minutes. Flip again and cook for 2 minutes more. Remove the sandwich to a cutting board. Cut into 9 equal squares.

Ladle the soup into bowls. Float the croutons on top and garnish with fresh chives.

Capturing Essence

FARMERS MARKET TIP

Just before summer gets into full swing, you'll see green tendrils of garlic scapes right next to the spring onions at the booths in the farmer's market. These are the flowering tippy tops of garlic bulb. The bud is removed in late June to encourage the bulbs to plump up. Scapes taste just like garlic, and they are delicious to eat! They can be used in exactly the same way as garlic in any recipe. If you are a garlic lover like I am, and you hit the market on just the right day, add a spoonful of chopped scapes to simmer in this soup.

Eggsactly

SAVORY EGG MUFFINS

makes 12 muffins

20 minute cuisine

One of the things we grandparents enjoy, visiting the North Carolina farmers' markets, is tasting some of the local favorites as we stroll the stalls. This takes on a whole new meaning when your grandchildren are in tow. There are hands to hold, baskets to carry and those cute little mouths to feed. My granddaughter is in love with the breakfast pizza food truck at our Boone Farmers Market. My grandson devours (in minutes) freshly baked cinnamon rolls that are the size of his head from a local baker! My favorite is the booth that sells breakfast sandwiches filled with eggs and everything else you can imagine, smooshed between biscuits, muffins, and artisanal breads. Fillings include assorted cheeses, prosciutto, Virginia ham, and so much more. My pick for a grab and go breakfast is the naked egg sandwich. No bread, just middle! While balancing a breakfast pizza, a huge muffin, and a basket full of produce, an easy-to-eat, delicious bite is the perfect answer for this busy, Nana. This is my home version of that fresh market breakfast treat.

½ pound fresh broccoli florets, cut into very small pieces, about 1 cup

1 bunch green onions, thinly sliced, about 1 cup

1 large red bell pepper, seeded, veins removed, diced, about 1 cup

4 ounces cooked ham, diced, about 1 cup

4 ounces white sharp cheddar cheese, grated, about 1 cup

6 large eggs

¼ cup half-and-half

1 teaspoon kosher salt

1 teaspoon coarse black pepper

FOR GARNISHING:

Salsa

Hot pepper sauce

Sour cream

Preheat the oven to 350°. Coat a 12-cup muffin tin with vegetable oil spray. Toss together the veggies, ham, and half of the cheese. Divide and place into the bottom of the muffin cups.

Whisk the eggs and half-and-half in a bowl until just combined. Season with salt and pepper. Pour the beaten eggs into the muffin cups. Top with the remaining cheese.

Bake until the eggs are set, and the cheese is melting, about 20 minutes. Remove the veggie egg muffins to a platter and serve warm or at room temperature. Garnish with salsa, hot pepper sauce, and sour cream.

COOK'S TIP

These eggy muffins are the perfect make-in-advance meal. I bake them on Sunday so that we can eat them in a flash on a busy weekday. After they come out of the oven cool the muffins to room temperature. Wrap them individually and place them in the fridge. the muffins will be good all week long in your refrigerator and, if you are very industrious, they will last up to 3 months in your freezer!

When you are ready to grab and go, simply plop a muffin into the microwave and cook on high for about 30 seconds. You have a breakfast treat that is ready to eat faster than you can navigate that corner drive through restaurant!

FARMERS MARKET ORZO SALAD

serves 4 to 6 as a side salad

30 minute cuisine

Sue and I live in the mountains of North Carolina in the summer. She loves to paint the lush, rural landscapes that surround us as the fields blossom. I like to reap the bounty of those blossoms by strolling through the markets, reaching for the freshest produce I can find. I usually over-do it, finding myself with a few extra peppers and tomatoes in the fridge. I can't stand to think of these treats going to waste, so I create salads and soups that take advantage of every last bit. Farmers market staples of crisp green onions, cool diced cucumber, and summer-sweet baby heirloom tomatoes, make this simple pasta salad the perfect side dish for every meal. Make it a main dish by adding slices of grilled chicken, or vegetarian entrée by serving it alongside a platter of grilled veggies.

1 cup uncooked orzo pasta

Juice of 2 medium lemons, about ¼ cup

3 large garlic cloves, peeled and minced, about 2 teaspoons

1 teaspoon yellow mustard

½ cup olive oil

2 teaspoons kosher salt

1 teaspoon coarse black pepper

1 large cucumber, peeled, seeded, and diced into ¼-inch pieces, about 1 ½ cups

4 to 5 green onions, thinly sliced, about ½ cup

1 pint baby heirloom tomatoes, quartered

2 tablespoons chopped fresh Italian parsley

Cook the orzo in 2 quarts salted, boiling water until tender, about 8 to 10 minutes. Whisk together lemon juice, garlic, and mustard in a bowl. Whisk in the olive oil in a slow steady stream. Season the dressing with some of the salt and pepper.

Drain the orzo through a colander and place into a large bowl. Pour half of the dressing over the orzo and stir. Cool to room temperature (or place into the fridge to chill for 5 minutes or so).

Add the cucumbers, onions, tomatoes, and parsley to the cooled orzo. Pour in the remaining dressing. Gently toss the salad together. Taste and season with salt and pepper if needed.

COOK'S TIP

Have extra orzo salad? Get creative! Stuff it into a pita with some chicken and feta cheese. Layer into bell peppers with some extra lemon vinaigrette. Add to your favorite meatball recipe. It's all good!!

FARMERS MARKET TIP

I have a black thumb. I can't grow anything. This is probably why i am enthralled with every farmers market that I visit. But then:my daughter-in-law, Kimber gave me the gift that keeps on giving, a Tower Garden®. This amazing upright tower allows me to grow my own herbs and veggies right on my back deck! All I have to do is keep the tub filled with water and plug in the motor. It's amazing: a scientific miracle in my book. You add a couple drops of nutrients to good old tap water, insert some seedlings into the holes in the tower and before you know it you have heads of lettuce, stems of herbs and fruits like tomatoes and zucchini ready for the picking. There are different types of towers and if you are a DIY crafter you can even rig one up on your own. any way you do it, you can unleash your inner farmer by finding a garden that is just right for you.

BEER BATTERED FRIED ONION RINGS WITH SPICY DIPPING SAUCE

serves a crowd

30 to 45 minute cuisine

Here's a little secret about traveling: as keen as your desire is to taste the local cuisine and dine on exotic ingredients, after a week or so, there's something about that little bit of American comfort food that lures you home. Burgers and fries aside, another all-time American favorite of mine are big, fat, puffy fried onions. They are a treat with every meal—especially when they're piled super high, in a cloth-lined basket. Ahhh, the perfect pass around, backyard appy! There's that Aussie restaurant (as close as I've gotten to Australia as of now) that serves a yummy dipping sauce to go alongside the perfectly fried onions. In early summer markets, you'll find smaller, tender spring onions with white or purple bulbs. You can use the same technique in this recipe to fry up these babies. They turn into crispy, golden strings, perfect for mounding on top of your favorite burger. It's all yummy!

FOR ONIONS:

2 large white sweet onions, cut into ¼-inch slices

2 cups buttermilk

FOR DIPPING SAUCE:

½ cup mayonnaise

2 tablespoons ketchup

2 tablespoons prepared horseradish

1 teaspoon paprika

½ teaspoon ground oregano

2 teaspoons kosher salt

1 teaspoon coarse black pepper

2 or more drops hot pepper sauce

FOR THE BATTER:

1 cup unbleached all-purpose flour

1 cup rice flour

2 cups club soda

1 (12-ounce) bottle beer

For dredging:

2 cups unbleached all-purpose flour

1 tablespoon chili powder

For big finish:

Vegetable oil for frying

2 tablespoons chopped fresh parsley

Flaky salt (like sea salt)

Separate the onion rings and place into a shallow bowl or baking dish. Cover with buttermilk pushing the rings down into the liquid while you get everything else ready to go.

Whisk together mayonnaise, ketchup, horseradish, paprika, and oregano. Taste and season with some of the salt and pepper. Stir in as much hot sauce as you like. Pour the dipping sauce into a bowl.

Whisk together 1 cup all-purpose flour with the rice flour in a shallow bowl or baking dish. Stir in the club soda and beer.

Place the remaining 2 cups all-purpose flour into a shallow baking dish. Whisk in chili powder and season generously with salt and pepper.

Heat about 3-inches of vegetable oil in a deep, large pot over medium-high heat to 350°. The vegetable oil should come no higher than one third up the side of the pot. Once you add the onion rings, the oil will bubble up. The temperature of the oil will go down when you add battered onion rings and then come up again as they cook. I use a candy thermometer to make sure that the temperature is hot before I add more onion rings to the oil.

Lift an onion ring out of the buttermilk and shake off the extra liquid. Dredge into the seasoned flour and then dip into the beer batter, again shaking off the excess liquid. Place the battered onion ring into the hot oil. Continue this process to fry several rings at a time, being careful not to place too many into the oil at the same time. You want them to swim freely as they fry. Use a slotted spoon or spider strainer to turn the rings in the oil until golden brown on both sides, about 3 to 5 minutes. Remove the rings to a paper towel lined baking sheet. Continue with the remaining rings until there are none left. Once you remove the onion rings from the oil, immediately sprinkle with parsley and flakey salt. Serve with dipping sauce.

COOK'S TIP

For a really FUN presentation at your next barbecue, serve these onion rings right out of the fryer and onto a foot-long wooden dowel mounted onto a wooden block. You won't find this in the restaurant supply store. Instead you'll have to get your best DIY buddy to make them for you. Your friends will love plucking a puffy onion ring right off the stick.

ANOTHER COOK'S TIP

When you find those spring onions in the market, grab them up! The ones that I like look like scallions, the green onions you see in the produce section of the grocery store. But, they differ because the white bulb of the onion is much larger, from the size of a gold ball to the size of a tennis ball! I find these onions to be sweeter, lovely to caramelize. For a very FUN presentation, slice these onions into thin rings. Place them into a pot. Cover the onions with vegetable oil and bring the oil to a boil over medium-high heat. reduce the heat to medium-low to simmer the onions until they turn golden, about 20 to 30 minutes. Use a slotted spoon to remove the onions to a platter lined with paper towels. the onions come out of the oil tender and limp and then crisp up as they cool. Use these to top your favorite burger. It's a YUM!

CAULIFLOWER STEAKS WITH GORGONZOLA COMPOUND BUTTER AND BALSAMIC STEAK SAUCE

serves 4 for a veggie main dish
30 minute cuisine

Hubby and I traveled to China on our way to Vietnam; we spent several nights in Beijing. The first night in our hotel, we saw long lines of tourists, queueing up outside the American steakhouse located in the lobby. This tourist smugly put her nose in the air, headed out to sample local Peking duck, feeling every bit the international foodie. We lapped up every dish we came across. It took us only three days of sampling authentic Chinese fare to find ourselves standing at the front of that American steakhouse line. The moral of the story . . . you can take the American out of a steakhouse, but you can't take the steak (even a cauliflower one) out of the American! This recipe brings together all the flare of the traditional steakhouse but offers a vegetarian take on the dish. Note the absence of soy sauce!

FOR COMPOUND BUTTER:

½ cup butter, softened
2 ounces Gorgonzola cheese, crumbled, about ¼ cup
¼ cup chopped fresh parsley
1 garlic clove, peeled and minced

FOR STEAK SAUCE:

¾ cup balsamic vinegar
½ cup ketchup
¼ cup honey
2 small shallots, peeled and finely diced
2 tablespoons Worcestershire sauce
1 tablespoon Dijon mustard
1 tablespoon brown sugar
¼ teaspoon allspice
1 to 2 teaspoons kosher salt
1 to 2 teaspoons coarse black pepper
2 tablespoons butter

Calling All Cauliflowers

2 heads cauliflower

2 (or more) tablespoons olive oil

Place the softened butter, Gorgonzola cheese, parsley, and garlic into the bowl of a food processor. Pulse to combine. Spoon the compound butter onto a sheet of plastic wrap. Use your hands to roll the plastic wrapped butter into a cylinder. Twist the ends of the wrap to make a tight tube. Chill in the fridge for at least 30 minutes and up to several days. Bring the butter to room temperature before serving.

Place the balsamic vinegar, ketchup, honey, shallots, Worcestershire sauce, mustard, brown sugar and all-spice into a small pot. Bring to a boil over medium-high heat. Reduce the heat to medium low and simmer until the sauce thickens, about 10 minutes. Remove the sauce from the heat. Season with some of the salt and pepper and swirl in 2 tablespoons of butter to give your steak sauce a rich shine.

Preheat the oven to 425°. Remove leaves and trim the stem end of cauliflower, leaving the core intact. Place one head of cauliflower, stem side down, on your work surface. Divide the cauliflower in half from top to bottom. Slice the cauliflower into four 1-inch "steaks" from the center to the outer edge. (You can save the outer slices to snack on!) Arrange steaks on parchment lined baking sheets. Repeat with the second head. Drizzle each side of the steaks with olive oil and season with salt and pepper. Bake until the top of the cauliflower steak is golden brown, about 10 to 15 minutes. Use a large spatula to flip the steaks and cook until the second side is golden brown, about 15 to 20 minutes more. Remove the baking sheets from the oven.

Top each steak with a round of gorgonzola butter and return to the oven until the butter begins to melt, about 1 to 2 minutes more. Serve the steaks with a drizzle of steak sauce over the top.

CHICKEN AND CAULIFLOWER CURRY WITH LIME-AVOCADO YOGURT AND FRIED CHICKPEAS

serves 4 as a main or 6 as a side

60 minute cuisine

One of the things that we love about London is the diversity of the many cultures and the resulting diversity of foodie experiences. I love to sample the authentic dishes from India mostly from small, family owned restaurants. Some like it hot, then there are Sue and I who like spicy dishes that don't burn the roof of your mouth. This bowlful of curry comfort is just the right temperature. India may be the one place that we haven't traveled to—yet. But, we are always inspired by local, fresh ingredients that whisk you away to cultural cuisines.

For curry:

2 tablespoon olive oil

2 boneless, skinless chicken breasts cut into 2-inch pieces

1 teaspoon kosher salt

½ teaspoon coarse black pepper

1 medium onion, peeled and diced, about 1 cup

4 garlic cloves, peeled and diced, about 2 tablespoons

2-inch piece fresh ginger, peeled and grated, about 2 tablespoons

1 medium jalapeno pepper, seeded, veins and stem removed, finely diced, about 1 tablespoon

2 tablespoons tomato paste

2 tablespoons curry powder

2 tablespoons garam masala

1 cinnamon stick

2 cups homemade chicken stock or prepared low sodium broth

1 head cauliflower, cut into small florets

1 (15-ounce) can diced tomatoes

½ cup coconut milk

FOR YOGURT:

1 cup plain Greek yogurt

1 ripe avocado, peeled, seed removed

2 small green onions, thinly sliced

Juice of 1 lime, about 1 tablespoon

2 tablespoons chopped fresh cilantro

FOR CHICKPEAS:

1 (15-ounce can) chickpeas

½ cup olive oil

1 teaspoon paprika

1 teaspoon kosher salt

Zest of 1 lime, about 1 teaspoon

Heat olive oil in a skillet with deep sides over medium-high heat. Place the chicken pieces into the skillet and cook until golden brown on all sides. Season with some of the salt and pepper. Transfer the chicken to a platter.

Reduce the heat to medium and add the onion, garlic, ginger, jalapeno, tomato paste, curry powder, garam masala and cinnamon stick to the skillet. Stir and cook for 2 to 3 minutes. Your kitchen should begin to smell like curry! Stir in the chicken broth. Add the cauliflower to the skillet and cook until tender, about 6 minutes. Add the tomatoes, sautéed chicken, and coconut milk. Cook for 5 minutes more. Reduce the heat and simmer until the chicken is cooked through and the cauliflower tender but not mushy, about 15 to 20 minutes more. Taste and season with salt and pepper.

Use a hand mixer, blender, or immersion blender to blend the yogurt and avocado until smooth. Stir in the green onions, lime juice and cilantro. Taste and season with salt.

Rinse, drain, and pat dry chickpeas. Heat olive oil in a skillet over medium-high heat. Place the chickpeas into the oil and fry until golden brown, about 4 to 5 minutes. If your pan is not very large you can do this in batches. Use a slotted spoon to transfer chickpeas to a baking sheet lined with paper towels. Sprinkle with paprika, salt, and lime zest. Toss to coat.

Serve the cauliflower and chicken curry in a bowl garnished with a spoonful of lime-avocado yogurt and sprinkled with fried chickpeas.

Meet Me at the Market

CAULIFLOWER RISOTTO WITH CINNAMON-ROASTED BUTTERNUT SQUASH

serves 6

30 minute cuisine

As with my pasta experience, when I sampled risotto in Rome, I was impressed by the lightness of the dish. The creamy texture comes from cooking the rice just perfectly, so there's just a bit of give when your tooth breaks the kernel, but the creaminess of the center shines through. I decided to substitute cauliflower for rice in my twist on a risotto dish. Just like the traditional meal, the creamy texture of the cauliflower is developed by slowly simmering in rich chicken stock. I couldn't help reaching for a whole butternut squash after admiring Sue's painting, Positano Pairings. I roast the squash with chili and cinnamon before I add it to the cauliflower risotto and the end result is . . . well, you check it out and see what I mean!

FOR SQUASH:

1 medium butternut squash, peeled and diced into ½-inch squares (about 3 cups)

2 tablespoons olive oil

1 tablespoon chili powder

2 teaspoons ground cinnamon

1 teaspoon garlic powder

1 teaspoon onion powder

1 teaspoon kosher salt

½ teaspoon coarse ground pepper

FOR RISOTTO:

2 tablespoons olive oil

½ yellow onion, peeled and chopped

1 head cauliflower, chopped to coarse crumbs, about 6 cups

3 cups homemade chicken stock or prepared low sodium broth

½ cup half-and-half

2 tablespoons butter

2 ounces Parmesan cheese, grated, about ½ cup

Preheat the oven to 425°. Place the butternut squash chunks onto a baking sheet. Drizzle with olive oil, sprinkle with seasonings and toss to coat. Bake until the squash is soft and golden brown, about 20 minutes. Heat 2 tablespoons olive oil in a skillet over medium-high heat. Add the onion and cook until soft, about 5 minutes. Add the cauliflower and cook for 5 minutes more, stirring so that the cauliflower does not burn. Add one cup of chicken stock and stir. When the liquid is absorbed, add another cup. Reduce the heat to medium and simmer the cauliflower for 5 minutes. Add the remaining cup of chicken stock and cook until most of the liquid is absorbed. Scrape the squash into the cauliflower. Stir in the half-and-half and butter. Season with salt and pepper. Swirl in the Parmesan cheese.

CAULIFLOWER FRIED RICE

serves 4 as a side dish

30 minute cuisine

Rice dishes are prevalent in East Asian countries. What I found fascinating is that rice is served with every meal—even breakfast. It's not a bad way to go since it takes on the flavors of whatever food you place beside it. Fried rice is a Chinese staple; one that we Americans love to make at home either in a skillet or wok. But here's a little twist on the dish for those veggie lovers out there. Cauliflower takes the place of rice in this riff on a traditional dish. Fresh peas, carrots and two types of onion take the veggie quotient to the upper limits! This is not 100% Beijing cuisine, but it's close enough for my taste!

1 large head cauliflower, stem and outer leaves removed

2 tablespoons sesame oil

1 medium white onion, peeled and diced

2 medium carrots, peeled, trimmed, and diced, about 1 cup

2 tablespoons soy sauce

¼ pound fresh shelled peas, 1 cup (substitute with thawed, frozen peas)

2 large eggs, beaten

1 teaspoon kosher salt

3 to 4 drops Sriracha hot chili sauce

4 to 5 green onions, thinly sliced, about ½ cup

Chop the cauliflower into pieces and place into the bowl of a food processor. Pulse until the cauliflower looks like rice. This will only take a few pulses.

Heat the sesame oil in a large skillet or wok over medium-high heat. Add the cauliflower, white onion, and carrots. Cook until soft, about 5 to 10 minutes. Stir in the soy sauce. Add the peas to the pan. Cook until the peas are tender, about 3 to 5 minutes.

Push the veggies to the side of the skillet. Pour in the eggs. Stir and cook the eggs until they are soft-scrambled. Stir back in the veggies from the side. Taste and season with salt and add a drop or two of hot chili sauce. Sprinkle green onions on top. Serve as a side dish or top with grilled shrimp or chicken to fill out a dinner meal.

BROCCOLI SALAD WITH CHERRIES, ALMONDS AND WARM BOURBON-BACON DRESSING

serves 4 as a side salad

30 minute cuisine

I think one of the things that I miss when we travel is a fresh, green salad. You just don't see it on menus abroad as much as we do here is America. Maybe we just love our farmers so much that we have to include veggies as much as possible. I bet you won't find a potluck supper in any region of this country that doesn't include a veggie salad. One of my favorites is a chilled broccoli salad with a warm dressing. You'll find all sorts of varieties and colors including golden and purple heads when you stroll the fresh market. I also like to take advantage of the tender stems of the stalks. Use a vegetable peeler to take off any tough outer skin, then slice the stems into thin rounds. Whether you steam or blanch the broccoli, don't leave out the ice water bath afterward. You want crisp broccoli in this salad to stand up to the warm sweet-sour dressing.

1 head broccoli, cut into florets, stems peeled and thinly sliced

¼ pound bacon, cut into ½-inch pieces, about 4 to 5 strips

2 tablespoons brown sugar

½ cup homemade chicken stock or prepared low sodium broth

1 sprig fresh rosemary

2 tablespoons bourbon

Juice of 1 medium lemon, about 2 tablespoons

1 tablespoon butter

½ small red onion, peeled and thinly sliced, about ¼ cup

¼ pound fresh sweet cherries, pitted, halved, about ½ cup

½ cup slivered almonds, toasted

Blanch the broccoli in boiling, salted water until crisp-tender, about 3 to 5minutes. Transfer to ice water to stop the cooking process. Drain and place in the fridge to cool. Cook the bacon in a large skillet over medium-high heat until just beginning to crisp, about 3 to 5 minutes. Use a slotted spoon or wire skimmer to transfer to a plate lined with paper towels. Pour off most of the bacon drippings. Return the skillet to the stove and add the brown sugar. Stir to melt and scrape up any brown bits left in the pan. Pour in the chicken broth and drop in the rosemary spring. Simmer until the dressing reduces and thickens to a syrupy consistency, about 5 to 7 minutes. Turn off the heat and stir in the bourbon and lemon juice. Add the butter and swirl in the pan to melt. Remove the rosemary sprig.

Place the broccoli and red onion into a serving bowl. Pour in the warm dressing. Season with salt and pepper. Add the cherries and bacon and toss. Top with toasted almonds.

Haute Cuisine

CREAMY BAKED SHELLS WITH ROASTED CAULIFLOWER

serves a crowd

60 minute cuisine

Here's another basically American dish that you won't find on a menu across the ocean—the casserole. Even in Italy, mac and cheese is a dish of macaroni pasta served with a light cream sauce and has no similarity to its namesake. I am a casserole lover. I just can't leave anything in the fridge that might go to waste. (It's a hand-me-down, Depression-era, grandmother thing.) I turn every last piece of veggie into something casserole-ish. When I told Sue, she let out a laugh and said, "Ha!" Having raised her six kids as vegetarians, she was all over this years before I came up with the idea! This recipe is a twist on standard mac and cheese in an effort to hide some of these healthy veggies in a traditional cheesy dish. I add fresh, farmer's market veg to the pasta and an added pile-on of cheese, cheese and more ever-lovin' cheese. I love the purple and golden cauliflower that's often offered at the market. But, if your trying to sneak veggies into mac and cheese, I'd stick with the white variety!

1 large head cauliflower cut into small florets, about 3 cups

2 tablespoons olive oil

2 teaspoons kosher salt

½ teaspoon coarse black pepper

¾ pound pasta shells, medium size

2 tablespoons butter, plus 2 more for breadcrumbs

2 tablespoon all-purpose flour

2 cups milk

½ teaspoon ground sage

¼ teaspoon ground nutmeg

4 ounces fontina cheese, grated, about 1 cup

2 large garlic cloves, peeled and minced

1 cup panko bread crumbs

2 ounces Parmesan cheese, grated about ½ cup

2 tablespoons chopped fresh Italian parsley

8 ounces ricotta cheese, about 1 cup

Preheat the oven to 425°. Steam or blanch the cauliflower florets until crisp tender. (You can do this using the fresh vegetable setting on your microwave oven). Place them onto a baking sheet. Drizzle with some of the olive oil, salt, and pepper and toss to coat. Roast the cauliflower until the edges are just beginning to brown, about 15 to 20 minutes. Remove from the oven, cool slightly and place into a large bowl.

Cook the pasta shells in boiling water until al dente, about 8 to 10 minutes. Drain and add to the bowl with the cauliflower.

Melt 2 tablespoons butter in a saucepan over medium heat. Whisk in the flour and cook until bubbly, about 2 minutes. Slowly whisk in the milk. Continue whisking and cooking until the sauce thickens, about 4 to 6 minutes. Season with salt, pepper, sage, and nutmeg. Remove the sauce from the heat and whisk in the fontina cheese until melted. Pour the sauce over the shells and cauliflower and toss to coat all the pieces.

Melt the remaining 2 tablespoons butter in a skillet over medium-high heat. Add the garlic and cook until golden, about 1 minute. Stir in the bread crumbs, Parmesan cheese and parsley. Cook until the crumbs are just golden, about 1 to 2 minutes more.

Reduce the oven temperature to 375°. Pour half of the shells, cauliflower, and sauce into a baking dish. Spoon the ricotta cheese over all. Pour the remaining shells over the ricotta cheese. Sprinkle the breadcrumbs over the top of the casserole. Cover the casserole with aluminum foil and bake until the casserole is bubbling, about 20 minutes. Remove the foil from the casserole and bake until the crumb topping is toasted and golden, about 5 to 10 minutes more.

FRUIT

/fro͞ot/

noun

1. the sweet and fleshy product of a tree or other plant that contains seed and can be eaten as food.
    "tropical fruits such as mangoes and papaya"

verb

2. (of a tree or other plant) produce fruit, typically at a specified time.
    "the trees fruit very early"

Basic Bounty

I came to Hoi An's Central Market in Vietnam as part of an all-day cooking class under the direction of the Red Bridge Cooking School. To begin, I had to find my way to the market through the busy streets of the village. This was a challenge. I had a map, I knew I had to get to the center of town and I can always find fresh food. But, this was not enough. It took a nice local with a cyclo (three-wheeled bicycle taxi) to get me to my group at the entrance to the market. It literally took the village for me to find my way! A tour of the market was followed by a boat ride down the Hoi An river and then a stroll through a stunning herb garden. A multi-course cooking class and a luxurious lunch followed. It was quite a day.

I was most impressed with the market. Not only is it the center of the village, but it is bustling with activity. Hoi An residents visit the market twice a day; in the morning for their midday meal and then again in the early afternoon for supper ingredients. The seafood is plucked from the water by fisherman with nets and then delivered to the stalls by fast-moving young men. Mostly women merchants clean the fish. They perch atop the tables that hold their wares, scaling and filleting as they carry on a conversation with the neighbor next door. There is no refrigeration in the stalls, no ice to keep things cold. So "fresh from the sea" takes on a whole new meaning!

Contrasting the busy seafood stalls are the pasta stalls on the outer sidewalks of the market. Older women sit on tables, chewing betel nuts while watching noodles of all shapes and grains dry and dry, and dry some more in the hot sun. Some of these noodles turn into Hoi An's unique dish, Cao lầu. Think noodle bowl with local greens and shredded pork or seafood. This dish is all about the broth.

If we're talking street food, then we're talking about Vietnamese pancakes, which is Hoi An's version of fast food. They are not really pancakes, as we Americans are used to, but thin, eggy, crepes studded with green onions and filled with herbs, leaves, and perhaps some delicate fish. Afterward, you mustn't pass up the paper sacks of fried and sugared Banh ran. The ones found in the market are perhaps a little more authentic than those you find being hustled by young peddlers on the streets. (These look and taste suspiciously like Dunkin' Donut holes.)

More than anything else, the central market is all about their fresh produce. Baskets, upon baskets are filled with varieties of herbs and spices; fruits like whole pineapples and multi-colored eggplants. There are all sorts of greens and legumes and exotics like dragon fruit and lychee. It's a sea of farm fresh bounty that is as picturesque as it is enticing.

Sue's painting *Basic Bounty* takes me back to the Hoi An Central Market and reminds me of the necessity of fresh food for local cultures. For us, fresh food is a hobby, a goal, something to be sought out. Fresh food is the upper crust of its canned or frozen counterpart. It requires more work than foods that are already chopped, partially cooked or previously sauced. But, for so many parts of the world, fresh food is the reality not a luxury. If we think about it, there is probably something we can learn from this.

WHIPPED EGGPLANT WITH GARLIC MARINATED ROASTED PEPPERS AND TOASTED PITA WEDGES

serves a crowd

45 minute cuisine

Sue's paintings capture the beauty of the eggplant. And the eggplant's beauty is in its diversity. There are at least ten types, many of them found in fresh markets. With names like Graffiti (also known as Sicilian eggplant), Italian, Chinese and Japanese, Fairy Tale Eggplant, white eggplant, Indian and Little Green eggplant, you can get lost in the selection. They come in all shapes, sizes and colors that range from deep purple to pink-striped to white. All of them will work well in this (and most) recipes. This dip is kinda like fluffy hummus whipped cream. The flavors of the peppers are sweet and smoky. The combo slathered onto a toasted pita wedge is perfect to serve as an appy or for a bread course for an alfresco lunch with pals.

FOR EGGPLANT:

1 large eggplant

4 ounces ricotta cheese, about ½ cup

2 ounces cream cheese, about ¼ cup

1 teaspoon kosher salt

½ teaspoon coarse black pepper

FOR PEPPERS:

4 large red bell peppers

¼ cup olive oil

6 large garlic cloves, peeled and thinly sliced, about 2 tablespoons

2 tablespoons chopped fresh parsley

FOR PITA BREAD:

4 pita flatbreads

2 tablespoons olive oil

1 ounce Parmesan cheese, grated, about ¼ cup

Preheat the oven to 400°. Cut the eggplant in half and place, cut-side-down onto a rimmed baking sheet. Roast the eggplant until soft, about 20 minutes. Cool to room temperature. Peel the eggplant and place the soft flesh into the bowl of a food processor. Add the ricotta and cream cheese into the bowl. Pulse until pureed. Season with some of the salt and pepper and pulse one more time.

While the eggplant is baking, roast the peppers, turning and turning over a direct flame on an outdoor grill, gas stove top or broiler until all sides are black and blistered. Transfer the peppers to a bowl. Cover with plastic wrap to steam for 15 to 20 minutes. Heat ¼ cup olive oil in a skillet over medium-low heat. Add the garlic slices. Cook until the garlic is softened, about 10 minutes. Remove the garlic infused oil from the heat. Peel the charred skin from the peppers. (You can do this by rubbing the skin with a clean cloth or paper towel.) Cut each one in half and remove the stem and seeds. Cut the peppers into strips. Place into a shallow bowl. Pour the garlic oil over top. Season with salt and pepper. Toss in fresh parsley.

Preheat the oven to 400°. Brush each pita bread with olive oil and sprinkle with cheese. Cut into 6 wedges. Place the wedges onto a parchment paper lined rimmed baking sheet. Bake until the bread is just golden, about 5 minutes.

Place the eggplant into a bowl, arrange the peppers onto a platter and lay the pita wedges all around. Top each pita wedge with a slather of whipped eggplant and a layer of roasted pepper.

After Market Leftovers

This eggplant spread is wonderful slathered onto a thick slice of whole grain bread for an ideal start to the perfect open-face sandwich. But, take it way, way over the top as the start for your perfect panini. Top your eggplant slathered bottom slice of bread with roasted eggplant and chicken slices. Top with some of the roasted peppers, your favorite cheese and another slathered slice of bread. Coat the outside of your sandwich with olive oil and cook in a panini maker, or crunched into a waffle iron, or smooshed into a cast iron skillet with another skillet on top. Now, this is one terrific panini sandwich.

GRILLED GUAC

serves a crowd

20 minute cuisine (plus 45 minutes for roasting garlic)

I visited Austin, Texas several years ago when my son and daughter-in-law chose it as their wedding destination. Tex-Mex food is a staple and after just a few days visit, I became a fan and vowed to "Keep Austin Weird." I love every aspect of their guac prepared tableside in almost every restaurant in town! This recipe, however, blows the doors off any guac I've ever had. Just by grilling the traditional ingredients, you change the depth of flavor to a rarified fired-up dish. Make it just for FUN or impress your guests by grilling all the ingredients, taking them to the table, and asking them to mash the guac for you. Serve on nachos, as a condiment on fish or chicken, or . . .how about frying a tortilla in oil for just a couple of secs. Break off pieces and dip into the grilled guac for a communal appy? It doesn't get any better!!

2 tablespoons olive oil

2 medium ripe avocados, halved, seed removed, peeled and diced, about 1 cup

4 medium plum tomatoes, halved

½ large red onion, peeled and cut into ½-inch rounds

2 large jalapeno peppers, cut in half and seeded

2 limes, cut in half

6 cloves roasted garlic (see the recipe for Roasted Garlic and Tomato soupon page 18 to learn about roasting garlic)

1 teaspoon ground chili powder

1 teaspoon kosher salt

½ teaspoon coarse ground pepper

Heat a grill pan over high heat. Drizzle with 2 tablespoons olive oil. Place the avocado, tomatoes, onion, jalapeno peppers and limes onto the grill pan, cut sides down. Cook until you see grill marks on all the food, about 3 to 5 minutes. Flip the veggies and limes and cook on the other side for about 2 to 3 minutes more. You want the onions to be fork tender, and the rest of the food firm, but not mushy.

Remove the food to your work surface and let cool so that you can handle each item. Scoop the flesh from the avocado into a bowl. Chop the tomatoes, onion, and jalapenos. Add them to the bowl. Squeeze the juice of one lime into the bowl. Add the roasted garlic. Season with chili powder, salt and pepper. Use a potato masher to mash all the ingredients to your desired consistency. Less mashing for chunky guac. More mashing for smoother guacamole. You can drizzle additional olive oil into the guac for added richness and more lime juice for extra smoothness.

COOK'S TIP

Roasted garlic is one of my most favorite things. I spread it onto crackers and toast, add it to soups and stews and blend it into sauces and dips. It's easy to prepare, so I roasted several heads at a time and save extras in a resealable plastic bag in the fridge. To prepare roasted garlic, preheat the oven to 400°. Cut the top third from the garlic bulbs. Place the bulbs onto a sheet of aluminum foil. Drizzle the cut side of the garlic with olive oil and season with dried oregano, salt and pepper. Close the foil to make a packet, leaving a small opening at the top. Place the packet onto a baking dish, and roast until the cloves are soft, caramelized and popping out thier skins, about 30 to 40 minutes. remove from the packet and cool to room temperature.

AVOCADO TOASTS WITH ROASTED TOMATO MAYONNAISE AND MANCHEGO CHEESE

serves a crowd

45 minute cuisine

On a visit to Cambodia, I was surprised to see that in addition to baskets and platters of fresh fruits, there was also an abundance of vegetables on breakfast buffet tables. Tomatoes and avocados were as common as oranges and bananas. I found myself piling on veggies on top of my traditional breakfast foods. Here in the states, I think avocados are in the limelight and as such people are finding all kinds of ways to include them in their meals. I've seen avocado boats holding everything from salads to baked eggs! My recipe for avocado toasts creates a great snack, a fun first course for lunch or my favorite, an open-faced choice for breakfast (reminding me of my trip to Cambodia). In that spirit, I like to top the toast with a poached egg for an elevated and filling breakfast. Give it a try!

FOR MAYONNAISE:

1 pound small, ripe plum tomatoes, about 8

1 tablespoon olive oil

1 teaspoon ground cumin

1 teaspoon kosher salt

1 teaspoon black pepper

½ teaspoon ground mustard

½ teaspoon ground fennel

½ cup mayonnaise

FOR TOASTS:

1 small (hoagie-size) artisanal 5-grain loaf, cut into ½-inch slices

1 medium ripe avocado, seed removed, peeled and sliced, about 1 cup

4 ounces Manchego cheese, grated, about 1 cup

Preheat the oven to 475°. Cut the tomatoes in half lengthwise. Toss the tomatoes with olive oil, cumin, salt, pepper, ground mustard and fennel on a rimmed baking sheet. Roast the tomatoes until the skins begin to blacken and blister, about 8 to 10 minutes. Remove the sheet from the oven and cool to room temperature. Place the tomatoes and their juices into the bowl of a food processor. Pulse to emulsify. Pour the tomato puree into a small bowl. Fold in the mayonnaise.

Increase the oven temperature to the broil setting. Place the bread slices onto a broiler pan. Place into the oven and toast on one side, about 2 to 3 minutes. Watch carefully, this goes fast! Remove the pan from the oven. Flip the toast to the other side. Slather each one with a generous spoonful of tomato mayonnaise. Fan avocado slices over the mayonnaise. Mound cheese on top. Place the pan back into the oven on the top rack and broil until the cheese is golden, melty and bubbling, about 3 to 4 minutes more. Remove the pan from the broiler and serve the warm toasts.

VIETNAMESE EGGPLANT STEW

serves 4 as a side dish

30 minute cuisine

The chef at the Red Bridge Cooking School in Hoi An, Vietnam, didn't speak much English. His toothy smile was enough to keep us interested as he demonstrated dish after dish. He stood in front of twenty or so students, each equipped with our own burners, utensils and ingredients. We copied his every move, chopping, stewing and seasoning while the cooking smells wafted around the open-air classroom. We made rice paper and then created a traditional spring roll filled with super thin slices of fresh veggies and bitty-sized shrimp. We made crispy pancakes and turned pineapple into a boat! One of the signature dishes that the chef demonstrated was a lemon grass infused eggplant stew that we prepared in individual clay pots. After the class we strolled through the fresh garden on our way to the restaurant's dining room where the meal we prepared was served. It was quite the experience. This is my version of the dish we created in the school. The eggplant is rich and velvety and delicious.

2 teaspoons peanut oil

1 garlic clove, peeled and minced, about 1 teaspoon

1 stalk lemongrass, outer layer discarded, sliced, about 2 tablespoons

1 (1–inch) piece fresh turmeric, peeled and grated, about 2 teaspoons (you can substitute with ¼ teaspoon ground turmeric)

4 plum tomatoes, peeled and seeded, chopped, about 2 cups

2 tablespoons fish sauce, divided

1 teaspoon granulated sugar, divided

1 medium eggplant, cut into 2-inch pieces, about 3 cups

1 small red chili, seeded, veins removed, cut into thin strips, about 1 teaspoon

1 teaspoon kosher salt

¼ teaspoon coarse black pepper

1 tablespoon chopped fresh basil

1 green onion, diagonally sliced, about 1 tablespoon

Heat the peanut oil in a deep pot with lid, over medium heat. Add the garlic, lemongrass and turmeric to the pot and stir. Add the tomatoes to the pot. Stir in 2 tablespoons water. Simmer until the tomatoes break down, about 2 minutes. Stir in 1 tablespoon fish sauce and ½ teaspoon sugar. Add the eggplant to the pot. Pour in 1 cup water. Add the remaining fish sauce and sugar. Stir in the chili and season with salt, and pepper. Simmer until the eggplant is soft, about 5 to 10 minutes. Garnish with fresh basil and sliced green onions.

Market Central

ZUCCHINI ENCHILADA BOATS WITH CHORIZO AND BLACK BEAN FILLING

serves 6 to 8

30 minute cuisine

Austin, Texas, holds as much of an allure for Sue as it does for me. Sue's hubby, Tom, has designed several golf courses in the area, and together we have played on many of them. But, if golf was not involved, we'd still love Austin. It's a fast-growing city drawing young people in droves. While the restaurants spring up to accommodate all the Austin dwellers, the food trucks are there in force. You just can't beat the meals that come from these teeny kitchens, some of which are equipped with their own smoking ovens and coal-fed grills. While you can find just about any nationality of cuisine, you just can't beat the local fare, Tex-Mex. I'm a fainting femme fatale when it comes to enchiladas. I love them covered in spicy sauce and slathered with melty cheese. This dish has all the flavors of enchiladas, but stars farm fresh zucchini in place of tortillas. Peppery chorizo sausage and meaty black beans are the heart of this fiery dish. The yummy enchilada sauce brings the whole thing together. It's pretty darn delicious! And, as they say in Austin, "Let's keep it weird!"

FOR FILLING:

2 tablespoons olive oil

1 medium onion, peeled and diced, about 1 cup

4 large garlic cloves, peeled and minced, about 2 tablespoons

1 pound ground beef sirloin

8 ounces fresh chorizo sausage

1 (15.5-ounce) can black beans, rinsed and drained

1 teaspoon kosher salt

½ teaspoon coarse black pepper

FOR ENCHILADA SAUCE:

¼ cup vegetable oil

2 tablespoons unbleached all-purpose flour

2 tablespoons chili powder

1 cup tomato paste

2 cups homemade chicken stock, or prepared low sodium chicken broth

1 teaspoon onion powder

1 teaspoon garlic powder

½ teaspoon ground cumin

½ teaspoon ground oregano

FOR BOATS:

4 large zucchinis, cut in half lengthwise, seeded

8 ounces pepper jack cheese

Fresh cilantro

pickled jalapeno

pepper slices

Prepared guacamole, sour cream

Preheat the oven to 400°. Heat 2 tablespoons olive oil in a skillet over medium-high heat. Cook the onion in the skillet until soft, about 3 to 5 minutes. Stir in the garlic and cook for 1 minute more. Add the sirloin and chorizo and stir, breaking up large clumps, until the meat is browned, about 3 to 5 minutes. Add the black beans. Season with some of the salt and pepper. Use a potato masher to break up the beans into the meat filling. Remove the skillet from the heat.

Whisk together the vegetable oil, flour and chili powder in a pot over medium heat to form a paste. Stir in the tomato paste and the chicken stock. Stir in onion powder, garlic powder, cumin and oregano. Simmer the sauce for 5 minutes to thicken and allow the seasonings to merge together. Taste and season with salt and pepper. If the sauce is too thick you can pour in a bit more stock. Remove the pan from the heat.

Spoon some of the enchilada sauce into the bottom of a 13 x 9 x 2-inch baking dish. Scoop the seeds from the center of each zucchini half leaving enough of the flesh to create a boat. Place the zucchini boats into the dish. Season zucchini with salt and pepper. Spoon the filling into the boats. It's okay if the filling spills out. Pour the remaining enchilada sauce over the top of the boats. Layer cheese over the top. Cover the dish with a sheet of aluminum foil and bake for 15 minutes. Remove the foil and bake until the cheese is melted and beginning to brown and the zucchini is fork-tender, about 20 minutes more. Garnish the boats with fresh cilantro, jalapeno slices, guacamole and sour cream.

Unsung Melodies

ZUCCHINI INVOLTINI WITH SUN-DRIED TOMATO RICOTTA FILLING

serves 4 to 6

30 minute cuisine

Involtini is a favorite first course on some of the most impressive menus in Rome restaurants. Traditionally it's made with eggplant or pasta wrapped around a light ricotta filling. This dish is designed as a main course. I'm using my favorite flavors again! Creamy ricotta cheese, tangy sun-dried tomatoes, rich, red tomato sauce and buttery béchamel . . . oh and yes, there is zucchini! Choose larger zucchini for this dish so that you can load them up with the yummy filling. Your family will volunteer you to make this involtini . . . (now that's cheesy)!

FOR ZUCCHINI:

3 large zucchinis, cut lengthwise into ¼-inch slices

2 tablespoons olive oil

1 teaspoon salt

½ teaspoon coarse black pepper

1 cup ricotta cheese

1 large egg

2 ounces Parmesan cheese, grated, about ½ cup

¼ cup sun-dried tomatoes in oil, drained and finely diced

2 tablespoons chopped fresh parsley

FOR TOMATO SAUCE:

2 tablespoons olive oil

4 large garlic cloves, peeled and minced, about 2 tablespoons

1 small onion, peeled and minced, about ½ cup

1 (28-ounce) can crushed tomatoes

2 tablespoons tomato paste

2 tablespoons, chopped fresh basil

2 tablespoons butter

2 tablespoons unbleached all-purpose flour

1 ½ cups milk

¼ teaspoon ground nutmeg

2 ounces Parmesan cheese, grated, about ½ cup, plus more for topping

Preheat the oven to 400°. Lay the zucchini slices on parchment lined baking sheets. Brush both sides with olive oil and season with some of the salt and pepper. Roast until the slices are pliable, about 10 to 15 minutes. Remove the baking sheets from the oven and cool the zucchini so that you can work with it.

Stir the ricotta cheese, egg and ½ cup Parmesan cheese together in a bowl. Stir in sun-dried tomatoes and parsley. Season with salt and pepper.

Heat 2 tablespoons olive oil in a sauté pan over medium-high heat. Add the garlic and onion and cook until the veggies begin to soften, about 3 to 5 minutes. Pour in the tomatoes and tomato paste. Taste and season with salt, pepper and stir in the basil. Remove the pan from the heat.

Melt the butter in a pot over medium-high heat. Whisk in the flour to make a paste. Cook for two minutes. Pour in the milk. Reduce the heat to medium. Stir until the sauce begins to thicken. Season with salt, pepper and nutmeg. Stir in ½ cup Parmesan cheese. Remove the pot from the heat.

Pour a ladle full of tomato sauce into the bottom of an 11 x 7 x 2-inch baking dish. Place a spoonful of the ricotta filling onto each zucchini slice. Roll the zucchini over the filling and lay seam-side down into the pan. Repeat until all the zucchini slices and all the filling is rolled and in the baking dish. Cover the rolled zucchini with the remaining tomato sauce. Spoon the béchamel sauce over the top. Reduce the oven temperature to 375°. Bake until the top of the casserole begins to brown, and the sauces are bubbling, about 20 to 30 minutes. Let the casserole rest for 10 minutes before digging in!

APPLE, SAUSAGE AND CHEDDAR STUFFED ACORN SQUASH

serves 4

30 to 40 minute cuisine

The story behind this recipe is a long one, but considering I survived, I am compelled to tell it! On a trip that started in Russia, continued through Denmark, and ended in the UK, Sue and I found ourselves on a day trip to visit the city of Cork in Ireland. The main attraction in Cork is the Blarney Stone, which we set off to see amid a swarm of fellow tourists. We arrived at the Blarney Castle, which is a tower that some describe as majestic or looming, depending on your mood. After traveling up the very narrow (I mean EXTREMELY narrow), four-story, windowless and very claustrophobic staircase, Sue coaxed me through my one and only panic attack. I hadn't even known I was claustrophobic until I met Blarney Castle.

When we finally burst out of the tower and onto the top of the castle, we found ourselves still in the queue to finally kiss the stone. Tradition has it that in order to receive the gift of eloquence, one has to bend over backwards to kiss the stone. This means lowering your head (backwards!) from the parapet walk over an opening in the tower that leads all the way down to the ground below. There were two very, very young and scrawny teens that were on either side of the hole in the floor—to make sure you don't fall through, but they were not enough to persuade me.

Needless-to-say, after narrowly escaping death in the tower (a bit of an exaggeration) I sprinted past Sue and that stone, down the castle's back stairs and found my way to the closest pub. I took refuge in a pint and comfort in a dish called Cheshire Pie, which combines chunky pork and sautéed apples in a flaky crust. My recipe for stuffed acorn squash is a twist on that pie (minus the flaky crust). The flavors are sweet, tart and rich. It's super for a mid-week meal and awesome for a brunch gathering. Actually, it's a pretty perfect dish if you are just in need of a bit of calm after the storm!!

FOR SQUASH:

2 medium acorn squashes, halved and seeded

1 tablespoon olive oil

1 teaspoon apple pie spice

FOR STUFFING:

1 tablespoon olive oil

1 small onion, peeled and diced

1 small poblano pepper, seeded and diced

1 pound mild Italian sausage

2 Granny Smith apples, peeled, cored and diced

1 teaspoon apple pie spice

½ teaspoon kosher salt

½ teaspoon coarse black pepper

4 ounces sharp cheddar cheese, grated, about 1 cup

Sour cream

Preheat the oven to 400°. Drizzle the cut side of the squash with 1 tablespoon olive oil and sprinkle with apple pie spice. Place the squash, cut-side-down into a baking pan. Bake until the squash is fork tender, about 20 minutes.

Heat 1 tablespoon olive oil in a skillet over medium heat. Add the onion and pepper and cook until the veggies are soft, about 5 minutes. Add the sausage and cook until brown and crumbly, about 5 minutes more. Add the apples to the pan. Season with 1 more teaspoon apple pie spice and some of the salt and pepper. Stir in the cheese.

Pull the baking dish from the oven. Turn the squash so they are cut side up. Stuff the squash with the apple-sausage filling. Place the dish back into the oven and cook until the cheese is melted, about 10 minutes more. Garnish the stuffed squash with a dollop of sour cream.

COOK'S TIP

As a postscript to my Blarney Stone story, I'll add that when Sue and the rest of our group caught up to me in the pub, our friend Marti handed me a tee shirt she'd purchased from the gift shop. It was black with bold white letters that stated, "I KISSED THE BLARNEY STONE." The joke was that there was a bright red slash through the word "kissed" which was replaced by the word "missed." I guess I wasn't the first tourist to pass up that stone-kissing experience! Tee shirt aside, the Cook's Tip is that you can find inspiration for dishes through all sorts of experiences and those dishes offer wonderful memories of good times.

Positano Pairings

Plaza Di San Marco

BUTTERNUT SQUASH FETTUCCINE ALFREDO

serves 4

40 minute cuisine

Several years ago, we took a trip to Italy landing in Rome and visiting the city over several days. For our special celebration we had dinner in a lovely hotel where the restaurant sat on the top of the building overlooking one of the beautiful parks. Our guide told us to get there early and grab a table on the veranda in order to see the setting sun set the park on fire, bathed in golden light. It was magical, as was the several-course dinner that followed the sunset. I still remember the pasta course, a beautiful plate of fettuccine alfredo. There is something about the fresh pasta that makes the dish so light and delicate. Even the richest sauces are more fluffy than weighty when served in traditional Italian style. So how do we home cooks make this Italian staple even better? We amp up the veggie quotient adding silky, butternut squash puree to the sauce. It's a beautiful pasta, with the squash adding a golden hue to the whole dish, reminiscent of sunset in the park. And, it's really, really delish!

½ medium butternut squash, halved and seeded

1 tablespoon olive oil

2 teaspoons chili powder, divided

2 teaspoons kosher salt

½ teaspoon coarse black pepper

2 tablespoons butter

1 small onion, peeled and diced, about ½ cup

2 tablespoons unbleached all-purpose flour

2 tablespoons sherry

1 cup half-and-half

1 cup homemade chicken stock or prepared low sodium broth

2 large fresh sage leaves

2 ounces Parmesan cheese, grated about ¼ cup

8 ounces fresh fettuccine pasta (you can substitute with dried pasta but cook it longer)

2 tablespoons chopped fresh parsley

Preheat the oven to 375°. Drizzle the cut side of the butternut squash with olive oil and season with 1 teaspoon chili powder and some of the salt and pepper. Place the squash cut-side-down into a rimmed baking sheet. Roast until the squash is soft, about 20 to 30 minutes. Scoop out the squash from the skin. Place the squash into the bowl of a food processor (or use an immersion blender) to puree.

Prepare the sauce by melting the butter in a saucepan over medium heat. Cook the onion in the butter until soft, about 5 minutes. Whisk in the flour and cook for 1 minute more. Whisk in the sherry until smooth. Stir in half-and-half, and chicken stock. Continue to stir until the sauce thickens, about 1 to 2 minutes. Add the sage leaves, cover the pot, and reduce the heat to the lowest setting for 2 to 3 minutes so that the sage infuses the sauce.

Remove the sage leaves from the sauce. Stir in the butternut squash puree and Parmesan cheese. Season with 1 teaspoon chili powder, salt and pepper.

Cook the pasta, in salted, boiling water until al dente, just a couple of minutes. Drain the pasta (reserving some of the cooking liquid) and toss in the sauce. At this point if the sauce is thicker than you like you can add a ladle or two of pasta water to thin.

Garnish with chopped fresh parsley.

COOK'S TIP

Gorgeous butternut squash come in several sizes. You can find smaller ones, but often you'll find squash that will yield you much more than you need for one recipe. Don't despair. We can figure this out!

Solution numero uno. Simply cut the squash in half, using half for this recipe and reserving half for another use. However, you and I both know that the chances you are going to use butternut squash twice in a week (about the lifetime of that other half of a squash banned to the vegetable drawer) is slim to none. So, let's look for another idea.

Solution duo. Just purchase the amount you need from the pre-packaged section of your grocery store's produce aisle. The problem is that this will cost you two or three times as much as purchasing the squash whole. This option also is not the freshest as the squash may have been peeled and chopped days before.

Problem solved! Cut up the whole dang thing. Roast half as described in this recipe. Peel and cut the other half into 1-inch chunks. Season and roast alongside the half that you are going to scoop. Reserve the chunks and use them in another recipe. For example, stir them into your chili con carne. Add them to your meatloaf mix. Sautée them with some onions, pour in some chicken stock and puree into a lovely soup. Mix them into your rice side dish and add them to your black beans. Creative cooking is easy when the ingredients are yummy to begin with!

GAZPACHO WITH STRAWBERRIES AND BASIL

serves 4 to 6

20 minute cuisine plus chilling

If you're in the heart of Madrid, you just might embark on a Tapas Pub Crawl, visiting the local taverns, and sampling their bar cuisine. It's not uncommon to see a produce stand, next to a tapas stand, next to a wine stand . . . all under the umbrella of a central market. One menu item you are sure to find is chilled shot glasses full of spicy vegetable soup called Gazpacho. Depending upon what part of the region you are visiting, the soup is thick and creamy or thin and brothy. My home version blends farmfresh sweet strawberries into the mix. The flavor combo is so good, you'll break into a Tango!

2 pounds small ripe plum tomatoes, about 16 (or about 8 medium to large plum tomatoes)

½ large English cucumber, cut into chunks, about 1 cup

1 large red bell pepper, seeded cut into chunks, about 1 cup

1 small red onion, peeled and cut into chunks, about ½ cup

1 pint fresh strawberries, stems removed and halved, about 2 cups

2 cloves garlic, peeled and minced, about 2 teaspoons

2 tablespoons chopped fresh basil

1 slice white bread, soaked in water

1 cup homemade vegetable stock, or prepared low sodium vegetable broth

½ cup red wine vinegar

¼ cup olive oil

½ teaspoon kosher salt

2 to 4 drops hot pepper sauce

Bring a pot of water to a boil on the stove top. Fill another bowl with ice water. Cut an "x" at one end of each tomato. Drop the tomatoes into the boiling water and cook until the skin begins to wrinkle at the "x", about 45 to 50 seconds. Use a slotted spoon to remove them from the pot and dunk into the ice water. Peel the skin from the tomatoes. Cut each in half and squeeze to remove the seeds. Place the tomatoes into the bowl of a food processor. Add the cucumber, red pepper and onion. Pulse until chunky. Pour the veggies into a large bowl.

Place the strawberries into the food processor and pulse. (You want them chunky not pureed.) Add the strawberries to the veggies in the bowl.

Pour the strawberries and veggies back into the bowl of the food processor, reserving one cup. Add the garlic and basil. Squeeze the excess water from the bread and add to the food processor bowl. Pulse to puree the soup and then pour back into the large bowl. Stir in the stock, vinegar and olive oil. Stir in the chunky, 1 cup blend that you reserved. Season with salt and hot pepper sauce. Chill the soup for several hours. Serve with a garnish of basil and a slice of strawberry.

CHEESY SUMMER SQUASH AND ZUCCHINI BREAD PUDDING

serves 6 to 8 as a Side Dish

45 minutes prep plus 1 hour chillin' and 45 minutes to bake

When you visit a fresh market, the one thing that you notice is the interaction of the farmers. They truly respect and enjoy each other. They want you to know that their passion is the food that you eat. They'll pass out recipes, offer you free samples, and encourage you to choose a food that may be out of your comfort zone. To know the efforts that growers expend as they lovingly tend to their gardens, is to know this: not using every last veggie is a sin against the farm! Not to despair, this simple, Southern casserole takes advantage of the last veggies left in the fridge allowing you a legit reason to hit the market again the next weekend!

2 tablespoons olive oil

1 large onion, peeled and cut into ½-inch pieces

2 medium zucchinis, halved lengthwise and cut into ¼-inch slices, about 2 cups

2 medium yellow squash, halved lengthwise and cut into ¼-inch slices, about 2 cups

1 (12 ounce) baguette, cut into ½-inch cubes, about 4 cups

2 ounces provolone cheese, shredded, about ½ cup, divided

2 ounces fontina cheese, shredded, about ½ cup, divided

2 ounces Parmesan cheese, shredded, about ½ cup, divided

4 eggs, beaten

1 ½ cup milk

1 tablespoon chopped fresh parsley

1 teaspoon ground oregano

1 teaspoon ground basil

½ teaspoon ground rosemary

1 teaspoon kosher salt

½ teaspoon coarse black pepper

2 to 4 drops hot pepper sauce

Heat the olive oil in a skillet over medium-high heat. Add the onion, zucchini and squash.

Cook until soft and beginning to turn brown, about 5 minutes. Remove the pan from the heat. Coat an 11 x 7 x 2-inch baking dish with vegetable oil spray. Pour the bread cubes into the baking dish. Top with the vegetables, and half of each of the cheeses. Whisk together the eggs, milk, parsley, spices, salt, pepper and as much hot pepper sauce as you like. Pour over the bread cubes and veggies smushing down the bread cubes to make sure everything is submerged in custardy goodness! Top with the remaining cheese. Cover the baking dish with plastic wrap and chill for at least 1 hour or as much as overnight.

Preheat the oven to 325°. Remove the plastic wrap and bake until the top is golden and puffy, about 45 to 50 minutes. Let the casserole rest for 10 minutes before serving.

MEYER LEMON-INFUSED SPAGHETTI WITH PROSCIUTTO AND PARMIGIANO REGGIANO

serves 4

30 minute cuisine

I find there is no better way to savor Italy than to enjoy a delicious dish while over-looking the rural fields and farms. The sounds and smells of the pastures add to the taste of the food. The simple flavors of al fresco dining in a Southern Italian villa are captured in this dish. Meyer lemons taste like a cross between lemons and oranges adding just a bit of sweet to their mouth-puckering flavor with a fragrance that transports you to the orchard. With the addition of salty prosciutto and earthy cheese, this is a perfect pasta dish, especially when you are in a bit of a rush.

2 tablespoons butter

2 garlic cloves, peeled and minced, plus 2 more for pasta sauce, about 2 tablespoons

4 (1-inch thick) slices whole grain bread, crust removed, processed into about 2 cups coarse crumbs

1 pound fresh spaghetti pasta (you can substitute with dried pasta but cook it longer)

¼ cup olive oil

Zest of 1 Meyer lemon, about 1 tablespoon

Juice of 1 Meyer lemon, about 3 tablespoons

3-ounces prosciutto, about 5 thin slices, cut into strips

1 teaspoon kosher salt

¼ teaspoon crushed red pepper flakes

2 ounces Parmigiano Reggiano cheese, grated, about ½ cup

2 tablespoons chopped fresh Italian flat leaf parsley

Melt 2 tablespoons butter in a large skillet over medium-high heat. Add half of the garlic and stir. Add the bread crumbs, stir and cook until golden, about 3 to 5 minutes. Remove the toasted crumbs to a bowl.

Cook the pasta in boiling salted water until al dente, just a couple of minutes.

Heat ¼ cup olive oil, in the same skillet that you cooked the bread crumbs, over medium heat. Stir in the remaining 1 tablespoon minced garlic. Add the lemon zest and juice. Stir in the prosciutto. Drain the spaghetti (reserving 1 to 2 cups liquid). Add the pasta and toss to coat. Pour in 1 cup pasta liquid. Season with salt and red pepper flakes. Add the cheese. Stir in additional liquid if the pasta is too sticky. Toss in the bread crumbs and parsley.

Market Commuters

HEIRLOOM TOMATO TART WITH GREEN GODDESS CREAM

serves 4 to 6

30 minute cuisine

Farmers markets have a personality all their own, dependent on the season and location. When I was in Vietnam, the central market I visited was dominated by fresh seafood. In Italy, I was overwhelmed by fragrances, strolling through orchards with lemon and olive trees, flanking every path. In Sue's and my summer hometown in the Carolina mountains, markets are rife with different kinds of heirloom tomatoes. My straw basket overflows with red, purple, orange and sometimes green ones. Fresh tomatoes are perfectly accented with a green goddess inspired cream sauce, featuring fresh herbs and a touch of citrus in this recipe.

2 tablespoons (or more) unbleached all-purpose flour for dusting and rolling

1 sheet frozen puff pastry, thawed

1 (8-ounce) package cream cheese, room temperature

½ cup sour cream

1/2 cup mayonnaise

Juice of 1 medium lemon, about 3 tablespoons

2 tablespoons chopped fresh tarragon

2 tablespoons chopped fresh parsley

2 tablespoons chopped fresh chives

1 (7-ounce) tin flat fillets of anchovies, packed in oil, discard oil

1 tablespoon tarragon vinegar

½ teaspoon kosher salt

½ teaspoon coarse black pepper

¼ teaspoon granulated sugar

2 pints assorted baby heirloom tomatoes, halved

1 tablespoon olive oil

Preheat the oven to 400°. Place a piece of parchment paper onto a baking sheet. Dust with flour. Unfold the puff pastry onto the dusted parchment paper. Dust the pastry with flour. Roll out the pastry to about a 9 x 11-inch rectangle. Use the tip of a knife to score a ½-inch border all around the side of the rectangle. Poke the middle of the puff pastry with the tines of a fork. Place the baking sheet into the oven and bake until the puff pastry is golden brown, about 20 to 25 minutes. Remove from the oven and cool to room temperature.

Place the cream cheese, sour cream, mayonnaise, lemon juice, tarragon, parsley, chives, anchovies and vinegar into the bowl of a food processor. Pulse to combine. Season with some of the salt, pepper and sugar. Pulse one more time. Spread the green goddess cream sauce over the pastry crust. Arrange the tomatoes on top. Season the tomatoes with salt, pepper and a drizzle of olive oil. Cut into squares and serve.

WORLD FAMOUS FARMERS MARKET DIP WITH SEASONED CRACKERS

serves a crowd

30 minute cuisine

I have two great Saturday morning loves. I love strolling the stalls at the Farmer's market and I love coffee shops with bagels. At the market I taste my way from stand to stand. At the coffee shop, I order a bagel slathered with seasoned cream cheese. This dish is the marriage of my Saturday morning faves. Reminiscent of the "Everything Bagel" the crackers topped with this yummy dip are perfect for late afternoon snacks or on an hors d'oeuvres tray. Spread the dip on party-size pumpernickel bread slices and top with thinly sliced cucumber and a sprig of dill for an instant take on upscale tea sandwiches

FOR CRACKERS:

1 sleeve soda crackers, about 3 dozen

4 tablespoons butter, melted, ½ stick

1 tablespoon dried oregano flakes

1 tablespoon garlic powder

1 tablespoon onion powder

1 tablespoon poppy seeds

1 tablespoon sesame seeds

FOR DIP:

½ red bell pepper, seeded and diced, about ½ cup

1 small carrot, peeled, trimmed and diced, about ¼ cup

½ small red onion, peeled and diced, about ¼ cup

1 celery rib, diced, about 2 tablespoons

2 green onions, diced, about 2 tablespoons

2 large garlic cloves, peeled and minced, about 1 tablespoon

1 tablespoon chopped fresh dill

1 tablespoon chopped fresh parsley

1 (8-ounce) package cream cheese, room temperature

½ cup sour cream

1 teaspoon kosher salt

2 to 4 drops hot pepper sauce

Preheat the oven to 350°. Lay the crackers on a parchment lined baking sheet. Brush the crackers with butter. Mix together oregano, garlic and onion powder, poppy and sesame seeds in a small bowl. Sprinkle the seasoning over the crackers. Bake until the crackers are golden, about 4 to 5 minutes. Cool to room temperature.

Place the veggies, herbs, cream cheese, and sour cream into the bowl of a food processor. Pulse to combine. Season with salt, pepper, and as much hot sauce as you prefer. Spoon the dip into a bowl and serve alongside the seasoned crackers.

SPICY PEPPER CHUTNEY ON PEAR AND GRUYERE TOASTS

serves 4

45 minute cuisine

Inspired by the flavors of the Caribbean, this small plate dish is a super movie-watching snack. Enjoy it with your bestie and a glass or two of the best red wine you have on hand. There's something decadent about melting cheese over sweet pears and a tart, fragrant chutney condiment. Let's face it, we're not talking about your mama's grilled cheese sandwich, are we?

FOR CHUTNEY:

4 large red bell peppers

2 orange Anaheim peppers (substitute with 4 medium jalapeno peppers)

1 tablespoon olive oil

1 large red onion, thinly sliced, about 1 ½ cup

½ cup brown sugar

1 cinnamon stick

3 bay leaves

1 tablespoon Dijon-style mustard

½ teaspoon paprika

1 cup homemade chicken stock or prepared low-sodium chicken broth

1 teaspoon kosher salt

½ teaspoon coarse black pepper

FOR TOASTS:

4 (1-inch thick) slices nutty artisanal bread

1 ripe pear, peeled, cored and thinly sliced

4 ounces Gruyere cheese, grated, about 1 cup

Roast the peppers on an outdoor grill, stove top or broiler, turning until blistered. Transfer the peppers to a bowl. Cover with plastic wrap for 20 minutes. Pull off the charred skin (use a cloth or paper towel for this) and remove the stems and seeds. Chop the peppers. Heat 1 tablespoon olive oil in a large skillet over medium-high heat. Add the onion and cook until soft, about 10 minutes. Add the chopped peppers, brown sugar, cinnamon stick, bay leaves, mustard, paprika, and chicken stock. Reduce the heat to medium-low and simmer until the chutney becomes syrupy, about 30 minutes. Remove the bay leaves and cinnamon stick. Taste and season with salt and pepper. Remove the skillet from the heat. Preheat the oven to 475° and position a rack a few inches away from the heating element. Place the bread slices onto a rimmed baking sheet lined with parchment paper. Toast the bread until golden on one side, about 2 to 3 minutes. Remove the baking sheet from the oven. Turn up the oven to the broil setting. Flip the bread and slather a spoonful of chutney on the untoasted side. Fan pear slices over the chutney. Mound the cheese over the top. Return the baking sheet to the oven and broil until the cheese is melted and bubbly, about 2 to 3 minutes. Cut each toast into diagonal pieces and serve warm.

Marche Couvert D'Avalon

GARLICKY SHRIMP AND SHISHITO PEPPERS

serves 4 as main 6 to 8 as appy

30 minute cuisine

On summer day, as I was strolling the market, I saw a farmer toasting peppers in what looked like a giant mesh drum. He used a handle to turn the drum over an open flame. The he removed the pinky finger-sized peppers and offered samples. I copied others and bit into the whole pepper. The taste was delish! Slightly tangy and definitely toasty, the peppery flavor bursts in your mouth hinting at heat, but just teasing you. Needless-to-say, I fell in love with his shishito peppers. Now, I buy them whenever I find them, usually in mid-summer. For this recipe, slow cooking garlic with paprika in olive oil does double duty. The oil becomes fragrant while the garlic becomes soft and sweet. Add the bite of shishito peppers and delicate shrimp to the herb-infused oil and you have a simple one-pan meal that comes together in minutes!

½ cup olive oil

1 whole head garlic, cloves peeled and thinly sliced, about ½ cup

1 tablespoon paprika

10 to 12 shishito peppers

1 bunch green onions, tops removed, halved and cut into 3-inch pieces

1 pound fresh extra-large shrimp, peeled and deveined, about 26 to 30

1 teaspoon kosher salt

½ teaspoon coarse black pepper

2 tablespoons chopped fresh parsley

Heat the olive oil in a skillet over medium heat. (I use a cast iron skillet for this dish.) Add the garlic and paprika and cook until the garlic is soft and just beginning to turn golden on the edges. Use a slotted spoon to transfer the garlic to a plate. Add peppers, green onion and shrimp to the skillet. Turn up the heat to medium-high. Toss the veggies and shrimp in the garlicky oil until the peppers begin to blister and the shrimp turn pink and are cooked through, about 3 to 5 minutes. Scrape the garlic back into the skillet. Season with salt and pepper. Sprinkle with parsley and serve.

FUNGI AND LEAVES

fun·gus

'fəNGgəs/

noun

fun·gi

'fən͵gē,'fən͵jē,'fən͵gī,'fən͵jī/

plural form of fungus.

1. any of a group of unicellular, multicellular, or syncytial spore-producing organisms feeding on organic matter, including molds, yeast, mushrooms, and toadstools.

leaf

/lēf/

Noun

/lēvz/

plural form of leaf.

1. a flattened structure of a higher plant, typically green and bladelike, that is attached to a stem directly or via a stalk. Leaves are the main organs of photosynthesis and transpiration.
   synonyms: leaflet, frond, blade, needle

Corner Market

The vivid colors of a bustling market depicted in Sue's painting *Corner Market* remind me of my trip to Beijing, China. Foodie that I am, my dream was to sample only authentic food during my short stay. I started with Peking Duck known for its robustly flavored, crackling skin and moist, tender flesh. It's pretty yummy. Then, we moved onto bamboo baskets of steamed buns—bao—filled with minced pork or veggies. It was all about the salty-sweet dipping sauce for this dish, as it was for the steamed bun's cousin, the pot sticker. Oh, and then there was that crispy fish.

As I worked down my list of Chinese food faves, I built a rapport with our tour guide, Jack. We spent hours traveling to and from sites and talking excitedly about food. Jack was not very open when the discussion led to politics, but he was rather effusive about the dishes he likes to cook at home. I asked him if he would take us to experience his favorite local Chinese restaurant meal, and the next thing I knew we were driving to a mall! Just when I thought he had misunderstood my request, the mall revealed itself as everything a foodie could hope for. Jack led us down the escalator to a group of restaurants and what awaited us was nothing like an American food court. Here, Jack explained, we would discover the joy of lunching over a traditional Chinese hot pot.

We gathered around a table with a cooking unit in the center. The server immediately topped the burner with a large pot, divided into curry and mushroom flavored broths. Another waiter placed food platters around the table and handed out chopsticks. First, there were trays of rolled, thin sliced beef (chicken and seafood were an option). Next came huge platters of veggies and tofu. On these were artistically displayed leaves of cabbage, spinach and lettuce, thinly sliced pieces of yam, cucumber and radishes, needle mushrooms and tiny delights like wedges, raw fish, and crab meatballs. Lastly, we were treated to dishes of noodles: oodles and oodles of noodles made from soy, green beans, or wheat.

There were two condiment bowls before us, brimming with sesame and peanut sauces. Jack instructed us to add a generous pinch of fresh cilantro, a pour of dark vinegar, fresh garlic and green onions to our sauces. While we waited for the broths to boil, he shared the history of the dish. The story goes that Mongolian soldiers during battle used their large, metal helmets for pots. They foraged for any ingredients they could find and cooked everything over a compact fire.

Our chopsticks poised, we placed the meat into the broth. Jack, ever patient, made us wait exactly four minutes, or until the "germs were killed", before we scooped the meat from the broth and plunged it into our condiment bowls. The taste is . . . daring. The meat was fatty and rich, but the broth was light and highly seasoned. The condiment bowl was sooo fresh. After relishing the meat, we plunged the veggies into the broth. Both the broth and the condiment bowl were utterly transformed by the constant dipping. The broth is a bit richer from the meat and the condiment bowl a bit lighter from the broth. Jack explained that the reason it all tastes so amazing, is the method and order to our dining. The meal, eaten in the correct order prepares your body for a crescendo of satisfaction.

The meal took hours to eat, and when I looked around me the tables were filled with young people eating, conversing and sharing the food. Sue and I firmly believe that food is meant to be communal, eaten with friends and family. This meal is a perfect example of this experience, one we can recreate in the States!

Marche Bastille

CHINESE HOT POT MADE IN THE USA

serves a party crowd

45 minutes to prep ingredients

In Beijing, our guide treated us to a traditional Hot Pot lunch. Picture a restaurant full of communal tables; at the center of each is a deep pot of fragrant simmering broth, surrounded by dishes of raw ingredients. Here, the chopsticks fly as fast as the conversation. The meal is meant to be eaten in a specific order. First, thin slices of raw meat or seafood are placed into savory, simmering broth. We eat the meat first, because it heats up and energizes the body. After the broth absorbs the flavors of the protein, we submerge pieces of vegetables. We eat the blanched veggies to cool down the system. Finally, we finish with a variety of noodles hydrated by the now, very flavorful broth. These are meant to satisfy and soothe. Each item is cooked in the broth and then dipped in a series of spicy sauces. This is my made-in-the-USA version of the very fun Chinese Hot Pot meal. Please invite your friends and family to share the food and create your own Beijing experience. The best vessel to use for your hot pot is an electric skillet but, a group of fondue pots will work just fine!

FOR GINGER SOY SAUCE:

½ cup soy sauce

2 teaspoons honey

2 teaspoons sesame oil

Juice of 2 large limes, about ¼ cup

1 (1-inch) piece fresh ginger, peeled and grated, about 1 tablespoon

FOR PEANUT SAUCE:

½ cup creamy peanut butter

Juice of 1 large lime, about 2 tablespoons

1 (1-inch piece) fresh ginger, peeled and grated, about 1 tablespoon

1 clove garlic, peeled and minced

2 tablespoons soy sauce

1 teaspoon light brown sugar

¼ teaspoon crushed red pepper

F O R   B R O T H :

2 quarts homemade beef stock, or prepared low sodium broth

4 to 6 green onions

4 cloves garlic, peeled and thinly sliced

6 to 8 shishito peppers, chopped (substitute with mild green peppers)

½ teaspoon crushed red pepper

F O R   D I P P I N G :

Chopped fresh cilantro

1 (12-ounce) sirloin beef steak, chilled, cut into very thin slices

1 pound fresh spinach or kale leaves, about 4 cups

1 medium head Bibb lettuce, leaves separated, about 4 cups

2 medium heads bok choy, separated into leaves, about 4 cups

½ pound fresh green beans, about 3 cups, ends trimmed

½ pound fresh assorted wild mushrooms, sliced, about 2 cups

5 to 7 medium carrots, peeled, trimmed and finely shredded, about 2 cups

½ pound medium fresh asparagus spears, about 16, sliced into 1-inch pieces, about 2 cups

1 pound thin wonton noodles

1 pound soba noodles

Whisk together ½ cup soy sauce with honey, sesame oil, ¼ cup lime juice and 1 tablespoon fresh ginger in a small bowl. Set the ginger soy sauce aside.

Place the peanut butter into the bowl of a food processor. Add 2 tablespoons lime juice, 1 tablespoon ginger, garlic, 2 tablespoons soy sauce, brown sugar and ¼ teaspoon crushed red pepper. Pulse to create a smooth paste. With the machine running, pour in ¼ cup water to thin the paste to dipping consistency. Pour the peanut sauce into a bowl and set aside.

Heat the broth in an electric skillet over medium heat. Add green onions, garlic, shishito peppers and ½ teaspoon crushed red pepper. Bring the broth to a boil, and then reduce the heat, so that the broth simmers.

Give each person a small bowl filled with some of each sauce. Place fresh cilantro on top of each bowl. Pass out the chopsticks!

Place all the dipping ingredients around the electric skillet, containing the simmering broth. As the meal continues, the broth will absorb all the flavors of the food as they cook. This meal is meant to take some time and has an order to its chaos.

Each person chooses one or two slices of beef and submerges it into the broth. *Wait, wait, wait* until the meat is cooked through, about 4 minutes. Use your chopsticks to remove the meat to your plate, dipping it in your sauce of choice along the way.

Everyone takes turns placing ingredients into the broth. Cook veggies until leaves wilt, stems relax, and mushrooms plump. Cook noodles until they soften. Keep dipping, keep submerging. Throughout the meal the broth becomes rich and concentrated, changing the taste of the food from beginning to end.

CELEBRATION TIME EGG ROLLS WITH CHICKEN, MUSHROOM AND CABBAGE

makes 20 egg rolls

30 minute cuisine

We traveled all through Beijing and tasted all sorts of authentic Chinese food and I was hard pressed to find a single eggroll. We found plenty of the delicious sauces that you dip those eggrolls into, but little to no eggrolls. Ah well, that's what creates recipe innovation . . . cravings! These little bundles of flavor are so much better than those frozen egg rolls, you find in the grocery store. You can use whatever ingredients you have on hand . . . OR make use of the fresh veggie you find in the market. The secret is to combine the spicy flavor of ginger and garlic, with the crunch of cabbage and onion. It's a celebration in your mouth!

FOR SAUCE:

¼ cup granulated sugar

¼ cup white wine vinegar

¼ cup soy sauce

1 tablespoon chili sauce

2 tablespoons cornstrach, mixed with ½ cup water

FOR EGGROLLS:

1 tablespoon olive oil

1 pound ground chicken

1 (2-inch piece) fresh ginger, peeled and minced, about 1 tablespoon

2 cloves garlic, peeled and minced, about 2 teaspoons

1 teaspoon kosher salt

½ teaspoon coarse black pepper

½ pound fresh assorted wild mushrooms, sliced, about 2 cups

1 (1-pound package) egg roll wrappers, about 20

¼ medium cabbage, shredded, about 1 cup

3 to 5 medium carrots, peeled, trimmed and finely shredded, about 1 cup

4 to 5 green onions, thinly sliced, about ½ cup

1 large egg, beaten with 2 tablespoons water

Canola oil for frying

Place the sugar, vinegar, soy sauce and chili sauce in a medium saucepan over medium-high heat. Stir in the cornstarch slurry. Bring the sauce to a boil. Reduce the heat to medium. Stir and cook until the sauce has thickened, about 5 minutes.

Heat the olive oil in a skillet over medium-high heat. Cook the chicken until browned and crumbly. Stir in the ginger and garlic. Season with some of the salt and pepper. Cook until fragrant, about 5 minutes total. Transfer the chicken to a bowl.

Add the mushrooms to the pan. Cook until just beginning to soften, about 2 to 3 minutes. Season with salt and pepper. Transfer to a bowl.

Lay one egg roll wrapper onto your work surface. Place a spoonful of chicken onto the bottom third of the wrapper. Top with a few slices of mushroom. Top these with a bit of cabbage, carrot and green onion. Roll the bottom of the wrapper over the filling. Fold in the sides. Roll once more to seal the filling in the wrapper. Brush with egg wash. Place onto a baking sheet, seam side down. Continue with the remaining wrappers and filling.

Pour enough canola oil into a deep pot (or a skillet) to cover about 2 inches deep. Heat the oil over medium-high heat. Carefully place the egg rolls into the hot oil, seam side down and fry until golden, about 3 to 5 minutes. Transfer the eggrolls to a platter lined with paper towels. Do this in batches, depending on the size of your pot or skillet.

Serve warm eggrolls with dipping sauce.

COOK'S TIP

Frying is not as tricky as you think. Just make sure that whatever size pot you use, that the oil comes no higher than one third up the side of the pot. Oil will expand when it's hot and expand again when you add your food for frying!

Wake up Little Suzi

GRILLED PORTOBELLO MUSHROOMS WITH SUN-DRIED TOMATOES, PANCETTA AND TOASTED BREADCRUMBS

serves 4 for a veggie main or 8 as an appy

30 minute cuisine

Spending quality time in the farmers market naturally leads to veggie-forward main meals. This is one of those. There's nothing better than meaty mushrooms, with a tangy, crunchy filling! You can serve these mushrooms as a first course, or as a late-night snack. The flavors are fantastic—everyone is a mushroom lover after tasting this dish!

1 cup panko breadcrumbs

2 tablespoons butter, melted, plus 2 more for sauce

1 (3.5-ounce) julienned sun-dried tomatoes packed in oil, drained, reserve 2 tablespoons of the oil

4 ounces pancetta, finely diced

4 large garlic cloves, minced, about 2 tablespoons

¼ cup Marsala wine

Juice of ½ medium lemon, about 2 tablespoons

1 teaspoon kosher salt

¼ teaspoon crushed red pepper flakes

2 tablespoons chopped fresh parsley

8 Portobello mushrooms, stem and gills removed

2 tablespoons olive oil

Preheat the oven to 350°. Mix the breadcrumbs with 2 tablespoons melted butter in a small bowl. Spread the crumbs onto a baking sheet. Toast the buttered crumbs until they begin to crisp, about 5 to 7 minutes. Remove and set aside.

Pour 2 tablespoons of the oil from the sun-dried tomatoes into a skillet over medium-high heat. Add the pancetta and cook until crisp. Use a slotted spoon to remove the pancetta to a platter lined with paper towels.

Add the sun-dried tomatoes to the skillet. Add the garlic and cook for 1 minute. Pour in the wine and simmer until most of the wine has disappeared, about 3 to 5 minutes. Pour in the lemon juice. Season with some of the salt and crushed red pepper. Turn off the heat and swirl in 2 tablespoons of butter. Stir in the parsley.

Heat a grill pan on high heat. Brush the mushrooms with olive oil on both sides. Season with salt and pepper. Grill the mushrooms, turning once, until they are just beginning to soften, about 5 minutes total. Transfer the mushrooms to a platter. Spoon the sun-dried tomato sauce into the mushroom caps. Sprinkle with pancetta and toasted breadcrumbs.

STEAK, PORTOBELLO, AND CARAMELIZED ONION SALAD WITH BLUE CHEESE AND WALNUTS

serves 4 to 6

45 minute cuisine

The unique foods sold at the farmer's market always pique my interest. You haven't seen it all until you see the "mushroom lady" at the farmer's market selling her mushroom log. Yes, log. It's a woodsy piece about the size of your forearm. The mushrooms grow out of the bark and you can pick them at will. For those of us that need our mushrooms . . . and need 'em now, for a couple dollars more you can purchase a small brown bag of mushrooms that just need a little cleaning. Which would you choose?

FOR MUSHROOMS:

2 tablespoons olive oil

6 Portobello mushrooms, stemmed, gills removed, cut into 1-inch thick strips, about 6 cups

1 teaspoon kosher salt

½ teaspoon coarse black pepper

¼ cup sherry wine

FOR ONION:

2 tablespoons butter

1 large red onion, peeled, cut in half and sliced, about 1 ½ cups

1 tablespoon balsamic vinegar

FOR STEAK:

1 tablespoon olive oil

1 (6 to 8-ounce) sirloin strip steak

FOR SALAD

1 large head romaine lettuce

1 pint baby heirloom tomatoes, halved

1 large shallot, peeled and finely diced, about 2 tablespoons

1 tablespoon Dijon-style mustard

1 tablespoon chopped fresh tarragon

¼ cup tarragon vinegar

½ cup olive oil

4 ounces blue cheese, crumbled, about 1 cup

1 (2-ounce) package walnut pieces, about 1/3 cup

Heat 2 tablespoons olive oil in a large skillet over medium-high heat. Add the mushrooms and DO NOT TOUCH them until they are golden brown on one side, about 3 to 4 minutes. Flip the mushrooms and cook until browned on the other side, about 3 to 4 minutes more. Season with some of the salt and pepper. Pour in the sherry. Continue cooking until the liquid disappears. Transfer the mushrooms to a platter.

Heat 2 tablespoons butter in the same skillet over medium heat. Add the onion and cook until soft and golden, about 3 to 4 minutes. Pour in the balsamic vinegar. Continue cooking until the onion is syrupy and the liquid disappears, about 15 to 20 minutes. Transfer the onion to the same platter as the mushrooms.

Heat 1 tablespoon olive oil in the same skillet over medium-high heat. Season the steak with salt and pepper. Place the steak into the skillet and cook until golden brown on one side, about 4 to 5 minutes. Flip the steak and cook on the second side until the steak is rare in the middle. Total cooking time is about 8 minutes per inch of thickness. Place the steak on the same platter as the cooked veggies.

Assemble the salad on a large platter. Slice the lettuce in half lengthwise and then cut into 1-inch strips. Lay the chopped lettuce onto the platter. Top with tomatoes.

Whisk together the shallot, mustard, fresh tarragon, and tarragon vinegar in a small bowl. Slowly whisk in ½ cup olive oil. Season with salt and pepper. Drizzle half of the dressing over the lettuce and tomatoes and toss.

Cut the steak, against the grain into thin slices. Lay the slices over the dressed salad. Top the steak with mushrooms and onions. Crumble the blue cheese over the top and scatter the walnuts over all. Drizzle the remaining dressing over the top of the salad.

COOK'S TIP

This is the perfect salad to use to clean out your produce drawer in the fridge. You can use leftover steak or chicken. Use Gorgonzola, feta, or Parmesan cheese. Switch romaine for Bibb or red leaf lettuce. Toasted pine nuts or almond slices work well and if you don't tell anyone, you can certainly sneak in bottled salad dressing. But, please, please cook those mushrooms to perfectly golden brown. It makes all the difference!

GRILLED CAP STEAKS WITH CREAMED SPINACH AND SAUTÉED MUSHROOMS

serves 4

30 minute cuisine

Much like Lucy and Ethel, sidekicks are meant to be fused together. Sue and I know this to be true! Traveling together bonds you heart and soul by discovering new experiences, becoming enthralled with new sights and digging into new cuisines. However, there comes that time when you look at each other and cry out, "There's no place like home!" You just gotta have a classic American-made meal. In my opinion, there's no greater combination of traditional American pairings than steak and creamed spinach. This dish elevates that friendship by adding perfectly cooked mushrooms to the spinach and hugging it to the most flavorful cut of beef you can find!

For steak:

4 (6 to 8-ounce) beef tenderloin steaks

2 tablespoons Worcestershire sauce

2 tablespoons soy sauce

1 tablespoon garlic powder

1 tablespoon onion powder

For spinach:

1 tablespoon olive oil

1 medium onion, peeled, cut in half and thinly sliced

2 pounds fresh spinach leaves, about 8 cups

1 teaspoon kosher salt

1 teaspoon coarse black pepper

2 tablespoons butter

2 tablespoons unbleached all-purpose flour

2 cups milk

½ teaspoon ground nutmeg

2 ounces Gruyere cheese, grated, about ½ cup

FOR MUSHROOMS:

2 tablespoons butter

½ pound fresh assorted wild mushrooms, sliced, about 2 cups

2 ounces Parmesan cheese, grated, about ½ cup

Marinate the steaks in a large bowl or dish by seasoning with Worcestershire, soy sauce, garlic and onion powders. (You can do this hours in advance and as much as overnight.)

Preheat the oven to 350°. Heat the olive oil in a large pan over medium heat. Add the onion and cook until soft. Add the spinach leaves and cook until they just begin to wilt. Season with some of the salt and pepper. Transfer the sautéed spinach to a colander and let it sit for several minutes to drain excess liquid. Pour the spinach into a medium size baking dish.

Melt 2 tablespoons butter in a saucepan over medium heat. Whisk in the flour and cook until bubbling, about 2 minutes. Slowly pour in the milk. Continue whisking until the sauce begins to thicken, about 5 minutes. Season with nutmeg, salt and pepper. Remove the sauce from the heat and stir in the Gruyere cheese. Pour the cream sauce over the spinach and toss to combine.

Use the same skillet that you used for the spinach to melt 2 tablespoons butter over medium-high heat. Add the mushrooms to the pan. DO NOT TOUCH THEM until they are deeply golden brown, about 4 to 5 minutes. Flip the mushrooms over and sauté on the second side until golden, about another 3 to 4 minutes. Sprinkle the mushrooms over the spinach. Season with salt and pepper. Top with grated Parmesan cheese. Bake the spinach casserole until the cheese is melted and the spinach is bubbling, about 20 minutes.

Prepare an outdoor grill, or heat up a grill pan on top of the stove to medium-high heat. Just before grilling, season the steaks with salt and pepper. Cap steaks will cook more quickly than their look-a-like filets. Grill for about 3 to 4 minutes per side and then check for doneness. Let the steaks rest for 5 minutes before serving. Scoop a generous portion of the mushroom topped cream spinach onto a plate. Set the cap steak alongside the veggies.

Nona's Garden

"KALE YEAH!" MUSHROOM AND CHILI PIZZA

serves 4

30 minute cuisine plus an hour to heat your pizza stone

You say flatbread, I say pizza, and whichever you choose, the result is gooey, cheesy, melty FUN! Prepared pizza crusts make the whole experience as easy as 1-2-3. Using a pizza stone heated as hot as you can get it helps to mimic those wood-fired oven crusts found in all the corner Italian trattorias. Everything tastes better on a pizza crust, but fresh veggies and artisanal cheeses take pizza to a whole new level. You can mix it up by using any variety of mushroom and your favorite green. It's all good.

2 tablespoons olive oil, plus more for garnish

½ pound fresh assorted wild mushrooms, sliced, about 2 cups

1 bunch kale leaves, sliced into 1-inch strips, about 4 cups

½ teaspoon dried red chili flakes

Zest of 1 medium lemon, about 2 teaspoons

1 teaspoon kosher salt

½ teaspoon coarse black pepper

Prepared whole wheat pizza dough

¾ cup ricotta cheese

2 tablespoons Pecorino cheese, grated, about ½ cup

Preheat the oven to 500°. Place a pizza stone into the oven and preheat for at least one hour.

Heat 2 tablespoons olive oil in a skillet over medium-high heat. Place the mushrooms into the pan and cook until golden on one side, about 5 minutes. Turn and cook until the mushrooms are well browned, about 2 minutes more. Add the kale and cook until wilted, about 5 minutes more. Stir in chili flakes and lemon juice. Season with some of the salt and pepper.

Roll the pizza dough into a 12 x 10-inch rectangle. Place the dough onto a pizza peel dusted with flour. Semolina flour or cornmeal will work well to keep the pizza from sticking to the peel. Or, sprinkle a baking sheet with a bit of olive oil and stretch your dough into the pan.

Spread the ricotta cheese onto the dough. Place the mushroom-kale topping over the cheese. Slide the pizza from the peel onto the preheated pizza stone. Bake until the crust is golden and cooked through, about 10 to 15 minutes for a large pizza.

Remove the pizza from the oven and sprinkle with Pecorino cheese and a drizzle of olive oil. Use a pizza cutter or sharp knife to cut into squares.

MUSHROOM BOLOGNESE SAUCE OVER PASTA RAGS

serves 4 to 6

45 minute cuisine

Drop into any Italian corner trattoria, and you will find Nona's family recipe for hearty Bolognese on the menu. The sauce is full of slowly simmering meats, stewed tomatoes, spices and cheese. This veggie-forward sauce has the same flavors, but we use mushrooms in place of meat and load the sauce full of diced up veggies. (It's a perfect way to use those extra veggies you find in the back of the fridge drawer.) This Bolognese benefits from low and slow simmering to encourage those spongy mushrooms to suck up all the flavors. All mushrooms work for this recipe, so don't turn away from the exotic ones you see in the farmer's market.

1 medium onion, peeled and cut into pieces, about 1 cup

3 medium celery stalks, cut into pieces, about 1 cup

2 large carrots, peeled and cut into pieces, about 1 cup

1 tablespoon olive oil

¼ pound bacon, cut into 1-inch pieces, about 4 to 5 slices

1 small zucchini, cut into pieces, about 1 cup

1 yellow squash, cut into pieces, about 1 cup

¾ pound fresh assorted wild mushrooms, about 3 cups

4 large garlic cloves, peeled and minced

1 teaspoon kosher salt

1 teaspoon coarse black pepper

½ cup red wine

2 cups homemade beef stock, or low sodium beef broth

1 (6-ounce) can tomato paste

1 tablespoon granulated sugar (shhhh! secret ingredient)

1 teaspoon ground oregano

1 teaspoon dried basil

1 teaspoon garlic powder

1 pound fresh pasta sheets, torn into 3 x 1-inch "rags" (substitute with fresh fettuccine)

2 ounces Parmesan cheese, grated, about ½ cup

Place the onion, celery and carrots in the bowl of a food processor and pulse to finely chop. Heat olive oil in a deep pot over medium-high heat. Add the bacon and cook until golden. Use a slotted spoon or wire skimmer to remove the bacon to a paper towel lined plated. Place the diced onion, celery and carrots into the pot. Place the zucchini and squash into the bowl of the food processor. Pulse to finely chop. Pour these veggies into the pot. Place the mushrooms into the bowl of the food processor and pulse to finely chop. Add the mushrooms and garlic to the pot. Season the vegetables with salt and pepper. Cook the veggies until they are soft and browned and just beginning to stick to the bottom of the pot, about 5 to 8 minutes.

Reduce the heat to medium-low and pour the wine into the pot. Stir, scraping the bottom of the pan and cook until the liquid disappears. Pour 1 cup of the broth into the skillet. Stir in the tomato paste and sprinkle the sugar over top. Season with oregano, basil and garlic powder. Stir in the bacon and remaining broth. Simmer the sauce for 5 minutes. Reduce the heat and simmer for at least 20 to 30 minutes. At this point you can cool the Bolognese to room temperature, cover the pot and chill overnight. This will also encourage those little spongy mushrooms to soak up the flavors. When you are ready to serve, reheat the sauce over low to medium-low heat.

Cook the pasta in boiling, salted water until just al dente, about 3 to 5 minutes for fresh pasta. Drain the pasta (reserving some of the liquid). Pour the pasta into a large shallow bowl. Ladle some of the Bolognese sauce over the top and toss. Top with Parmesan cheese. Serve additional sauce on the side. If the sauce is too thick, you can add some of the reserved pasta water to the pot.

. . . And Everything Nice

PAPPARDELLE WITH KALE PESTO, SPINACH, AND PORTOBELLO MUSHROOMS

serves 4 to 6
30 minute cuisine

Pasta dishes in Italy are lightly dressed and highly garnished. I am blown-away by the difference between an authentic Italian dish of pasta and the ones we get here in the states. I strive for that lightness and find that the secret is to work with the freshest ingredients you can find. Use fresh pasta when you can and add pasta water to thin heavier sauces. The other secret is to serve the dish as quickly as you can, so that the pasta retains its softness and is buoyed by the sauce, not drowned in it. This simple peasant-style meal comes together quickly, using whatever greens you have from the market and whatever cheese you have in the fridge.

FOR PESTO:

1 pound kale, about 4 cups
4 garlic cloves, peeled
½ cup pine nuts, toasted, plus ½ cup more for pasta
2 ounces Parmesan cheese, about ½ cup
½ cup olive oil
1 teaspoon kosher salt
½ teaspoon coarse black pepper

FOR PASTA:

2 Portobello mushrooms, stems and gills removed
1 tablespoon olive oil
12 ounces fresh pappardelle pasta
1 pound fresh spinach leaves, about 4 cups
2 ounces Pecorino cheese, grated, about ½ cup

Make the pesto by placing the kale, garlic, ½ cup pine nuts and parmesan cheese into the bowl of a food processor. Pulse to combine. With the blade running, slowly drizzle in the olive oil to form a thick paste. Season with some of the salt and pepper.

Preheat the oven to 400°. Brush both sides of the mushrooms with olive oil and season with salt and pepper. Place into a baking dish and bake until soft, about 10 minutes. Cut the mushrooms into thin slices.

Cook the pasta in a pot of salted, boiling water until al dente, just a couple of minutes for fresh pasta.

Place the pesto into a large bowl and add the spinach leaves. Reserving 2 cups of the pasta water, drain the pasta and place into the bowl with the pesto. Ladle in 1 cup pasta water into the pasta and toss to combine. (You can add more water if the sauce is too thick.) Place the mushrooms on top of the pasta. Sprinkle the dish with Pecorino cheese and top with extra pine nuts.

Stocked Market

KALE SALAD WITH STRAWBERRIES AND GOAT CHEESE AND A NUTTY TOPPER

serves 4 to 6 as a side salad

30 minute cuisine

When you think farmer's market, you think veggies. But, in truth the farmers are humanely raising animals and poultry too—using eggs and milk to create other wares for sale. One of my favorite stops are cheese stalls. All sorts of varieties are offered for tasting. There's a cheese maker at my favorite North Carolina Farmers Market, who produces so many variations of goat cheese, it's hard to choose. You can taste them all, if you are patient enough to wait your turn. This salad takes advantage of the freshest kale, sweetest strawberries and creamiest artisanal cheese at the farmer's market and tops it all off with a sugary, crusty nut blend.

FOR NUTTY TOPPER:

1 tablespoons butter

1 tablespoon brown sugar

¼ cup roasted, salted and shelled pistachios

¼ cup roasted, salted sunflower seeds

¼ cup roasted, and salted Pepitas (pumpkin seeds)

FOR DRESSING:

½ large lemon juiced, about 2 tablespoons

1 tablespoon Dijon-mustard

1 teaspoons honey

½ teaspoon kosher salt

½ teaspoon coarse black pepper

½ cup olive oil

FOR SALAD:

1 bunch kale, stems removed, leaves chopped, about 3 to 4 cups

1 pint fresh strawberries, stems removed and sliced, about 2 cups

4 to 5 medium radishes, sliced thin, about 1 cup

4 ounces goat cheese, crumbled, about ½ cup

Melt the butter and brown sugar in a medium skillet over medium-high heat. Stir in the pistachios, sunflower seeds and pepitas. Cook until the nuts are just beginning to toast, about 2 to 3 minutes. Pour the nuts and seeds onto a parchment paper lined rimmed baking sheet to cool. Place the lemon juice, mustard and honey in a small bowl. Season with some of the salt and pepper. Whisk in the olive oil. Place the kale into a salad bowl and pour the dressing over the top. Let the salad sit on the counter at room temperature for 20 to 30 minutes to allow the kale leaves to soften. Add the strawberries, radishes and goat cheese to the salad bowl. Toss with the dressed kale and sprinkle the nutty topper over the top.

FALL IN LOVE SLAW

serves 6 or more

30 minute cuisine

As with most American tourists, when Sue and I travel, we tend to visit different countries during the warmer months of their seasons. So, for me, when the weather begins to turn a little cooler and the leaves on the trees begin to change their colors, I most often find myself in autumn in the Carolinas. Fall farmers markets offer different veggies than spring or summer markets. You'll find pumpkins and gourds, large heads of cabbage, apples and beets and all varieties of root veggies. When fall knocks on the door and summer still has a hold on my heart, I tend to combine my love for both in the dishes I bring to the table. This recipe is just one of those. Summer slaw is crisp and bright and goes perfectly with grilled burgers and hotdogs. Fall slaw is a bit richer, earthier, and is an excellent side dish for slow-roasted, braised beef or pork. When you start to feel a chill in the air, it might be time to visit your local Farmers market to take advantage of the harvest root veggies and sweet apples.

FOR SLAW:

1 medium Napa cabbage

2 medium carrots, peeled

3 medium celery ribs

2 large apples, peeled and cored

½ pound kale leaves

FOR DRESSING:

1 cup mayonnaise

½ cup sour cream

1/3 cup apple cider vinegar

2 tablespoons granulated sugar

2 teaspoon ground fennel seed

2 teaspoons ground cumin

1 teaspoon kosher salt

½ teaspoon coarse black pepper

Cut the cabbage, carrots, celery and apples into pieces and shred using the shred blade of a food processor or a box grater. Place the shredded vegetables into a large bowl. Remove the shredding blade and insert the chopping blade in the food processor. Place the kale into the bowl and pulse to completely chop the leaves. Add the kale to the other veggies in the bowl. Whisk together the mayonnaise, sour cream, vinegar, sugar, fennel, and cumin. Taste and season with salt and pepper. Pour the dressing over the vegetables in the bowl and toss. Refrigerate for at least one hour to allow all the flavors to blend together and the sauce to soak into the veggies. The slaw is great right from the fridge, but I like it even better when it sits out on the counter for 20 minutes or so. You can taste all the individual components just a little bit more.

SWISS CHARD STRATA WITH ARTISANAL SAUSAGE

serves 8 to 10

20 minute cuisine plus 1 hour baking

Sue raised her six kids as vegetarians. While my three sons, hubby, and I . . . well, we loved us some meat! Today, one of my favorite finds at the local farmers market is the wide variety of artisanal sausages. It reminds me of the sausages and hams that you find hanging in the central markets in Spain and Italy. It's my goal to taste them all! I found myself with so many different types of sausage in my fridge, I was running out of ways to use them. Until . . . I remembered my holiday favorite brunch dish . . . strata! Here's a dish, ideal for using up all kinds of leftovers. In this recipe, leftover bread, greens and meats find their way to a light and fluffy casserole, sure to please.

2 tablespoons olive oil, divided

1 pound fresh artisanal sausage, casing removed

1 pound Swiss chard, trimmed and chopped, about 5 to 6 cups

1 teaspoon kosher salt

1 teaspoon coarse black pepper

10 large eggs

3 cups milk

4 to 5 green onions, sliced, about ½ cup

½ cup chopped fresh parsley

½ teaspoon ground nutmeg

1 (1-pound) loaf Artisanal bread, cut into 1-inch cubes

12 ounces Gruyere cheese, grated, about 3 cups

Heat 1 tablespoon olive oil in a large skillet over medium-high heat. Add the sausage and cook until browned and crumbly. Transfer to a paper towel lined platter. Heat 1 more tablespoon olive oil in the same skillet over medium-high heat. Add the chard and sauté until wilted, about 5 minutes. Season with some of the salt and pepper. Remove the pan from the heat.

Whisk together the eggs and milk in a large bowl. Stir in the green onions and parsley. Stir in nutmeg and season with salt and pepper. Place half of the bread cubes into a large 13 x

9 x 2-inch baking dish that has been coated with vegetable oil spray. Top with half of the sausage and half of the chard. Place 1 cup of the cheese on top. Layer the rest of the bread into the dish. Cover with the remaining sausage, chard and one more cup of cheese. Pour the milk and egg custard over all. Use your hands to gently submerge all the bread cubes. Toss the remaining cheese over the top of the casserole. Let the casserole sit on your counter for at least 30 minutes (or overnight in the fridge) allowing the bread to soak up the custard. Preheat the oven to 350°. Place the baking dish into the oven and bake until the top is golden, and the center is set, about 1 hour. Let strata rest for 15 minutes before cutting into squares.

ASIAN CHICKEN BIBB LETTUCE WRAPS

serves a crowd for an appy or 4 for dinner

30 minute cuisine

Whether you're gathering together the kids for a family supper or rounding up your friends for a beer on game day, finger food is the way to go. Tender, buttery Bibb lettuce heads are prevalent at your local fresh market and are the star for this flavorful dish. The sauce is truly a winning combination of Asian spices. But the real fun in the dish is its messiness. There is absolutely no way to wrap this lettuce around these yummy ingredients and guarantee a smooth passage from plate to mouth. If you are like Sue and me, you'll come to see that this is the best part of the dish. "Bib up" and get ready for a meal full of giggles.

FOR CHICKEN:

½ cup hoisin sauce

¼ cup soy sauce

2 tablespoons rice wine vinegar

1 tablespoon Sriracha (hot chili sauce)

1 (1-inch) piece ginger, peeled and grated, about 1 tablespoon

2 pounds boneless, skinless chicken thighs

FOR DIPPING SAUCE:

3 tablespoons soy sauce

3 tablespoons rice wine vinegar

1 tablespoon honey

1 (1-inch) piece ginger, peeled and grated, about 1 tablespoon

2 tablespoons sesame seeds

1 tablespoon sesame oil

FOR WRAPS:

2 tablespoons sesame oil

3 medium celery ribs, sliced, about 1 cup

4 to 5 green onions, thinly sliced, about ½ cup

2 tablespoons peanuts, chopped

Outer leaves from 2 large heads Bibb Lettuce, reserve smaller leaves for tomorrow's salad

Whisk together ½ cup hoisin sauce, ¼ cup soy sauce, 2 tablespoons rice wine vinegar, Sriracha sauce and 1 tablespoon ginger in a bowl. Chop the chicken into ¼-inch cubes and place into the bowl. Marinate the chicken in the sauce for at least 20 minutes or covered and refrigerated for several hours.

Whisk together 3 tablespoons soy sauce, 3 tablespoons rice wine vinegar, honey, 1 tablespoon ginger, sesame seeds, and 1 tablespoon sesame oil in a bowl. Set this dipping sauce on the counter while you move onto the chicken.

Heat 2 tablespoons sesame oil in a large skillet over medium heat. Add the chicken and the marinade. Stir in the celery. Cook, stirring occasionally, until the chicken is browned and cooked through, about 5 minutes. Add the green onions and peanuts. Toss to combine.

Tear the outer leaves from the heads of lettuce and stack them up on a platter. Serve the chicken in a bowl. Place a spoonful of chicken into the center of a lettuce leaf. Roll the lettuce around the filling like you would a burrito. Serve dipping sauce on the side. Encourage everyone to eat with their fingers and laugh out loud at all the dribbles.

COOK'S TIP

There are so many FUN versions of this dish that you can try out on your friends and family. Those lettuce leaves can wrap around taco spiced ground beef with diced cubes of avocado and tomato added in. You can also use barbecue-sauced pulled pork with some shredded carrots and cabbage as a filling. Why not try chili-seasoned shredded chicken with yellow rice and black beans? Then there is chopped, cooked shrimp flavored with a little Old Bay seasoning served with a little hot pepper sauce on the side. Oh, I could go on and on and on!! And, I do because it's all about the sloppy giggles in this dish!

DAINTY EGG SALAD TARTINES WITH SLICED RADISHES, BASIL AND WATERCRESS

serves 8

30 minute cuisine

I don't know why, but the snappy heat when you bite down on a crisp, farm fresh radish is just so much sharper than a grocery store radish. The taste is downright feisty! This is why fresh radishes are perfect on these simple open-face sandwiches. Tartines (the fancy French word for dainty sammies) are perfect for a light lunch, tea party or appetizer. In this version, the heat of the radish is tempered by creamy egg salad and mild, buttery greens. How about adding a sip of chilled Rosé wine? Now we have a little somethin', somethin'!

FOR EGG SALAD:

8 large eggs, hardboiled, peeled

¼ cup mayonnaise

¼ cup sour cream

2 green onions, white part only, minced, about 2 tablespoons

2 tablespoons pale green inner leaves of celery, chopped

1 small shallot, peeled and minced, about 1 tablespoon

2 teaspoons Dijon-style mustard

1 teaspoon honey

½ teaspoon kosher salt

½ teaspoon coarse black pepper

FOR TARTINES:

8 (1-inch thick) slices artisanal whole grain bread

1 cup watercress leaves

1 bunch fresh basil leaves

4 large radishes, thinly sliced

Place the eggs into the bowl of a food processor. Pulse to finely chop. Transfer to a medium bowl. Fold in the mayonnaise, sour cream, green onions, celery leaves, shallot, mustard and honey. Taste and season with salt and pepper.

Lay the bread onto your work surface. Mound the watercress onto the bread. Top with egg salad. Top the egg salad with basil leaves and radish slices. Cut each in half diagonally. Sprinkle a bit of additional salt over the radishes.

COOK'S TIP

To hard cook eggs perfectly, start with a pan of cold water. Lay the eggs into the pan in a single layer. Cover the pan, bring the water to a boil and then immediately turn off the heat. Turn on a timer and let the eggs sit, covered for exactly 11 minutes. Transfer the eggs to ice water to cool and refrigerate until you are ready to peel and eat.

GRAMMY'S CABBAGE ROLLS

serves 6 to 8

45 minute cuisine plus 2 hours in slow cooker

In the fall, you can find basketball-size heads of green cabbage at the farmer's market. These are so large, that it's hard to get them from market stall to straw basket to home without some help from a friend. When I see these humongous cabbages, I think of my delicate polish Grammy. I'm reminded of smaller heads lining her kitchen counter, preparing to be dunked in steaming pots of boiling water, in preparation for her favorite dish. She made savory, sweet cabbage rolls in large batches, and then "put them up" in jars to eat later. A slow cooker makes pretty easy work of the process today, guaranteeing that a lot less effort goes into preparing them, than when Grammy and I worked at the task. I haven't visited Poland . . . yet. But, I think I have the taste of Poland in my heart, because of my Grammy's cabbage rolls.

FOR CABBAGE:

1 large head cabbage, cored

1 tablespoon olive oil

1 large onion, peeled and finely chopped, about 1 ½ cup

2 cloves garlic, peeled and minced, about 1 teaspoon

1 pounds ground sirloin

2 cups cooked white rice

½ cup golden raisins

2 tablespoons chopped fresh parsley

1 teaspoon kosher salt

½ teaspoon coarse black pepper

FOR SAUCE:

1 (14.5-ounce can) crushed tomatoes

½ cup white grape juice

1 tablespoon white wine vinegar

Bring a large pot of water to boil over high heat. Drop the cabbage into the hot water and cook until the leaves begin to soften, about 3 to 5 minutes. Remove the cabbage to your work surface and remove the top leaves, about 16. Use a sharp knife to trim the thick vein so that it is even with the rest of the leaf. Do not remove the vein, you want a flat surface.

Heat the olive oil in a large skillet over medium-high heat. Add the onion and garlic and cook until soft, about 5 minutes. Add the ground sirloin and cook until brown and crumbly. Remove the skillet from the heat. Stir in the cooked rice, raisins and parsley. Season with salt and pepper.

Place one leaf onto your work surface. Spoon about ¼ cup of the sirloin-rice filling into the center of the leaf. Fold the edges up and over the filling and roll up to small cylinders. Place into the bottom of a slow cooker. Continue with the remaining rolls.

Stir together the tomatoes, grape juice and vinegar. Season with salt and pepper. Pour the sauce over the rolls. Cook on the high setting for 2 hours (or the low setting for 6 to 8 hours) and keep warm until ready to serve.

After Market Leftovers

Since you are only using the top leaves for this dish, you'll have some extra cabbage left over. To use up those leaves, here are a couple of my favorite cabbage dishes.

My dad's all-time favorite dish was slowly braised pork (usually spareribs) served with mashed potatoes that are topped with sauerkraut. Sure, you can open a bag or jar of sauerkraut and add it to the pan, but my favorite way to serve sauerkraut is to add sautéed onions and cabbage to the mix. Simply cook thin slices of onion and cabbage in olive oil until soft. Add these to prepared sauerkraut and place this mix into the bottom of a roasting pan. Place the spare ribs on top and cook in a low and slow oven. You can add a cup of beer to the pan for an extra little bit of yumm!

Buttered cabbage is a Southern side that goes perfectly with fried chicken. Cut the cabbage into thin slices. Cook in butter and toss with some bacon and black pepper before serving.

I actually ate Colcannon when we visited Ireland. It was served with some perfectly poached salmon and was memorable! Colcannon is a mix of potatoes and cabbage. To prepare the dish, stir sautéed cabbage into whipped potatoes. Add in some bacon and fresh parsley. It's pretty darn good!

Cabbage Commute

BRAISED RAINBOW CHARD

serves 4

30 minute cuisine

Trust me, farmers markets across these great United States are thrilled to offer you huge piles of gorgeous chard. The leaves are large, and the stems are vibrantly colored. Slow braising in a lemony flavored broth adds depth, flavor and ensures that both the leaves and the delicate stems are tender and delicious! This is a perfect side dish for meat, chicken or fish, but I just love, love, love it served with a poached egg on top for a good-for-you breakfast. (Sue agrees!)

1 bunch rainbow chard, about 1 pound (substitute with Swiss chard, mustard or collard greens)

2 tablespoons olive oil

1 medium onion, peeled and thinly sliced

4 garlic cloves, peeled and smashed

¼ teaspoon crushed red pepper flakes

1 teaspoon kosher salt

½ teaspoon coarse black pepper

½ teaspoon ground nutmeg

Zest of 1 medium lemon, about 2 teaspoons

Juice of 1 medium lemon, about 3 tablespoons

2 cups homemade chicken stock or prepared low sodium broth

To chop the leaves, trim the tough bottom stems from the chard. The stems in the center of the leaves are tender. Chop these with the leaves. Roll the leaves around each other (like a cigar) and cut into 1-inch strips.

Heat the olive oil in a large skillet over medium heat. Add the onion and cook until soft. Add the garlic and crushed red pepper flakes and cook for 2 minutes more. Add the chard in batches using tongs to continually toss the leaves with the onion. Season with some of the salt and pepper. Stir in the nutmeg, lemon zest and juice. Pour in the chicken stock and bring to a boil. Reduce the heat to low and simmer the chard in the broth until the leaves are tender and most of the liquid disappears, about 5 to 8 minutes.

COOK'S TIP

There is little difference between Swiss chard and rainbow chard, except that the stems of the rainbow chard are vibrantly colored orange, red, and yellow. The tender parts of the stems are closest to the leaves. Make sure that you cook the chard long enough so that the colorful stem pieces are very tender.

ROOTS AND SEEDS

/ro͞ot/

noun

1. the part of a plant that attaches it to the ground or to a support, typically underground, conveying water and nourishment to the rest of the plant via numerous branches and fibers.
   synonyms: rootstock, tuber, rootlet
   "cacti have deep and spreading roots"

/sēd/

noun

plural noun: seeds

1. a flowering plant's unit of reproduction, capable of developing into another such plant.
   synonyms: pip, stone, kernel; ovule
   "apple seeds"

Sophia's Song

Sue and I have a lot in common. We love our families, fiercely. We love our friends, strongly. You could say we're spiritual. We're definitely foodies. Sue and I love traveling and we love golf. When we have the opportunity to combine any or many of our loves, we grab the bull by the horn and join in. Thus, when a group of our friends booked a river cruise to the South of France to sip wine and play golf . . . well, guess who were the first ones on deck?

The ship was small and quaint. The rooms were even smaller and not so quaint. Hubby and I had to take turns dressing by one of us leaving the room, so the other could move around. There were more than one bruise from bumping into things and each other. But we found that the allure of a river cruise is not the accommodations . . . it's the ability to get immersed in the local culture. We began our trip in the small city of Biarritz which sits alongside the two rivers we traversed, the Adour and the Nive. Because of its proximity to Spain and the river, we found the food to be light, fresh, and delicious. Specialties of the area included shellfish, like shrimp and mussels, in a spicy sauce studded with dried fruits. Veal and pork are the meats of choice and are most often accompanied by delicately diced root veggies.

The city boasted one or two luxurious hotels that are perched on the sea, and houses that serve as summer homes for wealthy Parisians. Here, we found rocky terrain with crashing waves that are both mysterious and alluring. Perhaps this is why surfers are drawn to the city.

We played golf among private vineyards that were set along the rivers. The landscapes are a contrast of lush, green grass and foliage on one side with stark grapevines in rows of dark soil on the other. Instead of the usual hot dog at the turn, we sipped crisp, white wine and tasted pungent goat cheese. Our scores didn't improve, but we certainly looked forward to the 19th hole!

Sue's painting *Sophia's Song* reminds me of the markets we passed on the streets in the small towns we visited. Less one central market and more commonly street vendors, groups of men sharing their wares while they smoked cigars and played checkers. Oysters and mussels were more common than potatoes and beets. Trays of pre-made croissant sandwiches, delicate, bite-size pastries and home-made cheeses are sold from card tables set up on the sidewalks next to the vendors' parked cars.

Our trip ended in the more cosmopolitan city of Bordeaux. There, the influences of French food were evident. We tasted delicate beef tartare served alongside pommes frites and creamy, velvety vichyssoise that was delightfully light and fresh. We tasted dishes rich with bone marrow and lamb loins, and simple dishes prepared with fresh seafood and hints of peppery spices. And then there was the wine . . .

Our trip was made special by the food and the golf games, but most importantly by the friendships we initiated and bloomed. One pal brought along his guitar and each night on deck we sang folk songs by the light of the moon and the scent of the sea. One pal was a true wine connoisseur and delighted us with tastes of obscure wines and the stories of their origins. One pal, and this was my favorite, led me through the pouring rain, through the streets and into a bistro that served the best darn cheeseburger I have ever eaten, just to feed my craving! Now that's what friends are for!

CHILLED BEET SOUP

Serves 4

60 minutes to roast beets, 20 minutes for soup plus some time in the fridge for chillin'

Sue and I met on a trip to Russia. We bonded over foie gras on the cruise ship, but Moscow was a different story. I found the tourist experience to be more subdued than the other countries we've visited. Sidewalks are policed in certain areas, and if you step off, a uniformed guard blows a whistle in your direction. Likewise, there was not a lot of English spoken in the local restaurants. I remember walking down the street from our cosmopolitan hotel and into a corner diner where no one spoke English and the menu had no pictures. The only food I knew was Borscht, so we ordered it. It was served with dense dark bread and a slather of creamy butter. It was delish! There was no language barrier in that delightful dish, just smiles all around.

1 pound beets, about 5 to 6 (red beets are traditional for this soup, but use any kind)

1 tablespoon olive oil

1 parsnip, peeled and diced, about 1 cup

1 medium onion, peeled and diced, about 1 cup

1 whole leek, cut in half, thoroughly rinsed, thinly sliced, tough dark green leaves, discarded, about 1 cup

3 celery stalks, sliced, about 1 cup

2 medium carrots, peeled, trimmed and chopped, about 1 cup

1 medium apple, peeled, cored and diced, about 1 cup

½ teaspoon ground marjoram

1 quart homemade vegetable stock, or prepared low sodium vegetable broth

¼ cup chopped fresh dill

2 to 3 tablespoons red wine vinegar

1 teaspoon kosher salt

½ teaspoon coarse black pepper

Sour cream

Preheat the oven to 400°. Wrap the beets in aluminum foil and place into a baking dish. Bake until soft, about 45 to 60 minutes. Remove the baking dish from the oven. Cool the beets to room temperature. Rub the peel from the beets using paper towels. Chop the beets.

Heat the olive oil in a deep pot over medium-high heat. Add the parsnip, onion, leek, celery, carrots and apple to the pan. Cook until the vegetables begin to soften, about 5 to 10 minutes. Add the chopped beets to the pot. Season with marjoram. Pour in the broth and simmer the soup until all the vegetables are soft, about 15 minutes more. Add the dill to the soup. Cool the soup to room temperature. Use an immersion blender, food processor or blender to puree the soup. Stir in the vinegar. Taste and season with salt and pepper. Place the pureed soup into the refrigerator and chill for at least four hours. Ladle the soup into bowls and garnish with a swirl of sour cream and additional fresh dill.

YOU LOOK RADISHING

SPICY THAI PESTO CROSTINI WITH PICKLED RADISHES

serves a crowd

40 minute cuisine

The fusion of different flavors is what tasting different cuisines is really about. Ingredients that don't appear together in our culture are often traditionally paired in others. If you take that concept into your home kitchen, you give yourself permission to become creative in your cooking. Just like Sue's creativity on canvas, your cuisine will have a taste all its own! For this dish, peppery, crisp radishes are elevated by pickling them in a quick brine. I put these together with an Asian-flavored pesto on some crunchy crostini and you have a first-course appy that makes you say, "Whaaaaaaat!"

FOR RADISHES:

⅔ cup white wine vinegar

½ cup granulated sugar

2 teaspoons kosher salt

1 bunch radishes, about 12, tops removed, thinly sliced

FOR PESTO:

1 pound baby spinach leaves, about 4 cups

1 medium sweet long red pepper, seeded and chopped, about 2 tablespoons

1 stalk lemongrass, outer layer discarded, chopped, about 2 tablespoons

1 (½-inch) piece fresh ginger, peeled and grated, about 2 teaspoons

1 serrano chili, seeded and chopped, about 2 tablespoons

2 tablespoons roasted, salted peanuts

4 large garlic cloves, peeled, about 1 tablespoon

2 tablespoons fish sauce

½ teaspoon ground coriander

½ teaspoon coarse black pepper

⅓ cup vegetable oil, plus more for baguette slices

For crostini:

1 small baguette cut into diagonal ½-inch slices

Whisk together the vinegar, sugar and 2 teaspoons salt and pour over the radishes in a small bowl. Set aside at least 30 minutes. Place the spinach, sweet pepper, lemongrass, ginger, serrano chili, peanuts, garlic, fish sauce, and coriander into the bowl of a food processor. Pulse to form a paste. With the machine running, slowly pour in the vegetable oil. Taste and season with salt and pepper. Heat a grill pan over medium-high heat. Brush each side of the baguette slices with vegetable oil. Grill until golden on both sides, about 1 to 2 minutes per side. Drain the radishes from the brine. Spread each baguette slice with pesto. Fan several radish slices on top.

Waltz of the Watermelon

PICKLED BEET AND WATER-MELON CARPACCIO

serves a crowd

30 minute cuisine plus 1 hour or so for roasting

I ordered this dish at a super fancy restaurant in Las Vegas. The chef de cuisine served it on a beautifully chilled plate that kept the beets and the fruit fabulously cold. It was presented with a flare and a high price tag. I must admit, it's a stunning first course offering, a burst of excitement in each bite. This is my home cook's version of the dish. Not only is it pretty darn delicious, but you can serve it to about twenty-five of your friends for the same price as that fancy, schmancy restaurant charges.

FOR PICKLED BEETS:

4 medium red beets, tops removed, scrubbed

4 medium golden beets, tops removed, scrubbed

½ red onion, peeled and thinly sliced

4 cups apple cider vinegar

1 cup granulated sugar

1 teaspoon kosher salt

1 teaspoon coarse ground pepper

FOR VINAIGRETTE:

¼ cup white balsamic vinegar

Juice from 1 large orange, about ¼ cup

1 medium shallot, peeled, about 1 tablespoon

1 tablespoon Dijon-style mustard

½ cup olive oil

FOR CARPACCIO:

6 thin slices prosciutto

¼ medium watermelon

½ fennel bulb, tough outer parts remove, (save a few of the top leaves for garnish)

Preheat the oven to 350°. Wrap the beets in aluminum foil and place them into a baking dish. Bake until the beets just begin to soften, about 1 to 1 ½ hours. Remove the baking dish from the oven and cool the beets to room temperature.

Remove the skin from the beets by rubbing with paper towels. Use a mandoline slicer to slice the beets as thin as possible. Place the beets into a bowl with red onion slices. Whisk together the apple cider vinegar and granulated sugar in a separate bowl until the sugar is completely dissolved. Stir in the salt and pepper. Pour this liquid over the beets and onions and gently toss so that all the slices are coated in the brine. Set the bowl aside for at least 30 minutes. (You can cover and refrigerate the beets at this point for several days.)

Pour the balsamic vinegar and orange juice into a blender. Add the shallot and mustard. Pulse to emulsify. With the machine running, slowly drizzle in the olive oil. Season with additional salt and pepper.

Place your serving platter into the freezer to chill.

Increase the oven temperature to 400°. Place the prosciutto slices onto a parchment line baking sheet. Bake until the prosciutto is crisp, about 5 to 8 minutes. Remove the baking sheet from the oven and cool the crisp prosciutto to room temperature.

Cut the watermelon into ¼-inch slices. Use a 3-inch round biscuit cutter to cut medallions from the watermelon slices. Use the mandoline slicer to thinly shave the fennel bulb.

Remove your serving platter from the freezer and brush it with olive oil. Remove the beet slices from the brine. Lay the beets and watermelon onto the plater, slightly overlapping each round. Break the prosciutto into pieces and scatter over the top. Scatter thin slices of fennel over all. Drizzle just a spoonful or two of vinaigrette over the carpaccio. Garnish with the fresh green leaves cut from the fennel.

CELERY ROOT VICHYSSOISE WITH GREMOLATA OIL AND CHOPPED HAZELNUTS

serves 4 to 6

60 minute cuisine

Classic Vichyssoise is a cold French soup that begins with leeks, adds potatoes, and then doubles itself with rich cream. It's hubby's favorite, and we sipped it in every French bistro we visited. Interestingly enough, unlike the variations of Spanish gazpacho, no matter where you order Vichyssoise, you are pretty much guaranteed to get the exact same soup as the time you ordered it before. My take on the French soup is a tad less rich than its namesake. I like the addition of celery root (different from stalks of celery) because it is less dense, with brighter flavor than that good ole' American spud. I use the ingredients found in "gremolata", a pretty word for lemon zest, parsley and garlic, to make a flavorful oil and add a crunch of toasted hazelnuts as a special touch. Do the same and make this soup the headlining event of your farm-fresh supper.

FOR SOUP:

2 teaspoons butter

1 whole leek, washed, white parts only, chopped, about 1 cup

6 cloves garlic, peeled and crushed

2 celery roots, peeled and cut into 1-inch pieces, about 4 cups

2 large Idaho potatoes, peeled and cut into 1-inch pieces, about 4 cups

1 ounce Parmesan cheese rind, about a 2-inch piece

6 cups homemade chicken stock or prepared low sodium broth

1 teaspoon kosher salt

½ teaspoon white pepper

½ cup heavy cream

FOR GARNISH:

2 tablespoons chopped fresh parsley

Zest of 1 medium lemon, about 2 teaspoons

2 cloves garlic, peeled and minced

¼ cup olive oil

2 tablespoons hazelnuts, toasted, chopped

Melt the butter in a large pot over medium heat. Add the leek and crushed garlic and cook until the leeks are soft, about 5 minutes. Add the celery root, potatoes and chunk of cheese. Pour in the chicken stock and bring to a simmer. Cover the pot and simmer the soup until the celery root and potatoes are tender, about 20 to 30 minutes. Season with salt and pepper. Turn off the heat.

Mix together the parsley, lemon zest, and minced garlic with a small whisk. Slowly whisk in the olive oil to form a loose paste.

Remove the Parmesan rind from the soup and discard. Use a food processor, blender or immersion blender to puree the soup. You want the soup to be very smooth. If you are one of those crazy perfectionist types, you can pass the pureed soup through a fine sieve to get rid of any large pieces. Pour the soup into a large bowl. Cover with plastic wrap and chill for at least four hours or overnight.

Remove the chilled soup from the fridge. Stir in the cream. Taste and season with additional salt if needed.

Ladle the soup into bowls. Use a spoon to drizzle the gremolata oil on the top of the soup. Sprinkle with chopped toasted hazelnuts.

COOK'S TIP

Celery root is also called celeriac (although they are really not the same thing) and are usually found near the turnips and beets in the grocery store. The bulb is browned and craggy looking and has a flavor that is a cross between celery and parsley. Today, you can find celery root that has already been peeled and diced for you. But, chopping your own, fresh from the market, is the way to go!

Green Tears for You

TEX-MEX EGG ROLLS WITH ROASTED TOMATILLO SALSA

makes about 20 eggrolls

45 minute cuisine

Just like Sue's and my crazy friendship, and our travels to and from all the great destinations the world has to offer, we're all about fusion. Fusion is a mash-up of flavors, styles and ingredients. And that's what Sue's art and my food have in common . . . a mash up! This dish offers a fusion of East meets west when we combine a Tex-Mex filling into an Asian-style roll-up. The filling is spiced with jalapeno peppers, savory black beans and sweet toasted corn. Tangy, roasted tomatillo salsa is the perfect dipping sauce. Mixing it up is a great way to get creative on your canvas and in the kitchen.

FOR SALSA:

6 medium tomatillos, husks removed, cut in half

1 small white onion, peeled and cut into quarters

2 garlic cloves, peeled

1 small jalapeno chili, cut in half, seeded and deveined

1 teaspoon kosher salt

1 ½ teaspoon coarse black pepper

1 teaspoon honey

3 tablespoons chopped fresh cilantro

FOR CHICKEN:

2 large boneless, skinless chicken breasts

2 tablespoons chili powder

1 tablespoon onion powder

1 tablespoon garlic powder

FOR FILLING:

1 tablespoon olive oil

1 small red onion, peeled and diced, about ½ cup

1 (15.5-ounce) can black beans, rinsed and drained

4 ears fresh corn, kernels removed from cobs, about 1 cup

1 (1-pound) package egg roll wrappers, about 20

2 ounces sharp cheddar cheese, grated, about ½ cup

Vegetable oil for frying

Preheat the oven to 375°. Place the tomatillos, white onion, garlic and jalapeno pepper onto a baking sheet that has been coated with vegetable oil spray. Season with some of the salt and pepper. Roast the veggies until soft and just beginning to brown, about 10 to 15 minutes. Remove from the oven and scrape the veggies into the bowl of a food processor. Pulse to combine. Add the honey and cilantro. Pulse once more. Taste and season with additional salt and pepper if needed. Pour the salsa into a bowl. Set the bowl on the counter while you move on to the chicken.

Butterfly the chicken breasts to create 4 pieces. Mix together chili powder, onion powder, garlic powder and 1 teaspoon pepper. Season the chicken on both sides with about ¾ of the seasoning mix. Sprinkle the seasoned chicken with additional salt. Heat 1 tablespoon olive oil in a grill pan over medium-high heat. Grill the chicken breasts until golden on one side, about 4 to 5 minutes. Turn and cook until golden on the second side, about 4 to 5 minutes more. Transfer the chicken to a plate and tent with foil while you move on to the filling.

Heat 1 tablespoon olive oil in a skillet over medium-high heat. Add the red onion and cook until soft, about 2 minutes. Add the black beans and fresh corn. Season with the remaining seasoning mix and additional salt. Cook until the corn begins to toast, about 3 to 5 minutes more.

Slice the chicken breasts into thin pieces. Place 1 egg roll wrapper onto a cutting board. Place one or two pieces of chicken onto the bottom of the wrapper. Top with a spoonful of black beans and corn. Top with a bit of the cheddar cheese. Roll the wrapper once over the filling. Fold in the sides and continue wrapping. Brush the top of the wrapper with water to seal it together. Place the egg roll onto a baking sheet, seam side down. Continue with the remaining filling and wrappers.

Pour vegetable oil into a pot about 3-inches deep. The oil should not reach higher than one third up the sides of the pan. Hot oil will bubble up when you fry the eggrolls. Heat the oil to 375°. You can use a candy thermometer to monitor the temperature of the oil. Place a baking rack into a baking sheet with rim (to catch the drips!). Place one eggroll into the hot oil. Add one or two more, depending on the size of your pot. Cook until golden, about 2 to 3 minutes. Use a slotted spoon or wire skimmer to transfer the eggrolls to the rack. Continue until all the eggrolls have been fried.

Serve warm eggrolls on a platter with the salsa in a bowl on the side.

CORN ON THE COB WITH GARLIC SCAPE AND MACADAMIA NUT PESTO

serves 4

20 minute cuisine

In the early summer at the farmers market, you can find long, green, circles of thin stalks that look like skinny ropes. These are garlic scapes, the flowering bud of garlic plants. They are cut off the plant so that the bulb grows fatter and fatter, creating that papery globe of cloves we see most commonly. These strands of garlicky goodness can be used in the same way as garlic cloves with no peeling of course! I use them to make pesto and then I spread that pesto on everything from warm pasta, to toasted crostini to sautéed veggies. Melting, fragrant, nutty pesto is delicious on summer sweet corn. Give it a try to see what I mean!

3 to 4 garlic scapes, chopped, about ½ cup

½ pound spinach leaves, about 2 cups

1 bunch fresh basil, about ½ cup

¼ cup macadamia nuts

2 ounces Parmesan cheese, grated, about ½ cup

1 teaspoon kosher salt

½ teaspoon coarse black pepper

½ cup olive oil

4 large ears of corn, shucked

Place the garlic scapes, spinach leaves, basil leaves (no need to chop any of these, just dump them right in), macadamia nuts, and Parmesan cheese into the bowl of a food processor. Pulse several times until all the ingredients are ground together. Season with salt and pepper. With the machine running, slowly pour in the olive oil to make a paste. (You can store the pesto in an airtight container in the fridge for up to a week.)

Place the corn into a pan and cover with water. Bring the water to a boil over high heat and cook until the corn is tender, about 8 to 10 minutes. Drain the water from the pan. Place several spoonsful of the pesto into the pan with the corn. Cover with the lid and swirl the pan so that the hot corn melts the pesto and all the kernels are generously coated. Serve the corn with additional salt and pepper and another sprinkle of Parmesan cheese!

After Market Leftovers

For a salsa that is great with grilled guac, remove the kernels from the cobs and place into a bowl. Drain and rinse a can of black beans and pour into the same bowl. Add chopped tomatoes, onion and a bit of fresh jalapeno pepper. Sprinkle with fresh cilantro, kosher salt, and pepper. Drizzle with a bit of olive oil.

JALAPENO CORN BISQUE

serves 8
60 minute cuisine

Creamy and sweet with a touch of heat, this soup is fabulous served after a brisk walk on a cold day; I like my soup bowls served fireside! I was introduced to this dish, by a super chef in Banner Elk, North Carolina. It was that kind of bone-chilling autumn day when you just need a big bowl of soup to warm you from the inside out. It didn't hurt that the corn is grown right down the street from the restaurant. This is the sort of soup that Sue kept simmering all day long, so that her kids could ladle out a bowl full anytime during the day, after school, for a snack, and of course for supper.

2 tablespoons olive oil
1 large onion, peeled and chopped, about 1 cup
1 whole leek, white part chopped, about 1 cup
4 large jalapeno peppers, seeded, veins removed, diced, about 1 cup
8 ears of corn, kernels removed from cob, about 6 cups
1 teaspoon kosher salt
1 teaspoon coarse ground pepper
1 teaspoon ground cumin
1 teaspoon garlic powder
1 cup sherry
3 cups homemade chicken stock or prepared low sodium broth
4 cups half-and-half
1 tablespoon all-purpose flour mixed with 1 tablespoon room temperature butter (this is called a beurre manié)
Fresh chopped cilantro

Heat the olive oil in a deep soup pot over medium-high heat. Add the onion, leek and jalapeno peppers and cook until beginning to soften, about 2 to 3 minutes. Add the corn and cook for 5 minutes more. Season with salt, pepper, cumin and garlic powder. Pour in the sherry. Cook until the liquid is almost all evaporated, about 3 minutes. Pour in the chicken broth. Cover the pot and reduce the heat to medium. Cook until the veggies are soft, about 20 minutes. Remove the pot from the heat. Use your gadget of choice (food processor, blender, or immersion blender) to emulsify the soup.

Return the soup to the pot, if you have used a blender or food processor. Heat the soup over low heat. Stir in the half-and-half. Drop small pieces of the beurre manié (flour mixed with butter) into the soup. Stir until the soup thickens to your desired consistency. You can add more cream to thin the soup or more of the beurre manié to thicken it.

Garnish with fresh cilantro.

Bright and Early

VEGGIE FRITTO MISTO WITH BLUE CHEESE DRIZZLE AND HOT SAUCE

serves a crowd

45 minute cuisine

It just seems to me that other cultures run at a slower pace than we madcap Americans. Maybe it's because we're visiting these cultures as tourists, but I don't think so. It's a quality of life thing, reminding us to embrace, embrace, embrace the moment! For example, sitting in an outdoor café in a seaside village in Positano, watching the sun slip down and listening to the waves crash, I watch my fellow diners and note that they are more local to the neighborhood than one might imagine. The dishes are served family style and the meal is luxuriated over, not table-turned. It was here that I first sampled one of my favorite dishes, Fritto Misto, an Italian first course. It is a large platter of lightly battered and fried seafood or veggies, often served with a lemony aioli. This is my all-American, beer-drinkin', game-day version of the dish. It takes advantage of farmer's market veggies and is the perfect vegetarian foil to wings! It's a great dish to share with a rowdy crowd that's not going to necessarily slow down to luxuriate over the dish but, will find it just delicious enough to last through the first half!

FOR BLUE CHEESE SAUCE:

½ cup mayonnaise

½ cup sour cream

2 ounces blue cheese, crumbled, about ¼ cup

Juice of ½ medium lemon, about 1 tablespoon

2 (or more) tablespoons half-and-half

FOR HOT SAUCE

½ cup butter, 1 stick

4 cloves garlic, peeled and minced, about 1 tablespoon

½ cup hot pepper sauce

2 tablespoons red wine vinegar

For veggies:

Vegetable oil for frying

1 cup unbleached all-purpose flour

1 cup corn starch

1 teaspoon baking powder

1 teaspoon kosher salt

2 cups club soda, cold

1 small head cauliflower, cut into 1-inch florets

2 fennel bulbs, tops trimmed, cored and cut into 1-inch pieces

4 ounces green beans, trimmed and halved, about 1 ½ cups

½ teaspoon coarse black pepper

2 tablespoons chopped fresh Italian flat leaf parsley

Lemon wedges

Whisk together mayonnaise, sour cream, blue cheese and lemon juice in a small bowl. Add enough half-and-half to thin the sauce so that it will easily flow through a squeeze bottle.

Melt the butter over medium-low heat in a large skillet. Stir in the garlic, hot pepper sauce and vinegar. Simmer the hot sauce on low heat while you prepare the veggies.

Pour vegetable oil about a third of the way up the side of a deep pot. Heat the oil to 350°. You can use a candy thermometer to monitor the heat of the oil. Remember not to pour too much oil in the pot as it bubbles up quite a lot once you begin to fry the veggies.

Whisk together the flour, corn starch, baking powder and ½ teaspoon salt in a bowl. Stir in the club soda. Dip a cauliflower floret into the batter. Shake off the excess so that it drips back into the bowl. Use a wire skimmer basket to transfer the veggie into the oil. Repeat with the remaining florets. Do not overcrowd the pot. Fry until golden, about 3 to 4 minutes. Transfer the fried cauliflower florets to a baking sheet lined with paper towels. Season with additional salt and pepper. Keep the fried cauliflower warm in a warming drawer or oven set on the lowest temperature, while you fry the fennel and green beans. Drop just a couple strips at a time, so that they don't clump together.

When all the veggies are fried, transfer them to a large platter. Drizzle some of the blue cheese sauce over the top. Garnish with fresh parsley and lemon wedges. Serve the hot sauce in a bowl on the side for dipping.

FRESH CORN, GREEN BEAN AND ARUGULA SALAD WITH LEMON BALSAMIC VINAIGRETTE

serves 6 to 8

30 minute cuisine

Driving in the Appalachian Mountains, from Boone to Cashiers, you pass hundreds of acres of farmland. As early as June, you can see the corn stalks rising from the ground. Just watching the stalks sway in the wind makes me hanker for the crunch of sweet corn on the cob. I usually over-buy at the farmer's stand, ensuring I come up with multiple ways to use up the corn. Here's a hearty, summer salad, I serve all the time. The fresher the corn, the better the salad!

FOR DRESSING:

2 medium shallots, peeled and finely diced, about 2 tablespoons

1 tablespoon honey

Zest of 2 medium lemons, about 2 tablespoons

Juice of 2 medium lemons, about   cup

cup white balsamic vinegar

½ cup olive oil

1 teaspoon kosher salt

½ teaspoon coarse black pepper

FOR SALAD:

4 ears of corn, shucked

1 pound green beans, trimmed and cut into 1-inch pieces, about 4 cups

1 pint cherry tomatoes, halved

2 tablespoons chopped, fresh basil

2 large bunches fresh arugula leaves, about 6 cups

2 ounces feta cheese, chunked, about ½ cup

Place the shallots, honey and lemon zest into a small bowl. Whisk in the lemon juice followed by balsamic vinegar. Slowly whisk in olive oil. Season with some of the salt and pepper.

Blanch the corn in a pot of salted, boiling water until crisp-tender, about 5 minutes. Use a slotted spoon or tongs to transfer the corn to a bowl filled with ice water. Repeat the process to blanch the green beans. You can use the same pot! Cut the corn from the cobbs and place into a large bowl. Drain the green beans and transfer them to the same bowl. Add the tomatoes and basil. Season with salt and pepper.

Places the arugula on top of the vegetables in the bowl. Drizzle with some of the dressing. Toss the salad. You want to have everything lightly coated with dressing not drowning in it! You can add additional dressing if you like or store extra dressing for another day. Toss in feta cheese.

TUSCAN WHITE BEAN STEW WITH SMOKED SAUSAGE AND SWISS CHARD

serves 4 to 6

45 minute cuisine

The open-air markets in Tuscany are nothing short of enticing. Filled with the freshest produce and most fragrant fruit and cheese, you are inspired to eat farm to table. I love the little brown bags filled with heirloom beans, and I love the hearty stew that these beans turn into. Here is my shortcut version (don't judge—there's nothing wrong with using canned beans) of this peasant dish you can easily make during the week.

2 tablespoons olive oil, divided

½ pound pancetta, diced

1 medium white onion, peeled and diced, about 1 cup

2 medium carrots, peeled, trimmed and chopped, about 1 cup

3 medium celery ribs, sliced, about 1 cup

4 medium garlic cloves, peeled and minced, about 1 tablespoon

1 (15-ounce) can cannellini beans, drained and rinsed

1 (15-ounce) can white navy beans, drained and rinsed

1 (14.5-ounce cans) diced tomatoes

1 pound smoked sausage, diced

1 cup homemade chicken stock or prepared low sodium broth

1 teaspoon kosher salt

1 teaspoon coarse black pepper

2 to 3 sprigs fresh rosemary

½ pound Swiss chard, chopped, about 2 to 3 cups leaves

Parmesan cheese, grated

Heat 1 tablespoon olive oil in a deep pot over medium-high heat. Add the pancetta and cook until golden and crispy, about 3 to 5 minutes. Use a slotted spoon to transfer the pancetta to a platter lined with paper towels. Pour in 1 more tablespoon olive oil. Add the onion, carrots, and celery and cook until the vegetables are soft, about 5 minutes. Stir in the garlic.

Pour in the beans and tomatoes. Add the smoked sausage and pancetta. Pour in the chicken stock. Season with salt and pepper. Submerge the rosemary sprigs. Cover the pot, reduce the heat to medium low, and simmer for 15 minutes. Remove the lid and add the Swiss chard to the stew. Cover and simmer for 5 minutes more. If the stew is too thick, add more chicken stock. If the stew is thinner than you like, turn up the heat, take off the lid and cook until some of the liquid is reduced. Serve with a garnish of Parmesan cheese.

What's Your Pleasure

MEXICAN-STYLE STUFFED BELL PEPPERS

serves 4

45 minute cuisine

The Southwest is an area that Sue and I visit all the time, as we both have children who live there. After the margaritas, we love the flavors of Mexican food and we love them even more when we can elevate the dish by upping the veggie quotient. This is an easy to prepare veggie entre or a simple side with grilled pork and a spoonful of yellow rice.

4 large bell peppers, slice off stem tops, seeded and veins removed

1 tablespoon olive oil, plus 2 more for filling

1 teaspoon kosher salt

1 teaspoon coarse black pepper

1 large onion, cut into ¼-inch pieces, about 1 cup

1 large zucchini, cut into ¼-inch pieces, about 1 cup

2 ears of corn, kernels removed, about 1 cup

1 (15-ounce) can black beans, drained and rinsed

1 large jalapeno pepper, seeded, veins removed, diced, about 2 tablespoons

1 (14-ounce) jar prepared enchilada sauce (or check out the homemade version on page 57

1 small chipotle chili in adobo sauce, seeded, minced, about 2 teaspoons

2 tablespoons chopped, fresh cilantro

4 ounces Monterey Jack cheese, shredded, about 1 cup

1 cup tortilla chips, crushed

Preheat the oven to 375°. Place the peppers into a baking dish. Drizzle the inside with 1 tablespoon olive oil and some of the salt and pepper. Bake until the peppers are just beginning to soften, about 20 to 30 minutes. Remove the dish from the oven.

Drizzle 2 tablespoons olive oil in a large skillet, over medium-high heat. Add the onion and zucchini and cook until the veggies are softened, about 5 to 8 minutes. Stir in the corn, black beans and jalapeno pepper. Cook for several minutes more. Pour in the enchilada sauce. Stir in the chipotle pepper and cilantro. Reduce the heat to low and simmer until the veggies are soft and the sauce is reduced by half. You want a thick stew of veggies, not a soupy sauce. Taste and season with salt.

Fill half of each pepper with veggies. Top with some of the cheese and top that with some of the chips. Place the remaining veggies over the chips. Top with the rest of the cheese and the chips. Place the baking dish back into the oven and cook until the cheese is melted, and the chips are golden, about 15 minutes.

MOROCCAN SHEET PAN CHICKEN WITH SWEET 'N SALTY CARROTS AND CHICKPEAS

serves 4 to 6

30 minute cuisine

One place we have not yet been is Morocco, but that region of the world is definitely on our bucket list! I'm in love with the flavors of North African food: one that pairs sweet with tart, better than most anywhere else. Salty olives with sweet dates, hot spices with cooked brown sugar . . . I can't think of a bigger treat for dinner. This is a one-pan meal, ideal for serving with a bowl of lemon-infused jasmine rice.

SPICE BLEND:

1 tablespoon paprika

1 tablespoon brown sugar

2 teaspoons ground turmeric

2 teaspoons ground cinnamon

2 teaspoons ground ginger

1 teaspoon ground allspice

1 teaspoon ground coriander

1 teaspoon ground cumin

½ teaspoon cayenne pepper

FOR CHICKEN:

1 whole orange, cut into thin slices

8 large boneless, skinless chicken thighs (you can mix and match with boneless breasts)

2 tablespoons olive oil, plus 2 more for veggies

1 teaspoon kosher salt

½ teaspoon coarse black pepper

1 large red onion, peeled and cut into ½-inch wedges

1 pound baby carrots, about 12 to 14, cut in half

1 whole head of garlic, cloves peeled

1 (15-ounce) can chickpeas, drained and rinsed

½ cup Kalamata olives, pitted and chopped

½ pound pitted dates, about 1 ½ cups

1 cup dry white wine

2 tablespoon chopped fresh cilantro

Mix together all the spices in a small bowl. This will make more spice mix than you need, but it will keep well in an airtight container. Place the chicken pieces into a resealable plastic bag. Add two to three tablespoons of the spice blend into the bag. Seal and shake the bag to coat the chicken. Add the orange slices. Place the bag into the refrigerator and marinate for at least 2 hours and as much as overnight.

Preheat the oven to 400°. Remove the chicken from the bag and place into a baking dish that has been coated with vegetable oil spray. Drizzle 2 tablespoons olive oil over the top of the chicken. Season with some of the salt and pepper.

Place the onion, carrots, garlic and chickpeas into a large bowl. Sprinkle with 1 tablespoon of the spice blend and 2 more tablespoons olive oil. Season with salt and pepper. Lay the veggies around the chicken. Plop the olives and dates in and around the chicken and vegetables. Pour the wine over everything.

Bake until the chicken is cooked through (when the internal temperature reaches 165°) about 30 to 45 minutes. Pluck the chicken pieces from the sheet pan and place onto a serving platter. Spoon the pan juices, fruits and veggies over the chicken pieces. Garnish with fresh cilantro.

COOK'S TIP

The best way to ensure all the chicken cooks at the same time is to make sure that the pieces are of similar size. If you have chosen to cook chicken breasts, you might cut each breast in half to match the size of the thighs.

Wordless Wellness

NAVY BEAN VEGGIE BURGERS WITH MAPLE ONION JAM

serves 4

60 minute cuisine

You simply can't visit the farmers market without succumbing to the temptation of jars and jars of homemade jams and jellies. My favorites are the savory combinations that you can pour onto warmed cheeses, or spoon onto roasted meats. Inspired by Sue's roots in vegetarian cuisine, I pair this maple onion jam, as the world's best topper, with an inspired veggie burger.

FOR JAM:

1 tablespoon olive oil

2 large onions, peeled and chopped

2 tablespoons brown sugar

1 ½-inch piece ginger grated, about 1 teaspoon

½ teaspoon ground cardamom

½ teaspoon ground cinnamon

1 teaspoon kosher salt

½ teaspoon coarse black pepper

1 tablespoon maple syrup

2 teaspoons apple cider vinegar

FOR BURGERS:

1 tablespoon chopped fresh basil

1 clove garlic, peeled

1 ounce Parmesan cheese, grated, about ¼ cup

1 (15-ounce) can navy beans drained and rinsed, divided

½ cup panko breadcrumbs, divided

1 large egg

2 tablespoons butter

4 hamburger buns, split

2 tablespoons olive oil

Heat the olive oil in a skillet over medium-high heat. Add the onions and cook until soft, about 5 minutes. Stir in the brown sugar, ginger, cardamom and cinnamon. Season with salt and pepper. Reduce the heat to low and cook until the onions are syrupy, about 20 minutes more. Stir in the syrup and vinegar. Cool the jam to room temperature.

Place the basil, garlic and cheese into the bowl of a food processor. Pulse to combine. Add half of the beans, half of the breadcrumbs and the egg and pulse. Place the remaining beans into a bowl and mash with a potato masher. Scrape the bean mixture from the food processor into the bowl of mashed beans. Season with salt and pepper. Mix well. Use wet hands to form the bean mixture into four ¾-inch patties.

Place the remaining bread crumbs onto a plate. Coat each patty with the crumbs. Place the bean patties into the fridge to chill for 10 minutes.

Heat the butter in a large skillet over medium heat. Place the buns, cut sized down into the skillet to toast. Transfer the buns to a platter.

Pour 2 tablespoons olive oil into the skillet. Cook the bean burgers in the skillet until golden brown on one side, about 3 to 4 minutes. Carefully flip the burgers and cook until golden on the other side, about 4 minutes more. Place the burgers onto the buns and top with maple onion jam.

AFTER MARKET LEFTOVERS

Make a BIG batch of the maple onion jam and store it in an airtight container for up to two weeks. It's the perfect condiment for an instant appy atop room temperature cream cheese. Serve alongside roasted pork or spread over your almond butter toast.

SLOW COOKER WHITE BEAN CASSOULET

serves 6 to 8

30 minute prep and 8 hours in your slow cooker

Cassoulet is a French peasant dish, cooked for hours and hours atop the stove, in a huge covered pot. The original recipe for this stew features duck confit, which is an additional time-consuming task, that delivers a tender, really succulent bite of dark, rich poultry. For my made-in-the-USA version, I exchanged duck confit for chicken thigh meat, and let the slow cooker do much of the work. It's not authentically French, but it's darn good!

1 large onion, peeled and chopped, about 1 ½ cups

4 to 6 medium carrots, peeled, trimmed and cut into thin diagonal slices, about 1 ½ cups

1 parsnip, peeled and cut into thin diagonal slices, about 1 cup

2 cloves garlic, peeled and minced

2 (15-ounce) cans white beans, rinsed and drained

1 (28-ounce) can diced tomatoes

1 cup homemade chicken stock or prepared low sodium broth

2 tablespoons tomato paste

1 to 2 tablespoons olive oil

4 boneless, skinless chicken thighs, cut into ½-inch pieces

1 pound smoked sausage, cut into rounds

1 teaspoon kosher salt

½ teaspoon coarse black pepper

½ teaspoon dried thyme

1 bay leaf

½cup panko bread crumbs

1 ounce Parmesan cheese, grated, about ¼ cup

2 tablespoons chopped fresh parsley

2 tablespoons butter, melted

Place the onion, carrots, parsnip and garlic into a slow cooker. Pour in the beans, tomatoes, chicken stock and tomato paste. Heat 1 tablespoon olive oil in a skillet over medium-high heat. Cook the chicken in the skillet until golden on all sides, about 5 minutes. Add the chicken into the slow cooker. Cook sausage in the skillet until golden, about 5 minutes, adding more oil if needed. Add the sausage to the slow cooker. Season with salt, pepper and thyme. Submerge the bay leaf into the liquid. Cover and cook on low for 6 to 8 hours. About 30 to 60 minutes before serving, place the breadcrumbs, Parmesan cheese, parsley and butter into a sauté pan. Use a fork to combine. Cook over medium heat until golden and crispy. Crumble this on top of the cassoulet and continue to cook, in the slow cooker, uncovered. Spoon the cassoulet directly from your slow cooker into bowls and garnish with additional fresh parsley.

SPANISH-STYLE BRAISED CHICKEN THIGHS

serves 4 to 6

45 minute cuisine

When I traveled to Spain, I went to not one but two cooking schools. Both featured traditional paella, yet each dish was very unique. They were similar in that they were cooked over an open flame in a circular, shallow pan. They were different in their spiciness and ingredients, one had seafood, one had chicken. Both were delish! My made-in-the-USA dish is similar to those paellas but takes less time to prepare. There's a kick to it that might take the Spaniards by surprise; I ramped up the flavor with piquillo and banana peppers, straight from a jar in my pantry.

2 tablespoons olive oil

8 bone-in chicken thighs

1 teaspoon paprika

1 teaspoon kosher salt

½ teaspoon coarse black pepper

1 pound fresh chorizo (if you are using links remove casings)

1 large onion, chopped

6 cloves garlic, peeled and thinly sliced

1 (7-ounce) jar whole piquillo peppers, drained, about 1 cup

½ cup sliced marinated banana peppers

1 cup red wine

2 tablespoons tomato paste

Zest of 1 medium lemon, about 2 teaspoons

1 cup rice

1 (10-ounce) package frozen peas, thawed

3 cups homemade chicken stock or prepared low sodium broth

Juice of 1 medium lemon, about 3 tablespoons

2 tablespoons chopped fresh cilantro

Heat the olive oil in a large cast iron skillet over medium-high heat. Season both sides of the chicken with paprika, salt, and pepper. Place the chicken into the skillet, skin side down and cook until golden, about 4 to 5 minutes. Turn the chicken and cook on the second side until golden, about 4 to 5 minutes more. Transfer the chicken to a platter. Add the chorizo to the skillet and cook until browned and crumbly, about 4 to 5 minutes. Add the onion and garlic and cook until the veggies are soft, about 5 minutes more. Stir in the piquillo and banana peppers. Pour in the wine. Reduce the heat to medium and simmer until most of the liquid disappears. Stir in the tomato paste and lemon zest. Sprinkle the contents of the skillet with rice and stir in the peas. Pour in the chicken broth. Tuck the chicken pieces back into the skillet. Cover the skillet with aluminum foil and simmer until the chicken is cooked through and the rice is tender, about 15 to 20 minutes. Remove the aluminum foil from the skillet. Sprinkle with lemon juice and chopped fresh cilantro.

STEMS AND TUBERS

/stem/

noun

1. the main body or stalk of a plant or shrub, typically rising above ground but occasionally subterranean.
   synonyms: stalk, shoot, trunk, stock, cane, bine
   "a plant stem"

tu·ber

/ˈt(y)oobər/

noun

1. a much thickened underground part of a stem or rhizome, e.g., in the potato, serving as a food reserve and bearing buds from which new plants arise.

Mercat de la Boqueria

What's better than an evening spent nibbling and sipping? Well, how about a day spent nibbling and sipping. It seems to me that nibbling and sipping is what Spain is all about. A summer trip took us around the coast, with a detour through Seville and Madrid. The quaint coastal towns had one thing in common with their mountainous cousins . . . it's hot! Which, in my opinion, leads to the languid lifestyle of Spain. Things don't start happening until the sun goes down. Oh sure, we tourists start out in the morning for a tour of a cathedral or stroll through the shops, but those shops don't open 'til sometime after two and those cathedrals, even though cooled by marble and stone, were only open to pass through,

The one contrast are the cafes. Notably, there is a café at every other storefront. Even more notably, they are always open. There may be only two people in each café, but they're open. Each café offers tapas, small plates of local favorites. I have a theory about this. It's so hot, that you can barely move from place to place without needing a siesta to gather more strength. This might not be totally true, but it sure is a great excuse to visit more than one eatery in a very short amount of time!

A further illustration to develop my theory, is the evening experience of the tapas crawl. It's exactly what you think it is. You start at one café. The sipping and nibbling commences and before you are quite settled, it's time to move on to the next. This continues until you crawl into bed . . . at least it did for me! Those Spaniards are quite a bit more resilient than this tourist!

Fresh markets in Spain are housed under one roof, forming central markets (Mercado Central). The vendors have stalls that are organized in rows similar to the ones you find in American grocery stores. The meats and Iberian Ham (a prized product) are in one section and the seafood in another. Fresh produce lines rows and rows and rows of the market. But, in between the rows of fresh food are vendors serving everything from coffee, to pastries to skillet-roasted barnacles. Don't laugh, they're much better than they sound.

Our Tapas Crawl began with a guide who took us to a café, where we ordered small plates of everything—from braised short ribs, to a rich, velvety salmorejo (a cold soup similar to thick gazpacho), to fiery, garlic shrimp, to a wedge of potato tortilla. Just when we settled in, passing the plates around for each of us to taste, our guide stood up and motioned us to our next stop. We walked the brick roads to the Mercado Central and entered the building to find energetic shoppers next to wine or coffee sipping patrons—all on their way out for the evening. It was way, way after dark and the market was alive with activity. We had a glass of wine and walked around, while we sampled different tapas. I loved the bites of charred octopus! Afterward we wound our way to a churro shop. This churro shop had the allure of a Krispy Kreme with all the style of a bustling bistro! We ordered churros and chocolate sauce for dipping and sat (and drooled) until our order arrived. Even though it was late, we came alive with the sweet taste of cinnamon sugar slathered on beautifully fried dough. Yum oh yum!

When I look at Sue's painting *Mercat de la Boqueria*, I'm taken back to the central markets in Spain. The vibrant produce shines in dishes rich in peppers, spices and citrus. The heat of the sun sparkles and flares through every bite. There's something to be said for the Spanish way of life—something to be experienced and incorporated into our hectic American routine.

OVEN BAKED ASPARAGUS WITH GLAZED EGGS

serves 4

30 minute cuisine

Sue raise her six kids as vegetarians, so she was quite adept at turning veggies into meals. This is a dish she created for her daughter and three of her (seventeen) grandchildren. I was blown away to see a very similar dish on a very fancy Paris bistro menu. The asparagus were huge, and meaty and soft. They were served with rich, creamy hollandaise sauce and the combination was just absolutely delicious. This recipe reminds me of that French first course with a little bit of boldness added . . . just like Sue's painting!

½ pound medium fresh asparagus spears, about 16, choose the fattest spears you can find

Juice of 1 medium lemon, about 3 tablespoons

1 teaspoon kosher salt

½ teaspoon coarse black pepper

½ cup mayonnaise

2 tablespoons Dijon-style mustard

2 cups panko breadcrumbs

2 ounces Parmesan cheese, grated, about ½ cup

2 tablespoons olive oil

2 tablespoons butter

4 large eggs

1 tablespoon chopped fresh chives

Preheat the oven to 375°. Lay the asparagus onto a cutting board. Cut off the tough end at their natural break points. Peel the stems. Drizzle the lemon juice over the asparagus. Season with salt and pepper.

Whisk together the mayonnaise and mustard in a shallow bowl. Stir the bread crumbs with the Parmesan cheese in another bowl. Roll an asparagus spear first in the mayo blend and then in the breadcrumbs. Place onto a baking sheet. Continue with the remaining spears. Drizzle with olive oil. Bake the asparagus until the coating begins to turn golden, about 15 to 20 minutes. Turn off the oven and keep the asparagus warm while you prepare the eggs.

In a large non-stick skillet with a lid, melt 2 tablespoons butter over medium heat. Crack an egg into a small bowl or cup. Gently pour the egg into the skillet. Repeat with the remaining eggs. Immediately turn down the heat to low. Drizzle 2 tablespoons water around the eggs and cover the pan with the lid. Cook until the eggs are just beginning to set, about 3 to 4 minutes. Remove the lid and season with salt, pepper, and chopped chives. Place three or four spears on a plate. Slide a glazed egg over the top.

Bunches of Potential

ASPARAGUS FRIES WITH THOU- SAND ISLAND DIPPING SAUCE

serves 4

30 minute cuisine

I'm not crazy about those skinny little twig-looking asparagus you find in the grocery stores. However, I'm a big fan of the thick, plump asparagus spears you find at the farmers market. Trim them by bending the spear at its natural breaking point. This will preserve the tips and tender stalks. Now, what you do next is just a little bit naughty. Batter those bad boys and fry them just like the Italians do in the classic dish Fritto Misto. Then dip these into a spicy, creamy sauce that is just the perfect compliment. There's nothin' skinny about this!

FOR DRESSING:

1 ½ cups mayonnaise

½ cup ketchup

1 teaspoon white balsamic vinegar

3 tablespoons sweet pickle relish

1 large shallot, peeled and minced, about 2 tablespoons

1 teaspoon kosher salt

½ teaspoon cayenne pepper

1 large hard-boiled egg, peeled

1 teaspoon diced pimento

1 teaspoon chopped fresh chives

Hot pepper sauce

FOR FRIES:

Canola oil for frying

2 large eggs, beaten

¾ cup unbleached all-purpose flour

1 cup panko breadcrumbs

1 pound thick asparagus spears, tough ends trimmed, stems peeled, about 30

Whisk together the mayonnaise, ketchup, vinegar, relish and shallot. Season with some of the salt and cayenne pepper. Press the egg through a fine-mesh sieve into the bowl. Add the pimento and chives and stir to combine. Stir in as much hot pepper sauce as you like.

Heat 2 inches oil in a deep pot over medium-high heat reaching 375°. (I use a candy thermometer for this.) Pour the eggs into a shallow bowl. Place the flour on a plate and season with salt and pepper. Place the breadcrumbs on a separate plate. Dredge one asparagus spear, first in the flour, then in the egg and finally into the breadcrumbs. Place the battered asparagus into the hot oil. Repeat until you have several asparagus frying. Cook until golden, about 3 to 4 minutes. Transfer the asparagus to a paper towel lined baking sheet. Continue until all the asparagus has been fried. Serve asparagus fries with thousand island dipping sauce.

Revive Yourself Asparago!

ITALIAN-STYLE GREEN BEANS WITH POTATOES AND SUN-DRIED TOMATOES

serves 4

20 minute cuisine

This superb dish is a staple of the most frequented restaurants in Italy. Until you actually visit, you might think that all Italian food is pasta and pasta with a tad more pasta. But, in reality there are a great deal of peasant-style, comfort food dishes on a typical trattoria menu. This family style side is a combination of crisp tender green beans, with stewed tomatoes with tender potatoes. I find you can (and should) serve these green beans with everything. This is my quick home cooked version of one of my favorite Italian finds.

½ pound fresh green beans, about 3 cups, ends trimmed

8 baby Yukon Gold potatoes, cut into quarters, about 2 cups

3 tablespoons julienned sun-dried tomatoes with oil

2 garlic cloves, peeled and minced

Juice of 1 medium Meyer lemon, about 3 tablespoons (substitute with orange juice)

½ cup homemade chicken stock or prepared low sodium broth

1 teaspoon kosher salt

½ teaspoon coarse black pepper

Steam or blanch the beans and potatoes until they are just crisp tender using a steamer basket or microwave oven.

Heat the sundried tomatoes in a skillet over medium heat. Stir in the garlic and pour in the lemon juice. Pour in the chicken broth. Simmer for 5 minutes until the liquid reduces and you have a syrupy sauce. Add the beans and the potatoes. Toss to coat. Season with salt and pepper.

COOK'S TIP

It's easy to find packages of microwave veggies that are ready to steam in the bag they are sold in. These will work perfectly for this recipe. Simply place the bag of trimmed green beans in the microwave and press the fresh veggie setting. The microwave does all the work. You can find the same package of baby potatoes. Steam them first and then cut them into wedges.

A RAINBOW OF GRILLED VEGGIES WITH HERBED RANCH DRESSING AND SPICY PEANUT SAUCE

serves a Crowd

30 minute cuisine

Eat a rainbow! It's easy to do when you stroll through the market and see the expanse of fresh vegetable stands, boasting veggies in their most natural state. A hot grill caramelizes the veggies producing a combination of sweet with char. A drizzle of creamy ranch dressings kissed with fresh herbs brings the farm stand to your table in every amazing bite. But why stop there? Let's add a second drizzle of a spicy Asian peanut sauce to make this platter of veggies the star of your meal.

FOR RANCH DRESSING:

2 cloves garlic

1 cup mayonnaise

½ cup sour cream

2 tablespoons tarragon vinegar

2 tablespoons chopped fresh parsley

2 tablespoons chopped fresh dill

1 tablespoon chopped fresh chives

1 teaspoon Worcestershire sauce

½ teaspoon paprika

2 to 3 drops hot pepper sauce

¼ to ½ cup half-and-half

1 teaspoon kosher salt

½ teaspoon coarse black pepper

FOR SPICY PEANUT SAUCE:

1 tablespoon red curry paste

¾ cup coconut milk

¼ cup peanut butter

2 teaspoons fish sauce

Juice of ½ large lime, about 1 tablespoon

FOR VEGGIES:

½ pound medium asparagus spears, about 16

½ pound medium carrots, peeled, about 4 to 5

1 large fennel bulb, tops removed, cored and cut into ½-inch slices

2 large zucchinis, cut lengthwise into ½-inch slices

4 large yellow squash, cut lengthwise into ½-inch slices

1 large red onion, peeled and cut into ½-inch slices

1 medium eggplant, cut into ½-inch slices

½ cup olive oil

Place the garlic, mayonnaise, sour cream, tarragon vinegar, herbs, Worcestershire sauce, and paprika into the bowl of a food processor. Pulse to combine. Season with as much hot pepper sauce as you like. Pour in ¼ cup half-and-half and pulse. If the dressing is too thick you can add additional half and half. Taste and season with salt and pepper. Pour the dressing into a squeeze bottle and place onto the counter while you move on to the peanut sauce.

Whisk the red curry paste in a saucepan over medium heat for 1 minute. Whisk in the coconut milk, peanut butter, and fish sauce until smooth. Turn off the heat and whisk in the lime juice. If the sauce is too thick to flow through a squeeze bottle add more lime juice or thin with water. Cool to room temperature and pour into a squeeze bottle. Set the bottle on the counter while you move onto the vegetables.

Lay the vegetables onto baking sheets lined with parchment paper. Brush both sides with olive oil and season with salt and pepper. Heat a grill (or grill pan) over high heat. Grill the vegetables until they begin to soften and char, about 1 to 2 minutes per side depending on the veggie.

Place the veggies onto a platter and serve warm or at room temperature with a drizzle of ranch dressing, a drizzle of spicy peanut sauce and additional fresh parsley.

FARMER'S MARKET TIP

If you are grilling veggies for a week night dinner, do double duty by roasting more than you need! You can easily reserve half of the vegetables for later use. Cool to room temperature and place into a resealable plastic bag in the refrigerator. For a quick soup, pulse the grilled veggies in a food processor with chicken or vegetable broth. Voila! Grilled Veggie Soup.

SLOW COOKER CARIBBEAN STEW WITH HERB OIL AND YELLOW RICE

serves 6 to 8

30 minute cuisine plus 4 hours in the slow cooker

There is just something sexy-lazy about the Islands. The sun makes clothes-wearing an after-thought, since the lifestyle is languid and sensual. The killer is that as warm as the air is, the food in the Islands is as hot and spicy as it is flavorful. You'd expect to find ice cream and snow cones, but instead you are inundated with hot peppers and jerk seasoning. It doesn't make sense . . . but then, you're in the Islands, so "don't worry . . . be happy." In my version of a tropical dish, sweet potatoes face off with spicy sausage. Home cooks will revel in a stew that is not only crazy-fresh tasting, but delightfully easy to prepare, using your slow cooker. The accompanying scoop of yellow rice and a citrussy herb oil drizzle, make this Island staple an upscale supper.

FOR STEW:

2 tablespoons olive oil

2 boneless chicken breast halves, cut into ½-inch pieces

1 pound fresh chorizo sausage, casing removed if you have links

2 medium sweet potatoes, peeled and cut into ½-inch cubes, about 3 cups

1 large onion, peeled and diced, about 1 ½ cups

4 cloves garlic, peeled and minced, about 1 tablespoon

1 (28-ounce) can diced tomatoes with liquid

1 (15-ounce) can black beans, drained and rinsed

2 tablespoons tomato paste

1 teaspoon paprika

1 teaspoon thyme

1 teaspoon kosher salt

1 teaspoon coarse black pepper

½ teaspoon allspice

½ teaspoon cumin

FOR HERB OIL:

1 bunch cilantro, stems removed, about ½ cup leaves

Zest of 1 large orange, about 1 tablespoon

½ cup olive oil

Cooked yellow rice

Heat 2 tablespoons olive oil in a skillet over medium-high heat. Add the chicken to the skillet and cook until golden on all sides, about 3 to 5 minutes. Use a slotted spoon to transfer the chicken to your slow cooker. Do this in batches depending on the size of your skillet. Add the chorizo to the skillet and cook until browned and crumbly, about 5 minutes. Use a slotted spoon to transfer the sausage to the slow cooker.

Add the sweet potato, onion, and garlic to the slow cooker. Pour in the diced tomatoes and black beans. Stir in the tomato paste. Season with paprika, thyme, some of the salt and pepper and the allspice and cumin. Set the slow cooker on high and cook until the veggies are soft, and the chicken is cooked through, about 4 hours.

Place the cilantro leaves and orange zest in the bowl of a food processor. With the blade running, slowly pour in ½ cup olive oil. Season the herb oil with salt and pepper.

Place a spoonful of yellow rice in the bottom of a bowl. Ladle the stew over the top. Garnish with a drizzle of herb oil.

COOK'S TIP

Here's a "who knew?" kinda tip. It turns out, that spicy food like peppers and hot spices are prevalent in cuisine found in warmer climates for a reason. Eating spicy food can, in fact, cool you off. Your body perspires as a reaction to the heat and, therefore, your skin cools off. Contrarily, ice cream can warm you up. Foods with carbohydrates, fats, and proteins will cool you for a bit, but the energy your body expels digesting will warm you up. So, when you are luxuriating in the Caribbean sand, ask the waiter for a bowlful of peppers rather than an ice cream cone.

Bio Mercato

STUFFED HASSELBACK POTATOES

serves 4

60 minute cuisine

In my humble opinion, roasted potatoes are perfect with every meal. My eyes were opened to an even better roasted potato when I tasted an authentic Hasselback potato in Sweden, where the dish originated, in a restaurant with the same name. (Sue and I were on the first leg of our most memorable trip and were dining at the US Ambassador's residence. It was quite the experience to hear the Ambassador's tale of raising teenage girls in a very, very liberated country. The Swedish coming-of-age experience is quite different than ours. After the conversation, Sue and I agreed that we were happy to have raised our impressionable teens in the states!) My version of a Hasselback potato is based on a Junior League appy that I have made forevah. In that dish, you slice a round loaf of bread and stuff it with cheese and a rich seasoned, buttery sauce. Who knew it's even better in a potato!

4 large Idaho potatoes, scrubbed

1 cup butter, 2 sticks

4 garlic cloves, peeled and minced

1 teaspoon Beau Monde seasoning

1 teaspoon kosher salt

½ teaspoon ground white pepper

4 ounces Fontina cheese, shredded, about 1 cup

2 ounces Parmesan cheese, grated, about ½ cup

4 slices bacon, cooked and crumbled

Chopped fresh parsley

Preheat the oven to 425°. Lay two wooden skewers parallel on your work surface. Place one potato lengthwise on the skewers. Cut thin slices in the potato from top to bottom. Your knife will hit the skewers before it cuts all the way through, giving you an intact potato with accordion-type slices. Place the sliced potato into a baking dish. Repeat this technique on the remaining potatoes.

Melt the butter in a pot with the garlic and Beau Monde seasoning. Season with salt and pepper. Spoon some of the butter between the slices in the potatoes. Place shredded fontina cheese in between each slice. Pour the remaining butter over top of each potato and sprinkle with Parmesan cheese. Bake the potatoes until tender with the cheese melted, about 1 to 1 ½ hours depending on the size of your potato. Remove from the oven and garnish with crumbled bacon and fresh parsley.

COOK'S TIP

Beau Monde seasoning is a blend of celery and onion with a hint of sweetness. You can use it in rubs and marinades, but it's especially delicious in this dish.

RHUBARB CHUTNEY ON GOAT CHEESE CROSTINI

makes about 2 cups chutney

30 minute cuisine

Our first experiences with fresh markets were in our own backyards. Sue grew up on a farm in Ohio and grew a huge garden when she was raising her kids in Hendersonville, NC. My Irish grandparents had a lush garden in their backyard in rural Pennsylvania. Rhubarb was a staple in our gardens and is easily found in present-day fresh markets. You have to cook it down to really enjoy it. It also needs a bunch of sweetness to make is summery good. I love rhubarb chutney. You can make it in advance as it will keep for up to two weeks. When friends drop by, you're all set. Simply spread out some soft cheese and dollop the chutney over top. Serve it on crackers for an impromptu appetizer. It's also a great accompaniment to roast meats and works just fine over cream cheese, if your goat cheese has gone missing!

2 tablespoons olive oil

1 small onion, peeled and diced, about 1 cup

1 teaspoon ground mustard

1 teaspoon ground coriander

1 teaspoon ground cumin

¼ teaspoon crushed red pepper flakes

½ cup cider vinegar

2 bay leaves

1 cinnamon stick

1 teaspoon kosher salt

½ cup honey

¾ pound rhubarb, trimmed and cut into ½-inch pieces, about 2 ½ cups

½ cup golden raisins

Goat cheese, room temperature

Crostini

Chopped fresh mint

In a large skillet with lid, heat 2 tablespoons olive oil over medium-high heat. Add the onion and cook until soft, about 3 to 5 minutes. Stir in ground mustard, coriander, cumin, red pepper flakes and vinegar. Add the bay leaves and cinnamon stick. Season with salt. Pour in the honey. Add the rhubarb and raisins. Stir everything together. Reduce the heat to low, cover the skillet with the lid and simmer until the rhubarb is soft and falling apart, about 10 minutes. Remove the skillet from the heat and discard the bay leaves and cinnamon stick. Cool the chutney to room temperature.

Spread goat cheese onto some crostini. Spread chutney over top. Sprinkle with a bit of fresh mint.

BANGERS 'N MASH HAND PIES WITH MUSTARD DIPPING SAUCE

makes 8 small pies

45 minute cuisine

Visiting small towns in Ireland and England in the same trip, showed both the similarities and the differences of the countryside. It seems to me that the pastures are more lush and emerald green in Ireland, while the Brits embrace their high-rise housing options. Instead of finding differences, what Sue and I embraced were their similarities, specifically the social gathering places—pubs! While Londoners may boisterously "discuss" current political issues, Irish pub visitors are laughing a bit too loudly and discussing who just fell off the stool rather than who stole the election! It's the food found in the pubs that impress me the most. The pubs of England offer specialty dishes that go hand-in-hand with their fine ales. Bangers and mash: a combination of hearty sausages and creamy mashed potatoes, usually topped with onion gravy, is just one of those dishes that us tourists greedily lap up! In Irish pubs, to go along with their bold stouts, you will be tempted by meat pies of all varieties, including the peasant favorite, shepherd's pie. My mashed-up version of the two dishes combines potatoes and sausage in a hand-held pie. It is the best of both worlds and is easily prepared and enthusiastically accompanied by an all-American brewski, here in the good old US of A.

FOR HAND PIES:

1 tablespoon olive oil

1 pound mild Italian sausage

1 small russet potato, grated, about 1 cup

1 small onion, peeled and grated, about ½ cup

½ cup frozen peas, thawed

2 garlic cloves, peeled and minced

2 tablespoons chili sauce

1 tablespoon Worcestershire sauce

1 teaspoon kosher salt

1 teaspoon coarse black pepper

1 (1-pound) package frozen puff pastry, 2 sheets, thawed

3 tablespoons mayonnaise

2 tablespoons stone ground mustard

1 tablespoon Worcestershire sauce

Heat the olive oil in a skillet over medium heat. Cook the sausage until browned and crumbly. Use a box grater to grate potato and onion. Add the potato, onion, peas and garlic to the sausage and cook for 2 minutes. Stir in the chili sauce and 1 tablespoon Worcestershire. Season with salt and pepper. Remove from the heat and cool to room temperature.

Preheat the oven to 425°. Roll out the pastry crust and cut each sheet into approximately 4-inch squares, creating 8 pieces. Place about 2 tablespoons of the filling in the middle of each square. Brush the edges of the square with water. Fold over one side of the pasty to form a triangle. Seal the edges by crimping with the tines of a fork. Cut three small slits in the top of each pastry. Place the pies onto a baking sheet lined with parchment paper. Bake until the pies are golden, about 18 to 20 minutes.

Whisk together the mayonnaise, mustard and 1 tablespoon Worcestershire sauce. Serve the warm pies with the mustardy sauce for dipping.

GARLIC-PARMESAN FRIES WITH ROASTED TOMATO KETCHUP

serves a crowd

30 minutes for fries and an hour to simmer ketchup

True confession: I cannot resist tomatoes at the farmer's market. I don't know why, but they are sweeter, more fragrant, and all around more delicious than the ones we find in the grocery store. What then happens is I end up with a whole bunch of tomatoes and find myself looking for ways to use them. Truer confession: This is just an excuse to give you a really, really good French fry recipe. Somehow eating that fry is just a little less guilty when you use real tomatoes to make the ketchup you dip it into. Right?

FOR KETCHUP:

2 pounds ripe plum tomatoes, about 12 to 16

1 tablespoon olive oil

1 medium white onion, peeled and diced, about ½ cup

1 clove garlic, peeled and minced, about 1 teaspoon

½ cup cider vinegar

⅓ cup brown sugar

½ teaspoon kosher salt

¼ teaspoon coarse black pepper

¼ teaspoon ground mustard

¼ teaspoon ground all spice

¼ teaspoon ground cloves

¼ teaspoon ground ginger

FOR POTATOES:

4 large Idaho potatoes, scrubbed

Canola oil for frying

2 ounces Parmesan cheese, grated, about ½ cup

2 tablespoons chopped fresh parsley

2 cloves garlic, peeled and minced, about 2 tablespoons

Preheat the oven to 450°. Slice the tomatoes in half. Place cut-side down onto a baking sheet, coated with vegetable oil spray. Bake until the tomatoes are tender and wilted, about 10 to 15 minutes. Pass the tomatoes through a food mill, first using the course blade and second using the fine blade. (Alternatively, you can pulse the tomatoes in the bowl of a food processor. Then pour the tomatoes through a sieve and into a bowl.) Whatever method you use, the goal is a smooth-textured tomato puree free of tomato skins and seeds.

Heat 1 tablespoon olive oil in a skillet over medium heat. Add the onion and garlic and cook until the onion is soft and translucent. Add the tomato puree and remaining seasonings. Reduce the heat to low and simmer the ketchup until the flavors merge and the liquid reduces to about 2 cups. This will take at least an hour. Watch and stir your ketchup often to prevent burning.

Peel the potatoes. Cut each lengthwise into ¼-inch slices. Cut each slice into ¼-inch strips. Place the strips into a bowl of cold water for at least 30 minutes. Drain the potatoes through a colander. Transfer to paper towels and pat completely dry.

Pour enough canola oil into a deep pot or skillet to come one-third up the side. Heat over medium-high heat to 325°. Use a candy thermometer to monitor the temperature. Fry the potatoes in batches, until they just begin to turn golden, about 5 minutes. This will cook the inside of the fries. Use a slotted spoon to transfer the potatoes to a platter lined with paper towels. You can hold the fries at this stage for several hours.

Mix together Parmesan cheese, parsley and garlic in a small bowl. Set this seasoning mix aside.

When you are ready to serve, heat the oil to 375°. Cook the fries in the oil until they are golden brown and crisp on the outside, about 5 minutes. Transfer to a platter lined with paper towels and season with Parmesan seasoning, salt and pepper. Serve the fries with homemade ketchup.

Felice Navidad

POTATO PANCAKES WITH SAUTÉED APPLESAUCE

serves 4

30 minute cuisine

Sue and I met on a three-week trip, that included a visit to Moscow and a cruise in the Baltic Sea. Onboard, when we weren't eating foie gras, we identified our alternate favorite dish to be caviar. Yes, it's decadent, but when in Rome . . . I mean Russia . . . anyway, we ate caviar from pearl spoons, on blinis, on deviled eggs and on our other favorite thing: potato pancakes! You just can't beat a wafer-thin pancake with crisp little bits on the edges. Foie gras and caviar may not be your thing, but these potato pancakes are pretty darn good, especially when you top them with a sweet sauté of fresh apples. Serve these with a grilled pork chop for a fun family side dish!

FOR APPLESAUCE:

2 tablespoons butter

2 Granny Smith apples, peeled cored and diced, about 2 cups

¼ cup brown sugar

1 teaspoon ground cinnamon

1 teaspoon Chinese Five Spice

FOR POTATO PANCAKES:

2 large russet potatoes, about 1 pound, peeled and grated

1 medium white onion, peeled and grated

2 tablespoons unbleached all-purpose flour

1 egg, beaten

1 teaspoon ground nutmeg

1 teaspoon kosher salt

½ teaspoon coarse black pepper

Canola oil

Confectioners' sugar

Heat the butter in a skillet over medium heat. Add the apples, brown sugar, cinnamon and Chinese five spice. Cook until the apples are soft and syrupy, about 10 to 15 minutes. Keep the applesauce warm.

Use a box grater, potato ricer, or shredding blade of your food processor, to grate the potatoes into a large bowl. Grate the onion into the bowl. Sprinkle the flour over the top. Pour the egg into the bowl. Season with nutmeg, salt and pepper and stir to combine.

Heat enough canola oil to coat the bottom of a skillet over medium heat. Drop a medium-size ice cream scoop full of batter into the oil. Flatten the batter with the back of the scoop to form circle-shaped pancakes. Do this in batches depending on the size of your skillet. Cook until the pancakes are golden brown on one side, about 2 to 3 minutes. Carefully flip the pancakes and cook for 2 to 3 minutes more. Transfer to a platter lined with paper towels. Continue, using all the batter, adding more oil as needed.

Serve warm potato pancakes with a sprinkle of confectioners' sugar and a spoonful of applesauce.

COOK'S TIP

Soooooo, if you want to pretend you are on a cruise ship traversing the cool Adriatic Seas, serve these potato pancakes topped with thin slices of smoked salmon. Better yet, dollop the pancakes with a tad of sour cream, a sprinkle of fresh chives, and a pearl spoonful of caviar. It's oh so decadent!

HOMEMADE GNOCCHI WITH SAUSAGE AND BUTTERNUT SQUASH

serves 6 to 8 crowd

60 minute cuisine

When in Rome, we ordered what we thought would be a hearty Italian meal starring gnocchi: delicate puffs of pasta, usually made with potato. Turns out we were amazed by the lightness of the dish. You would think that gnocchi are heavy and totally tummy-filling, but I found them to be airy, less dense than our Southern dumplings. This recipe combines the flavors of fall, butternut squash and sausages, to make a sauce that the gnocchi swim in. Homemade gnocchi are fun to make! Use light hands to blend the ingredients together and you will create an airy puff. If you are a little daunted, don't turn away from this dish. You can always purchase prepared gnocchi in the grocery store. We don't judge!

FOR GNOCCHI:

1 ½ pounds Yukon Gold potatoes

2 cups unbleached all-purpose flour

1 large egg

½ teaspoon kosher salt

FOR SAUCE:

2 tablespoons olive oil

1 medium onion, peeled and diced

1 ½ pounds mild Italian sausage

2 tablespoons butter

4 garlic cloves, peeled and thinly sliced, about 2 tablespoons

2 cups butternut squash chunks, cut into ½-inch squares

½ teaspoon coarse black pepper

½ teaspoon nutmeg

1 cup dry white wine

1 cup homemade chicken stock or prepared low sodium broth

2 tablespoons chopped fresh Italian parsley

4 ounces Parmigiano-Reggiano, grated about 1 cup

Boil the whole potatoes until they are soft, about 30 to 45 minutes, depending on their size. Remove the potatoes and cool slightly. When they are cool enough to handle, peel the potatoes and pass them through a food mill, potato ricer, or pulse them in the bowl of a food processor and place into a large bowl.

Bring a large pot of water to a boil. Place ice and cold water into a separate large bowl.

Make well in center of the potatoes and sprinkle all over with the flour. Place the egg and salt in center of well. Use a fork to stir the egg into the flour and potatoes. Bring the dough together by kneading gently to form a ball and then continue kneading until the dough is dry to the touch, about 4 to 5 minutes more.

Break off a baseball-size piece of dough. Roll first into a ball and then into a log about ¾-inch in diameter. Cut the log into 1-inch long pieces. Roll one piece over the back of the tines on a fork, pushing down slightly. This creates the little ridges that gnocchi are famous for. Place the gnocchi onto a parchment lined baking sheet. Continue the process until all the dough has been used.

Once all the gnocchi are formed, drop them in batches into the boiling water. When they float to the top, the gnocchi are done. Use a slotted spoon, to transfer the cooked gnocchi to an ice water bath, to stop the cooking process. Once all the gnocchi have been cooled in the bath, use a slotted spoon to remove them to a platter and discard the water. Set aside while you make the sauce, or you can toss with a bit of olive oil and store in an airtight container for up to 48 hours in the refrigerator.

Heat 2 tablespoons olive oil in a large skillet over medium heat. Add the onion and cook until soft, about 5 minutes. Add the sausage and cook until crumbled and brown. Transfer the sausage and onion to a bowl.

Heat 2 tablespoons butter in the same skillet. Add the garlic and butternut squash. Season with salt, pepper and nutmeg. Add the wine and cook until the liquid is reduced, about 2 to 3 minutes. Pour in the chicken broth and continue cooking until the squash is fork tender, about 5 to 8 minutes more. Add the sausage and onion back to the skillet. Stir in the gnocchi and parsley. Cook until the gnocchi are warmed through. Sprinkle the cheese over the top. Serve the dish right from the skillet!

Turn Up the Volume

VERY VEGGIE POT PIE WITH CHEESY DROP BISCUIT CRUST

serves 6 or more

45 minute cuisine

The streets of Paris are lined with bistros that offer elevated peasant fare featuring farm fresh veggies enhanced with seasonings like herbes de Provence and wine-laced sauces. Pot pie is inherently American but, there is a hint of Paris that makes its way into this casserole-style dish. The sauce is infused with root veggie flavors and a cheesy topping that is just too good to resist. Viva la Veggie!

FOR FILLING:

2 tablespoons olive oil

2 tablespoons butter

2 large yellow onions, peeled and diced, about 2 cups

4 medium carrots, peeled, trimmed and diced, about 2 cups

2 medium turnips, peeled and diced, about 2 cups

3 medium celery ribs, sliced, about 1 cup

½ medium butternut squash, peeled and diced, about 1 cup

4 cloves garlic, peeled and minced

1 teaspoon kosher salt

½ teaspoon coarse black pepper

½ cup all-purpose flour

½ cup dry sherry

2 cups homemade chicken stock, or low sodium chicken broth

½ cup whipping cream

¼ pound fresh shelled peas, about 1 cup (you can substitute with thawed, frozen peas)

2 tablespoons chopped fresh parsley

1 teaspoon herbes de Provence

½ teaspoon ground nutmeg

FOR TOPPING:

2 ¼ cups all-purpose flour

1 tablespoon baking powder

1 teaspoon kosher salt

6 tablespoons butter, chilled, cut into pieces

4 ounces Swiss cheese, grated

1 to 1½ cups buttermilk

Heat the olive oil and 2 tablespoons butter in a large pot over medium-high heat. Add the onions, carrots, turnips, celery and butternut squash to the pot. Cook until the veggies begin to soften, about 5 to 10 minutes. Stir in the garlic and cook 2 minutes more. Season with some of the salt and pepper. Sprinkle the veggies with ½ cup flour and stir. Stir in the sherry and cook for 2 minutes. Pour in the broth and whipping cream. Simmer until the broth is quite thick, like the texture of gravy. Stir in the peas and parsley. Season with herbes de Provence and nutmeg. If your sauce is too thick, you can add more broth. If it is too thin, you can add a bit of flour combined with a bit of butter (beurre manié) to the sauce. Turn off the heat.

Preheat the oven to 400°. Place 2 ¼ cups flour into the bowl of a food processor. Add the baking soda and 1 teaspoon salt. Pulse to combine. Add 6 tablespoons cold butter and pulse to form crumbs. Add the cheese and pulse. With the blade running, pour in 1 cup buttermilk until the dough just comes together. You can add more buttermilk if you need to. The dough should be very wet.

Pour the veggies into a 13 x 9 x 2-inch baking dish that has been coated with vegetable oil spray. Use a large spoon to drop the dough onto the veggies. Bake until the biscuit-like topping is crusty and golden brown, and the veggies are bubbling, about 25 to 30 minutes.

FIERCE POTATOES (PATATAS BRAVAS)

serves 4 as appy or side dish

45 minute cuisine

Sue sees a basket of freshly dug potatoes, and they become the centerpiece of her painting. I see her painting, and my taste buds scream for this reincarnation of Madrid's Patatas Bravas: a fiery Spanish fried potato dish. It's a tapas classic in España! The accompanying spicy sauce coats the crispy potato chunks, with just enough creaminess to tame the heat from the cayenne pepper. It's a dish for sharing and can easily replace fries on your next burger platter. All this from a basket of spuds!

FOR SAUCE:

2 garlic cloves, peeled and minced, about 1 teaspoon

1 teaspoon kosher salt

1 tablespoon olive oil

1 teaspoon ground paprika

½ teaspoon cayenne pepper

½ cup crushed tomatoes

1 tablespoon sherry vinegar

¼ cup mayonnaise

Juice of 1 small lime, about 1 tablespoon

FOR POTATOES:

1 large russet potato, peeled and cut into ½-inch dice, about 3 cups

½ teaspoon baking soda

Vegetable oil for frying

Chopped fresh parsley

1 small lime, cut into wedges

Use the flat blade of a large knife to make a paste out of the garlic and 1 teaspoon salt by squishing the two together while scraping back and forth across your cutting board. Heat 1 tablespoon olive oil in a skillet over low heat. Add the garlic paste to the skillet with the paprika and cayenne pepper. Cook for 3 minutes. Raise the heat to medium. Stir in the crushed tomatoes and sherry vinegar. Simmer for 2 to 3 minutes more. Remove the sauce from the heat and cool to room temperature. Fold in the mayonnaise and lime juice. Scrape the sauce into a bowl.

Bring a large pot of water to boil over high heat. Add the potatoes and baking soda to the water. When the water begins to boil again, cook the potatoes for 2 more minutes. Drain the water from the pan and reduce the heat to low. Stir and cook for another minute to thoroughly dry out the potatoes. Transfer the potatoes to a platter.

Pour vegetable oil about a third of the way up the sides of a deep pot. Heat the oil to 375°. You can use a candy thermometer to monitor the heat of the oil. Remember not to pour too much oil into the pot as it bubbles up quite a lot once you start frying the potatoes. Add the potatoes to the oil using a slotted spoon or wire skimmer. Do this in batches depending on the size of your pot. Fry until the potatoes are golden brown and crispy. Use a slotted spoon or wire skimmer to transfer the potatoes to paper towel lined baking sheets. Season with salt.

To serve, place a spoonful of potatoes into a small bowl. Stir a dollop of sauce into the potatoes. Garnish the dish with fresh parsley and a wedge of lime.

Cook's Tip

Adding a bit of baking soda to the boiling water helps to plump the potato cubes. The centers are puffy so that when we fry these little pieces, we don't have to fry twice like in the other fried potato recipes. I use this method when I sauté zucchini slices. Just a bit of added baking soda to the pan helps to plump up the slices creating soft little pillows. Give it a try!

WARM PARSLEY POTATO SALAD

serves a BIG crowd

20 minute cuisine

I am drawn to the baskets of baby new potatoes at the market. They come in colors like red, golden, and purple. I'm also a strong believer in potluck suppers. I find potlucks to be a naturally easy way to entertain, and thus and incentive to share a meal with friends and family. This dish fits the bill for potluck, while taking advantage of my favorite bitty baby potatoes. Choose golf ball size potatoes for this recipe, and don't forget to grab a bunch of fresh parsley (although cilantro or dill would be just as good) while you are strolling the market. Parsley potatoes are a favorite for Sunday suppers. This recipe takes that homey potato dish and boosts it to new flavor heights with a warm bacony dressing. It's pretty yummy!

6 tablespoons butter

1 ½ pounds baby potatoes, rinsed and dried

1 teaspoon kosher salt

1 teaspoon coarse black pepper

3 tablespoons chopped fresh parsley

¼ pound bacon, cut into ½-inch pieces, about 3 to 4 slices

½ medium red onion, peeled and chopped, about ½ cup

¼ cup white balsamic vinegar

2 teaspoons Dijon-style mustard

¼ cup olive oil

4 to 5 green onions, thinly sliced, about ½ cup

Melt the butter in a large pot (with lid) over low heat. Add the potatoes. Season with salt and pepper. Cover the pot with the lid and cook the potatoes for 20 minutes. Shake the pot every few minutes so that the potatoes brown evenly on all sides. Turn off the heat. Add the parsley to the potatoes. Place the lid on the pot and let stand for 5 minutes to finish steaming the potatoes while you move on to the dressing.

Cook the bacon in a large skillet over medium-high heat until crisp. Remove the bacon with a slotted spoon and transfer to a platter lined with paper towels. Reduce the heat to medium. Add the red onion to the rendered bacon fat left in the skillet and cook until soft, about

3 to 4 minutes. Remove the skillet from the heat. Carefully stir in the vinegar and mustard and cook for 2 more minutes. Stir in ¼ cup oil. Pour the warm dressing into the pot with the potatoes and toss gently to coat. Fold in the bacon and green onions. Serve the salad warm or at room temperature.

FARMERS MARKET TIP

So…what makes a potato a "baby" or "new" potato? These terms are used to describe a potato that is plucked from the soil before it has matured. Baby potatoes tend to be sweeter, less dense. The skin is not as thick as a mature potato. Therefore, you need not cook the potato as long as you would a fully grown one, which is why this particular cooking method works so well in this recipe. Basically just a few minutes of steaming, cooks the potato to the soft-tender stage. Adding butter to the mix? Well, that's just an extra bit of YUM!

TORTILLA ESPAÑOLA (POTATO TORTE)

serves a crowd

40 minute cuisine

There are a lot of fiery bites on tapas plates. I guess the thought is the more blazing your taste buds, the more you require a swallow of chilled aperitif to put out the flames. This tapas wedge, has no fiery ambitions at all. It's made up of thinly sliced potatoes that you cook in oil before you assemble them into a torte held together with beaten eggs. It's a nice change to our all-American spud dishes and will fit in very nicely on either your brunch or dinner buffet table. It feeds a crowd, so it will also work well for your take-along potluck suppers. I describe this truly Spanish dish as a mash up of potatoes au gratin and a potato frittata with a definitely leaning toward good old-fashioned comfort food.

5 to 6 medium Yukon Gold potatoes

2 teaspoons kosher salt

Vegetable oil for frying

2 large yellow onions, diced, about 3 cups

6 large garlic cloves, peeled and minced, about 3 tablespoons

6 large eggs, beaten

½ teaspoon coarse black pepper

Chopped, fresh parsley

Use a mandoline slicer or very sharp knife to slice the potatoes into thin rounds. Place the potatoes into a colander and toss with salt. Pour enough oil to come one-third up the side of a deep skillet. Heat the oil over medium-high heat. You will know that the oil is ready when you place the end of a wooden spoon into the oil and you see bubbles. Fry the potatoes in the oil until they are tender in the middle and just beginning to brown on the edges, about 5 to 8 minutes. You can do this in batches so that you don't crowd too many slices into the pan. Use a slotted spoon or wire skimmer to transfer the potatoes onto a paper lined baking sheet.

Carefully add the onions and garlic to the oil. Lower the temperature to medium low and cook until the onions are soft and beginning to turn golden, about 5 to 8 minutes. Use a slotted spoon or wire skimmer to transfer to the baking sheet holding the potatoes.

Remove the skillet from the heat and carefully pour all but 2 tablespoons of the oil into heat resistant bowl. (When cooled, you can strain and reuse the oil for another recipe.)

Place the eggs into a large bowl. Gently slide the potatoes, onions and garlic into the bowl. Sprinkle with a bit more salt and pepper. Use a wooden spoon to gently toss everything together, trying not to break the potato slices. Some will break, so don't fret.

Heat the oil that remains in the skillet over medium heat. Pour in the potato and eggs using a spatula and spread evenly in the pan. Cook for 30 seconds to brown the (soon-to-be top) of the torte. Reduce the heat to medium low and cook until the center is set, about 5 to 8 minutes. Use the spatula to gently loosen the edges from the pan as it cooks. Shake the skillet to make sure the center is setting. Turn off the heat. Take a plate that is larger than the skillet and place it upside-down over the skillet. With one hand on the plate and the other on the skillet handle, invert the pan so that the torte comes out and onto the plate. There might be a little loose egg around the edges. Use your spatula to scrape any bits back into the torte. Gently slide the inverted torte back into the pan and turn the heat to medium. Cook until a tester inserted into the center of the torte comes out clean, about 5 to 6 minutes more. Transfer the torte to a clean platter and keep warm. The torte can be served warm or at room temperature. Sprinkle with a bit of fresh chopped parsley. Slice into wedges.

Cook's Tip

One of the easiest and most FUN parties to host is a Tapas Party. It's easy because you can make all of the food in advance and serve it on a buffet table. Offer small plates and let your guests graze all evening, while you refill their Sangria glasses! My tapas buffet table includes this torte, ham croquettes, my garlic shrimp and shishito pepper dish and of course paella. All of the recipes can be found in this book. Giving your party a FUN theme is an excellent way to entertain.

SWEET POTATO FRIES WITH CRISPY BUFFALO CHICKEN WITH BLUE CHEESE GRAVY

serves a crowd

45 minute cuisine

We're going way, way beyond that bag of frozen fries right here, right now! This is a mash-up of all my favorites. Canadian Poutine meets Jersey Disco fries and brings along Buffalo wing flavor in this elevated French fry dish. Poutine starts with a plate of fries. It's topped with cheese curds and then soaked in brown gravy. Disco fries slather fries with brown gravy and then pile on Mozzarella cheese. Then there's my fave, Buffalo wings that are fried and then submerged in melting garlic butter and hot sauce. If you crave a decadent French fry dish, then any one of these will do. But if you are looking for the absolute ultimate fry dish . . . give this a try!

FOR FRIES:

3 medium sweet potatoes, scrubbed and cut into ½-inch thick spears

Oil for frying

FOR BLUE CHEESE DRESSING:

4 tablespoons butter, ¼ cup

¼ cup unbleached all-purpose flour

2 cups milk, room temperature

1 teaspoon onion powder

1 to 2 teaspoons kosher salt

½ teaspoon ground white pepper

2 ounces blue cheese, crumbled, about ½ cup

FOR CHICKEN

2 boneless, skinless chicken breasts

½ teaspoon coarse black pepper

½ cup seasoned breadcrumbs

2 tablespoons olive oil

4 tablespoons butter, ¼ cup

2 to 3 garlic cloves, peeled and minced, about 1 tablespoon

1 (5-ounce) bottle hot sauce

2 tablespoons balsamic vinegar

3 celery ribs, thinly sliced

Soak the sweet potato spears in cold water for 20 minutes. Drain and pat dry. Heat enough oil to come one-third up the side of a deep pot to 325°. (Use a candy thermometer for this). Cook the fries in the oil until they just begin to turn golden, about 5 minutes. Use a slotted spoon to transfer the fries to a sheet pan lined with paper towels. Cover with clean paper towels until ready to assemble the dish.

Place 4 tablespoons butter into a sauté pan over medium-high heat. When the butter is melted, whisk in the flour. Cook the butter and flour until it bubbles. It will begin to color. Continue cooking until golden brown, about 8 minutes total. Slowly whisk in the milk. Reduce the heat to medium. Season with onion powder, some of the salt and white pepper. Continue cooking until the sauce becomes thick and gravy-like. Turn off the heat and stir in the blue cheese. It's okay if the gravy is not smooth. (The blue cheese crumbles resemble cheese curds like in the real deal poutine.) Cover the "gravy" with aluminum foil to keep it warm.

Season the chicken breasts with salt and black pepper. Put the bread crumbs onto a plate. Dredge the breasts in the bread crumbs until coated. Heat 2 tablespoons olive oil in a sauté pan, over medium-high heat. Cook the breasts in the oil, turning once until golden brown and crispy on both sides, about 8 minutes total cooking time. Transfer the chicken to a plate to rest.

Melt 4 tablespoons butter in the same pan that you used for the chicken, over medium-low heat. When melted, add the garlic and pour in the hot sauce. Stir in the balsamic vinegar. Simmer the sauce for 5 minutes. Place the chicken breast back into the pan and coat with the sauce. Simmer the sauced chicken over low heat while you finish the fries.

Fire up the oil to 375°. Fry the potatoes for a second time. The first frying cooks them, the middle. The second time you fry, the outside crisps. Cook until the fries are golden brown and crispy, about 5 minutes. Transfer to a paper-towel lined baking sheet and season with salt.

Assemble the dish by removing the chicken from the pan and slicing into thin strips. Lay the fries onto a platter. Top with slices of chicken. Pour the blue cheese gravy over the top. Drizzle some of the hot sauce from the skillet, over the gravy. Garnish with thin slices of celery.

MEATS AND CHEESES

/mēt/

noun

1. the flesh of an animal (especially a mammal) as food.
   "pieces of meat"
   synonyms: flesh, animal flesh

/CHēz/

noun

1. a food made from the pressed curds of milk.
   "grated cheese"

Sunday Morning Stroll

When Sue and I met on that once-in-a lifetime trip, we flew from a little town in Tennessee to Moscow on a private plane (thanks to Marti and Wayne) with about twenty other pals. Yes . . . it was quite a treat! We stayed in Moscow for a couple of days, while we toured the cathedrals and museums. We followed that stay with one in Copenhagen where we sample an appetizer of dark bread topped with thin slices of fresh cucumber, radish and dill for starters. After a couple of days of sightseeing and bike riding around the city, we embarked on a cruise ship that sailed the Baltic Sea. It's this part of the trip where Sue and I bonded over foie gras, champagne and caviar. Cruise ship fare was a far cry from the country fare served in the quaint bistros of Moscow. But, it is that contrasting food experience that stays with me all these years later.

We didn't visit any local markets when in Moscow. We were pretty much contained during our short visit. We did, however, manage to visit a couple of local bistros. Far different, than the bustling, vocal eateries that you find in other European cities, our experience was one that held sedate patrons and non-apologetic servers. The food was unique and delicious in its austerity and traditionalism. Of course, we tried Borscht, thick beet soup with toppings of fresh sour cream and even fresher herbs. On another evening, we sampled thick, rich beef stew. I still remember the tangy-sweet after taste that lingered, making you want more. It was only years later, when my book club read *A Gentleman in Moscow* by Amor Towles, that I discovered Latvian stew, which is probably the stew we sampled so many years earlier. As it turns out, that sweet, tangy taste is a result of adding dried fruits and a bit of cider to what would be an ordinary meat and root vegetable stew. Delicious!

By contrast to the austerity of Moscow streets, the markets in Copenhagen, were abundant with vendors offering wares of home-made items from jewelry to rag dolls. The foods offered by the locals are mostly pre-made sweets that just scream for you to taste as you stroll along the booths.

Our trip included a stop-over in Ireland, as we winged our way home. As I see Sue's painting of *Sunday Market Stroll*, I recall the lush, greenery of Ireland's fields and valleys and remember the fresh markets teaming with cheeses, lamb, root veggies and fresh seafood. We visited Cork, which offers indoor and smaller farmers' markets that have items like baked artisanal soda bread, pastries, chutneys and jams. I was surprised by the amount of fresh seafood available. I was more surprised by the vibrant green color of the valleys. The scenery in Ireland is spectacular. We saw fields and fields of goats and sheep with markings that denoted which farm they belong to, lest they stray away. No fences to spoil the landscape!

We spent no small amount of time in the local pubs, and enjoyed many versions of Irish stews, colcannon (a mash of potatoes and leafy greens), coddle (more potatoes, this time with sausage) and Shepherd's pie, a casserole of minced meats flavored with onions and garlic and topped with . . . well potatoes! There were a couple of ales that we managed to chug down and quite a bit of late night singing that fit right in with peasant comfort food.

Sue and I loved that trip. From the subtle restraint in Moscow, to the all-out love of life in Ireland, and the unreality of flowing champagne, caviar and foie gras on the ship, it was three weeks immersed in a life other than our norm. This is the trip that bonded us as friends, led to our love of traveling, taught us to respect the traditions of others and to treasure each day.

Rock 'n Roll

BEEF AND BROCCOLI NOODLE BOWL

serves 4

30 minute cuisine

Kind of a mash-up of Chinese take-out and the offerings from the farmers market, bowls are making their way to fast-dining menus quicker than, well quicker than a drive through! This fresh approach to a traditional Chinese take-out dish is filled with flavor and crisp veggie. The absolute best part of the broccoli flower is its edible stem. By peeling the tough outer layer from the stalk, you reach a crisp-tender bite that mimics sliced water chestnuts.

2 pounds skirt steak

½ cup soy sauce

3 tablespoons dry sherry

2 tablespoons dark brown sugar

3 garlic cloves, peeled and minced

1 (1-inch) piece ginger, peeled and minced

2 stalks broccoli, cut into florets, stems peeled and thinly sliced

2 tablespoons olive oil

2 tablespoons sesame oil

2 cups homemade beef stock, or prepared low sodium beef broth

¼ cup cornstarch whisked with 2 tablespoons cold water

8 ounces wide lo mein noodles

2 tablespoons hoisin sauce

2 tablespoons sesame seeds

Place the skirt steak into the freezer for 30 minutes to make it easier to carve. Slice the steak into very thin strips and place into a bowl. Whisk together the soy sauce, sherry, brown sugar, garlic and ginger. Spoon the sauce over the steak and marinate for 20 minutes.

Blanch (or steam) the broccoli and stem slices until crisp-tender. I use my microwave oven on the veggie setting to do this. Alternatively, you can blanch the broccoli in boiling water, or in a steamer basket. You want crispy, bright green florets.

Heat the olive oil and sesame oil in a large skillet (or wok) over medium-high heat. Add the beef and marinade and cook until the beef is browned on both sides, about 3 to 5 minutes.

You can do this in batches depending on the size of your skillet. Add the broccoli and cook for 2 minutes more. Pour in the beef stock. Stir in the cornstarch slurry and cook until the sauce thickens, about 3 to 5 minutes more.

Cook the noodles in boiling salted water according to the package directions, about 4 minutes. Drain the noodles and add to the skillet. Pour in the hoisin sauce and toss everything together. Top with sesame seeds. Serve the beef and broccoli with the noodles in shallow bowls.

LATVIAN STEW (PORK STEW WITH APRICOTS AND PRUNES)

serves 8

30 minute cuisine plus several hours for stewing

A simple peasant stew dish is found on many menus in Moscow, from the local mom and pop diners to the grandest hotel. Through the years of strife, stews were the way to stretch ingredients into meals. The addition of dark bread and rich, creamy butter adds to the substance of the meal. This recipe is based on the famous dish that fills the pages of the book club favorite, A Gentleman in Moscow. It differs from American stews with the addition of dried fruit which gives the dish a sweet depth of flavor. I'm not totally sure, but I think Sue and I sampled this dish when we were in a little restaurant right outside the door of our hotel on our first night in Moscow. It was a delicious combination of sweet and sour.

2 tablespoons butter

2 tablespoons olive oil

2 (1-pound) pork tenderloins, cut into 1-inch pieces

1 teaspoon kosher salt

1 teaspoon coarse black pepper

2 large onions, peeled and diced into ½ inch pieces, about 3 cups

3 medium Yukon gold potatoes, diced into 1-inch pieces, about 3 cups

1 medium sweet potato, peeled and diced into 1-inch pieces, about 1 cup

1 head garlic, cloves peeled and thinly sliced, about ¼ cup

¼ cup unbleached all-purpose flour

2 cups homemade chicken stock or prepared low sodium broth

1 ½ cups apple cider

1 cup dark beer

2 tablespoons Dijon-style mustard

1 teaspoon ground coriander

½ teaspoon ground cinnamon

8 ounces dried pitted prunes, chopped, about 1 ½ cups

6 ounces dried apricots, chopped, about 1 cup

Heat the butter and olive oil in a large pot over medium-high heat. Season the pork with some of the salt and pepper. Brown the pork in the hot oil, in batches. Use a slotted spoon to transfer the browned pork to a platter. Place the onions, potatoes, sweet potato and garlic in the pot. Cook until the veggies begin to soften, about 5 minutes. Sprinkle the veggies with flour and season with salt and pepper. Pour in the stock, cider and beer. Stir in the mustard, coriander, and cinnamon. Return the pork to the pot. Stir in the prunes and apricots. Simmer the stew until the pork and vegetables are cooked, and the sauce is thickened, about 1 hour.

Plum Crazy About You

SUNDAY GRAVY

serves 6 or more

all day cuisine

I'm not sure if this is an authentic Italian recipe or a Northeast American Italian recipe. But I know this: there are as many traditional family variations of this pasta sauce as there are Italian Nonas. What is common is that the sauce is rich, meaty, and benefits from simmering slowly all-day long. This can be accomplished in a large pot on the stovetop, in a slow cooker or my preference, in a covered Dutch oven placed in an oven, set on low heat. Whichever your choice, the freedom of this recipe, allows you to prepare it in the morning, and walk away for hours. When you take the top of that simmering pot, the rich sauce is done and ready to ladle onto your favorite pasta.

2 tablespoons olive oil

4 meaty beef short ribs

3 teaspoons kosher salt

2 teaspoons coarse black pepper

4 links Italian sausage

2 large white onions, peeled and diced, about 2 cups

6 garlic cloves, peeled and minced, about 2 tablespoons

2 teaspoons dried oregano

2 cups red wine

2 (28-ounce cans) crushed tomatoes

1 (6-ounce) can tomato paste

1 quart homemade beef stock, or prepared low sodium broth

2 teaspoons granulated sugar

12 (2-inch) meatballs (see Cook's Tip for recipe)

1 pound dried fettuccine pasta

2 tablespoons chopped fresh parsley

Parmesan cheese

Heat the olive oil in a Dutch oven (or large pot) over medium-high heat. Season the short ribs with salt and pepper. Cook the short ribs on all sides until they are well browned. This should take you about 10 minutes. Transfer the short ribs to a platter.

Cut the sausage links in half creating two smaller links. Cook the sausage in the oil until well browned, about 3 to 4 minutes. Transfer the sausage to the same platter as the short ribs. Reduce the heat to medium, add the onions to the oil and cook until softened and beginning to turn golden, about 3 to 5 minutes. Stir in the garlic. Pour in the wine. Simmer until the wine almost completely disappears. Pour in the crushed tomatoes. Stir in the tomato paste. Pour in three cups of the beef stock. Stir in the sugar and season with salt and pepper. Add the short ribs and and sausage back to the sauce. Cover and simmer on very low heat until the rib meat is falling off the bone, 4 hours or more on the stove top, 8 hours on low in a slow cooker, or 6 hours in a 250° oven.

Preheat the oven to 400°. Coat a rimmed baking sheet with 1 tablespoon olive oil. Place the meatballs onto the baking sheet and gently roll them in the oil. Bake until the meatballs are cooked through and the outside are golden brown, about 15 minutes. Gently place the meatballs into the sauce. Simmer for at least another 30 minutes. If your sauce is too thick, you can add more beef stock. If your sauce is too thin, you can stir in more tomato paste. Taste and add more salt if you like.

Cook pasta in salted boiling water according to the directions on the package. Drain the pasta and pour into a large bowl. Ladle some of the Sunday Gravy over the pasta and toss to coat the noodles. Ladle more sauce over the pasta and include the short rib meat, sausage and meatballs. Sprinkle with parsley. Serve family style with grated Parmesan cheese on the side.

Cook's Tip

You can purchase prepared meatballs in the butcher department of the grocery store. But, if you would like to make your own, it's easy to do. Soak 2 to 3 slices of bread with about ¼ cup milk for 10 minutes. Place ¾ pound of lean ground beef and ¾ pound ground pork in a small bowl. Season with ½ teaspoon dried oregano, 1 teaspoon chopped fresh parsley, 1 tablespoon of grated Parmesan cheese, salt and pepper. Add the soaked bread and any excess milk to the meat. Use your hands to gently combine all the ingredients and form into 2-inch balls. The gentler your hands, the fluffier the meatball.

VEGGIE STUFFED BEEF BURGERS WITH GORGONZOLA AND BALSAMIC GLAZE

serves 6

45 minute cuisine

Sue paints canvases of farm-fresh, picture-perfect veggies. But, you and I know that in real life our veggies can look a tad limp and droopy at the end of the week, stuck back there in the rear of your produce drawer. This is the perfect recipe to take advantage of those long forgotten ingredients. It blends rich cuts of beef with quick roasted veggies for a super burger filled with flavor. It's also a great way to sneak a little bit of fresh veg into you kids favorite meal!

1 small eggplant, peeled and finely diced, about 2 cups

1 medium zucchini, finely diced, about 1 cup

1 large red bell pepper, seeded, veins removed, finely diced, about 1 cup

1 small red onion, peeled, finely diced, about ½ cup

6 garlic cloves, peeled and minced, about 2 tablespoons

1 tablespoon olive oil

1 teaspoon kosher salt

½ teaspoon coarse black pepper

1 pound beef short rib meat, ground

1 pound beef brisket, ground

1 large egg, beaten

2 tablespoons chopped fresh parsley

½ cup ketchup

¼ cup balsamic vinegar

6 large burger buns

2 to 4 tablespoons butter, melted for brushing

2 ounces Gorgonzola cheese, crumbled about ½ cup

Preheat the oven to 400°. Place all of the vegetables and garlic onto a baking sheet. Drizzle with olive oil and season with some of the salt and pepper. Use your hands to toss the veggies together in the olive oil. Roast until the veggies are golden and tender, about 15 to 20 minutes.

The smaller the dice, the faster the veggies cook. Remove the veggies from the oven and cool to room temperature.

Place the beef into a large bowl. Add the beaten egg and roasted veggies. Season with salt and pepper. Add the parsley. Use your hands to blend all the ingredients together. Form into 6 patties.

Whisk together the ketchup and balsamic vinegar in a bowl. Set the bowl on the counter while you move on to the buns.

Brush the outside and inside of the buns with melted butter and toast in a 300° degree oven, butter side up, until just golden, about 5 minutes.

Heat a grill pan over medium-high heat and coat with vegetable oil spray. Place the burgers onto the grill pan. Cook on one side for 5 to 7 minutes. Flip the burgers. Brush the top of the burgers with the balsamic glaze. Continue cooking until the burgers reach an internal temperature of 145° for medium rare. Top with Gorgonzola crumbles. Turn off the heat. Tent the burgers with aluminum foil and let sit for 2 to 3 minutes to melt the cheese. Serve the burgers on the toasted buns.

Cook's Tip

Ask your butcher to grind the short rib and brisket together for you. Most butchers will be happy to respond to your request at no extra charge. If your purchase the beef from the farmers market you probably won't have this option. A meat grinder attachment for your electric mixer will work just fine. Remember to keep the meat chilled so that it goes through the grinder as easily as possible.

DOWN 'N DIRTY SOUTHERN BEEF WRAPS

serves 4

45 minute cuisine

Some of the very best food offerings at the farmers market are found at the food trucks. They hold the fare that gets you to the fair! Rustic breakfast pizzas in the morning markets, deeply Southern wraps for lunch, even artisanal brews offered in the late afternoons. It's all worth sampling. I try to have a different treat every time I go, but I always have something! This is my most favorite wrap from those I've sampled so far . . . but hey, there are so many more to come.

FOR STEAK BITES:

1 (12-ounce) sirloin beef steak

2 tablespoons Worcestershire sauce

1 teaspoon paprika

1 teaspoon onion powder

1 teaspoon garlic powder

1 teaspoon kosher salt

1 teaspoon coarse black pepper

FOR PIMENTO CHEESE:

3 ounces cream cheese

4 ounces cheddar cheese, grated, about 1 cup

4 ounces Monterey cheese, grated, about 1 cup

½ cup mayonnaise

1 (4-ounce) jar pimentos, drained

2 to 3 green onions, thinly sliced, about 2 tablespoons

¼ teaspoon garlic powder

¼ teaspoon paprika

For wraps:

2 tablespoons olive oil

4 (10 or 12-inch) flour tortillas

4 tablespoons prepared thousand island dressing (see tip below for making your own)

Baby lettuce leaves

Sliced tomatoes

Dill pickle rounds

Cut the steak into bite size pieces, about 1-inch cubes. Place them into a resealable plastic bag. Add the Worcestershire sauce, paprika, onion and garlic powder. Season with some of the salt and pepper. Seal and massage the meat to coat every bite with the seasonings. Place the bag on your counter to marinate while you move on to pimento cheese.

Place the cream cheese, cheddar cheese, Monterey Jack cheese and mayonnaise into the bowl of a food processor. Pulse until the cheese is a creamy mixture. Add the pimentos, onions, garlic and paprika to the bowl and pulse 1 or 2 more times. Taste and season with salt and pepper.

Heat 2 tablespoons olive oil in a large skillet over medium-high heat. A cast iron skillet is the best tool to use to get that really Southern flavor on the steak. Place the steak bites into the skillet and brown on all sides leaving the centers rare. Turn off the heat and start wrapping!

Lay one tortilla onto your work surface. Spread pimento cheese down the center of the tortilla leaving a 2-inch border on the top and bottom. Spoon one-fourth of the steak bites, including the juices in the skillet, down the center (from top to bottom) over the cheese, leaving a 2-inch border on the top and bottom. We're going to fold the tortilla around the filling, so we need to leave some room for the filling to spread out. Now dollop a tablespoon or so of thousand island dressing over the steak bites. Layer lettuce, tomatoes and pickles on top. Fold the sides of the tortilla half way in toward the center. You will still see the filling in the middle. Fold up the bottom third of the tortilla over the filling. Roll up the tortilla tucking in the filling as you go. Press down on the wrap to seal in the filling. At this point, I like to wrap the wrap in parchment paper. Continue with the remaining ingredients. When it's time to dig in, I cut the wrap in half, parchment paper and all, and just peel and bite my way through the sammich.

Cook's Tip

For a really quick thousand island dressing stir together ½ cup mayonnaise, 2 tablespoons chili sauce, 1 tablespoon sweet pickle relish, 1 teaspoon finely diced red onion, ¼ teaspoon garlic powder, ¼ teaspoon kosher salt and ⅛ teaspoon coarse black pepper.

ROASTED PORK TENDERLOIN WITH CILANTRO VINAIGRETTE, SMOTHERED ONIONS AND BOARD SAUCE

serves 6 to 8

45 to 60 minute cuisine

Let's face it, pork can be blah, blah bland. It is incumbent upon us cooks to flavor it up. This dish does just that. The pork is marinated and grilled and then rested on your cutting board in a sauce of melting butter, garlic and herbs. Then we slice the pork, smother it in sautéed onions, and drizzle a bit of citrusy vinaigrette over top. Now there's some flavor! The best thing about the dish is that it is so good, you will want to use the leftovers the next day for extremely yummy panini sandwiches. Simply layer the pork and veggies onto thick slices of artisanal bread. Slather or crumble some cheese in between the bread slices. Brush the outside of the sandwich with melted butter (or olive oil) and smash it down in the hot grill. It's a double dose of yumm.

FOR PORK:

2 (1-pound) pork tenderloins, trimmed

¼ cup Worcestershire sauce

¼ cup soy sauce

1 tablespoon steak seasoning (see Cook's Tip to make your own)

FOR ONIONS:

2 tablespoons olive oil

2 large red onions, peeled, cut in half and thinly sliced, about 2 cups

1 teaspoon Kosher salt

1 teaspoon coarse black pepper

FOR VINAIGRETTE:

Juice of ½ medium lemon, about 2 tablespoons

2 tablespoons white wine vinegar

1 tablespoon finely chopped fresh cilantro

4 large garlic cloves, peeled and minced, about 1 tablespoon

1 teaspoon Dijon-style mustard

¼ cup olive oil

FOR BOARD SAUCE:

2 tablespoons butter, cut into pieces

2 large garlic cloves, minced, about 2 teaspoons

2 tablespoons chopped fresh cilantro

2 tablespoons chopped fresh thyme

2 tablespoons chopped fresh rosemary

Place the tenderloins into a resealable plastic bag. Pour in the Worcestershire sauce, soy sauce and steak seasoning. Seal the bag and marinate for at least 30 minutes or in the fridge overnight.

Heat 2 tablespoons olive oil in a large skillet (I use a cast iron skillet) over medium-high heat. Add sliced onions. Cook until soft, about 5 minutes. Season with some of the salt and pepper. Reduce the heat to medium and cook until the onions are brown and syrupy, about 5 to 10 minutes more.

Whisk together the lemon juice, vinegar, 1 tablespoon cilantro, 1 tablespoon garlic and mustard. Slowly whisk in ¼ cup olive oil. Taste and season with just a bit of salt and pepper.

Place butter and garlic on a cutting board with a well around the edge. Sprinkle the board with cilantro, thyme and rosemary

Heat a grill pan (or outdoor grill) on high heat. Remove the tenderloins from the bag. Grill the tenderloins to an internal temperature of 145°. When you push down on the tenderloin, the flesh should have some resistance and not give in to your touch, about 8 minutes. Transfer the tenderloins to the cutting board and roll them in the "board sauce." Cover with aluminum foil and rest for 5 minutes. This will allow the pork to absorb the herb and garlic flavors.

Cut the pork into ½-inch slices. Pour about half of the vinaigrette over the meat. Top the meat with onions. Drizzle the remaining vinaigrette over the top. Serve the pork right from the cutting board.

Bathing in the Glory

COOK'S TIP

Score another mark on the cook's gold star chart by making your own steak seasoning, using the spices your family enjoys the most. Here's my favorite blend: 3 tablespoons kosher salt, 2 tablespoons paprika, 2 tablespoons coarse black pepper, 1 tablespoon dried minced onion, 1 tablespoon dried minced garlic, ½ tablespoon crushed red pepper flakes, ½ tablespoon dried thyme, ½ tablespoon dried rosemary, and 1 teaspoon ground mustard. Store the seasoning mix in an airtight container in the pantry.

FRIED PORK CHOPS WITH SAUTÉED DANDELION GREENS AND DIJON CREAM GRAVY

serves 4

45 minute cuisine

Nothin' says Southern like pork chops, gravy and dandelion greens. Make sure the pork chops are thin, the gravy is thick, and the greens are soft and syrupy. Dandelion greens, by their nature are slightly bitter, even the young, tender stems. They benefit from some tough love (boiling in salted water). Adding the sweetness of caramelized leeks and a bit of Balsamic vinegar brings them right to where they need to be in order to pair them with the richness of the pork and gravy. With this meal, you have all the fixin's for a back porch, Southern supper.

FOR GREENS:

2 bunches dandelion greens, stems trimmed, leaves chopped, about 6 cups

2 tablespoons olive oil

2 tablespoons butter

1 whole leek, cut in half, thinly sliced, tough dark green leaves discarded, about 1 cup

1 tablespoon balsamic vinegar

1 teaspoon kosher salt

½ teaspoon coarse black pepper

½ to 1 cup homemade chicken stock, or prepared low sodium vegetable broth

FOR PORK CHOPS:

4 (4 to 6-ounce) 1-inch thick, bone-in pork chops, pounded to ½-inch thickness

2 tablespoons Dijon-style mustard

2 cups breadcrumbs from about 6 slices day old bread

1 teaspoon dried oregano

1 teaspoon dried thyme

1 teaspoon garlic powder

1 teaspoon onion powder

¼ cup olive oil

2 tablespoons butter

For gravy:

1 tablespoon flour

¼ cup dry white wine

1 tablespoon Dijon-style mustard

1 ½ cups half-and-half

½ teaspoon ground nutmeg

Cook the dandelion greens in a pot of salted, boiling water for 5 minutes. Transfer to ice water to stop the cooking process. Drain and remove as much excess water as possible. Heat 2 tablespoons olive oil and 2 tablespoons butter in a large skillet over medium-low heat. Add the sliced leek and cook until golden, about 8 to 10 minutes. Add the balsamic vinegar and season with salt and pepper. Cook for 5 minutes more to caramelize the leeks. Add the dandelion greens. Season with some of the salt and pepper. Pour in ½ cup chicken broth. Reduce the heat to low and simmer until the greens are very soft, about 10 to 15 minutes. You can add additional chicken stock until you get the greens as tender as you like.

Brush both sides of the pork chops with mustard and season with salt and pepper. Stir together the breadcrumbs, oregano, thyme, garlic and onion powders in a shallow bowl. Melt ¼ cup olive oil together with 2 tablespoons butter in a large skillet over medium-high heat. Dredge the pork chops in the crumb mixture pressing down to thoroughly coat both sides. Place the chops into the hot oil and fry until golden on one side, about 3 to 5 minutes. Turn and fry on the second side until golden, about 5 minutes more. Transfer the pork chops to a platter, cover with aluminum foil and keep warm. (You can also place the chops into an oven set on low heat.)

Remove all but 2 tablespoons of the fat from the same skillet. Sprinkle the flour into the remaining oil in the skillet and whisk over medium heat until it is golden and bubbling, about 1 minute. Whisk in the white wine and mustard. Pour in half-and-half and stir until the gravy thickens. Stir in nutmeg. Taste and season with salt and pepper.

Puddle the gravy onto a plate. Lay the pork chops over the sauce and dandelion greens on top of the chop.

STUFFED COUSA SQUASH WITH CHORIZO, WHITE BEANS AND CHEDDAR

serves 4

30 minute cuisine

There are so many different types of squash grown by dedicated farmers. Depending on the climate and soil conditions, you'll find all sizes, shapes, and colors. All you have to do is thumb through the pages of this book to look at Sue's many depictions of this most versatile vegetable to get a glimpse of all the delicious variations. Cousa appears in the market in late summer. It is a round squash that is much like zucchini with sweeter, more tender flesh and a very thin skin. Often used in Mediterranean cuisine, it is a great vessel for stuffing with all your favorite things!

4 cousa squash

3 tablespoons olive oil, divided

1 teaspoon kosher salt

½ teaspoon coarse black pepper

½ medium eggplant, peeled and chopped, about 1 cup, (substitute with Japanese, Chinese, Indian or baby eggplants)

1 small white or purple spring onion, green top removed, diced, about 1 cup

1 small poblano pepper, veins and seeds removed, diced, about ½ cup

4 ounces fresh chorizo sausage

½ cup canned white beans, drained and rinsed

2 ounces grated cheddar cheese, about ½ cup

Preheat the oven to 350°. Cut the tops from the squash. Use a spoon to remove the inside flesh. Dice the flesh into small pieces and set aside. Place the squash into a baking dish and drizzle with 1 tablespoon of olive oil. Season with some of the salt and pepper. Bake until the squash is just tender, about 10 minutes.

Pour the remaining 2 tablespoons olive oil in to a skillet over medium-high heat. Add the diced squash, eggplant, onion and pepper to the pan. Season with salt and pepper. Cook until the veggies are tender and begin to turn brown, about 5 to 8 minutes.

Add the chorizo sausage to the veggies. Stir and cook until the chorizo is browned and crumbly, about 3 to 5 minutes. Stir in the beans and cheese.

Spoon the filling into the cousa squash. If you have extra filling, just spoon it around the squash . . . it's all good! Reduce the heat to 300°. Bake until the squash is completely tender, about 10 to 15 minutes.

Autumn's Answer

GRILLED STRIP STEAKS WITH HERBACEOUS CHIMICHURRI BOARD SAUCE

serves 4

45 minute cuisine

If you're like me, your summer garden is teaming with fresh herbs. A board sauce is the perfect way to highlight the freshness of the herbs, while adding to the flavor of grilled beef. You can prepare a puree like the one in this recipe or you can simply dump all your favorite herbs onto your cutting board. Chop, chop, chop your herbs, adding a bit of spice like minced garlic along the way. Douse everything in olive oil. Take your meat straight from the grill and roll it around in the herbs. Tent the meat and let it rest in the board sauce, while it absorbs all of those yummy juices. Yes . . . it's a fab presentation and it tastes really good too!

½ cup red wine vinegar

Zest of 1 medium lemon, about 1 tablespoon

Juice of 1 lemon, about 2 tablespoons

6 garlic cloves, peeled

1 small red chili, seeded, veins removed

½ cup chopped fresh Italian flat leaf parsley

½ cup chopped fresh cilantro

2 tablespoons chopped, fresh oregano

¾ cup olive oil

1 teaspoon salt

½ teaspoon coarse black pepper

4 (6 to 8-ounce) 1 ½-inch thick, sirloin strip steaks

4 tablespoons butter, cut into small pieces

Place the vinegar, lemon zest, and juice, garlic, red chili, parsley, cilantro, and oregano into the bowl of a food processor. Pulse to puree. With the blade running, slowly pour in the olive oil. The sauce will be the consistency of a thick paste like pesto. Season with some of the salt and pepper and pulse one more time.

Preheat a grill pan or outdoor grill to medium-high heat. Season the steaks with salt and pepper. Grill the steaks on one side until browned, about 4 to 5 minutes. Turn and grill on second side until a thermometer inserted in the center reaches 145° for medium rare, about 4 to 5 minutes more.

Spread half of the chimichurri sauce onto your cutting board. Drop small pieces of butter all over the board and sauce. Transfer the steaks from the hot grill to the board. Pour the remaining sauce over the steaks. Turn the steaks over one or two times to coat in the sauce and melt the butter. Tent the board with aluminum foil and let the steaks rest in the sauce for 5 minutes. Slice the steaks across the grain and transfer to a serving platter.

COMPANY'S COMIN' GUMBO

serves 6 to 8

40 minute cuisine

The Holy Trinity veggies found in most Cajun cooking are the combination of diced bell peppers, onions and celery. You can also see these as the Holy Trinity of the farmers market. Fresh peppers and onions are abundant in their varieties. Heads of celery are large, green, crisp and delicious. All three veggies find their way into your basket each week. What better way to start a dark, rich roux for Gumbo, than to dice up the trinity? I call this recipe "Company's Comin" because you can prepare this dish in advance and serve it when you're ready to call your pals to the table, with very little last-minute effort. It's really good!

1 cup unbleached all-purpose flour

1 cup butter, 2 sticks

1 red bell pepper, deveined and diced into ¼-inch pieces, about 1 cup

1 green bell pepper, deveined and diced into ¼-inch pieces, about 1 cup

2 tablespoons olive oil

1 large onion, peeled and diced into ¼-inch pieces, about 1 cup

4 stalks celery, trimmed and thinly sliced, about ½ cup

4 garlic cloves, peeled and minced, about 2 tablespoons

1 tablespoon Cajun seasoning

1 teaspoon kosher salt

½ teaspoon coarse black pepper

1 cup white wine

2 cups homemade chicken broth, or prepared low sodium chicken broth

2 (8-ounce) bottles clam juice

1 (14.5-ounce) can diced tomatoes

1 cup tomato paste

4 to 6 drops hot pepper sauce

14 ounces andouille sausage, sliced into rounds and cut in half

2 pounds uncooked jumbo shrimp (21 to 25 count), peeled, deveined with tails removed

2 to 3 cups cooked white rice

Preheat the oven to 350°. Spread the flour onto a baking sheet. Toast until the flour has a slight golden tinge, about 8 to 10 minutes. This step will help to remove any uncooked, floury taste from the sauce.

Melt the butter in a skillet over medium heat. Whisk in the toasted flour. Stir in the diced peppers. Cook the roux, stirring often, until it turns amber brown, about 10 to 15 minutes.

While you are cooking the roux, heat the olive oil in a soup pot over medium heat. Add the onion, celery and garlic to the pot. Add Cajun seasoning and add some of the salt and pepper. Cook until the veggies are soft, about 5 minutes. Pour in white wine and cook until the liquid mostly disappears. Stir in chicken broth, clam juice, diced tomatoes and tomato paste. Add the roux to the sauce and cook for 5 minutes. Taste the sauce and season with as much hot pepper sauce and additional salt and pepper as you like. Stir in the sausage and shrimp. Simmer until the shrimp is cooked through and the flavors meld, about 10 minutes.

Serve the gumbo by placing a scoop of rice in the middle of a bowl. Surround the rice with gumbo. Serve additional hot pepper sauce on the side!

MEATBALLS 'N PEPPERS OVER CREAMY POLENTA

serves a crowd

45 minute cuisine

A Sicilian picnic table, full of hand-waving, boisterous pals, is a totally communal experience. The food is laid in the center of the table and rather than dishes being passed, food is plucked from platters going directly into hungry mouths. Want to have some fun with a totally communal dish? Try this one. Start by finding a really, really big and very, very shallow bowl. Pour the creamy polenta into the bowl and top with the meatballs and all of that yummy, pepper-filled sauce. Give everyone a large spoon and a tiny dish and dig in. Bite by bite this just screams dinner party FUN!

FOR SAUCE:

¼ cup olive oil

2 large red bell peppers, seeded and cut into thin strips, about 2 cups

1 large green bell pepper, seeded and cut into thin strips, about 1 cup

1 medium red onion, peeled and sliced, about 1 cup

½ cup dry white wine

2 (28-ounce) cans crushed tomatoes

1 teaspoon dried oregano

1 teaspoon kosher salt

½ teaspoon coarse black pepper

FOR MEATBALLS:

4 slices sandwich bread, torn into small pieces

½ cup milk

1 pound ground beef sirloin

½ pound ground veal

½ pound ground pork

1 small yellow onion, peeled and diced, about ½ cup

3 large cloves garlic, peeled and minced

2 eggs, beaten

4 ounces Parmigiano Reggiano cheese, grated, about 1 cup

2 tablespoons chopped fresh flat leaf Italian parsley

FOR POLENTA:

3 cups homemade chicken stock or prepared low sodium chicken broth

1 cup polenta

½ teaspoon ground nutmeg

½ cup mascarpone cheese

Heat ¼ cup olive oil in a large pot over medium heat. Add the peppers and red onion to the pot and cook until soft, about 10 to 15 minutes. Pour in the wine and cook until most of the liquid has disappeared, about 5 minutes more. Pour in the tomatoes. Season with oregano and some of the salt and pepper. Reduce the heat to low and simmer the sauce for at least 20 minutes.

Preheat the oven to 375°. Soak the bread with milk for at least 10 minutes. Place the meats into a large bowl. Add the yellow onion, garlic, eggs, and cheese. Add in the soaked bread with any little bit of milk left in the bowl. Add the parsley. Use your very clean hands to gently combine all the ingredients. Scoop out enough mixture to fit into the palm of your hand. Roll into a ball about 2½ to 3-inches in diameter. Place the meatball onto a parchment-lined, rimmed baking sheet. Repeat with the remaining meat. Bake until the meatballs are just cooked through, about 20. minutes. It's okay if they are a bit rare in the center. Place the meatballs into the simmering sauce.

Heat 3 cups chicken stock in a deep pot over medium-high heat. When the stock begins to boil, stir in the polenta. Continue stirring until the polenta thickens, about 5 minutes. Season with nutmeg, salt and pepper. Remove the polenta from the heat and stir in the mascarpone cheese.

Pour the polenta into a large shallow serving bowl. Top with meatball and pepper sauce. Garnish with additional parsley and cheese.

MOUSSAKA STUFFED EGGPLANT

serves 4

60 minute cuisine

I made my first pan of moussaka as a newlywed. That dinner party was lightyears ago, but I remember explaining the dish to my perplexed guests. Apparently, moussaka, a traditional Greek dish, isn't well known here in the States. My dinner party guests assumed I'd messed with lasagna! Today, my friends know what moussaka is, and ask me to make it for them regularly. I love it because it combines several of my favorite ingredients; delicate lamb, roasted eggplant, and creamy béchamel sauce. In order to feature the eggplant in this farmer's market version of the dish, I turned moussaka upside down. Check it out!

2 large eggplants

1 tablespoon olive oil, plus 2 more for sautéing

1 teaspoon kosher salt

½ teaspoon coarse black pepper

1 pound ground lamb

½ teaspoon ground cinnamon

½ teaspoon ground ginger

½ teaspoon allspice

1 medium yellow onion, peeled and diced, about 1 cup

1 large bell pepper, seeded, veins removed, diced, about 1 cup

1 large jalapeno pepper, seeded, veins removed, diced, about 2 tablespoons

6 large garlic cloves, peeled and minced, about 2 tablespoons

1 cup red wine

2 tablespoons tomato paste

1 cup homemade vegetable stock, or prepared low sodium vegetable broth

¼ cup chopped fresh parsley

2 tablespoons chopped fresh oregano

4 tablespoons butter, ½ stick

¼ cup all-purpose flour

2 cups milk, room temperature

Take Your Pick

½ teaspoon ground nutmeg

4 ounces goat cheese, room temperature

3 large egg yolks

Zest of 1 medium lemon, about 2 teaspoons

4 ounces Parmigiano Reggiano cheese, grated, 1 cup

Preheat the oven to 400°. Cut the eggplant in half. Scoop out the center of the eggplant leaving about a ½-inch border all around so that the eggplant looks like a boat. Save the inside of the eggplant to add to the filling. Drizzle the interior of the eggplant boats with 1 tablespoon olive oil and season with some of the salt and pepper. Set the boats into a baking dish on the counter and move onto the sauce.

Chop the scooped centers from the eggplant boats into ¼-inch pieces. Place 1 tablespoon olive oil in a large skillet over medium-high heat. Add the lamb to the skillet and cook, stirring to break up large pieces. Season with cinnamon, ginger, allspice, salt and pepper. When the lamb is browned, scrape into a colander to drain and remove excess liquid. Transfer the lamb to a plate lined with paper towels.

Add 1 more tablespoon olive oil to the skillet. Add the chopped eggplant, onion, peppers and garlic. Cook until the veggies are softened, about 5 minutes. Add the lamb back into the skillet. Pour in the wine. Cook until most of the liquid disappears. Stir in the tomato paste and stock. Add in the parsley and oregano. Cook until the sauce thickens, about 5 minutes more. Taste and season with salt and pepper.

Melt the butter in a saucepan over medium heat. Whisk in the flour to create a paste. Cook for 1 to 2 minutes. Whisk in the milk and stir until the sauce thickens, about 5 minutes. Season with nutmeg, salt, and pepper. Remove the pan from the heat and cool for 5 minutes while you continue with the cheese part of the white sauce.

Whisk together the goat cheese, egg yolks, and lemon zest in a small bowl. Stir this into the white sauce in the pan.

Stuff the eggplant boats with lamb-eggplant filling. Spoon the goat cheese white sauce over the filling in the eggplant boats. Sprinkle the tops with Parmigiano Reggiano cheese. Place the baking pan into the oven and bake until the white sauce begins to brown, the filling is cooked through and the eggplant boats are softened, about 15 to 20 minutes. Garnish the moussaka-filled eggplant boats with additional chopped fresh parsley.

Make Them Pick You

CROQUETAS DE JAMÓN

serves a crowd

45 minute cuisine plus 4 hours chilling

Traveling through Madrid and Seville, we partook of a lot of tapas. Many of the small plates featured Iberian ham, which is the star of the region. In the different (and highly competitive stalls), the hams are displayed on their own cutting apparatus. Butchers compete to see how thinly they can slice their ham. Scuffles have occurred when one claims his ham slice is better than the guy's in the next stall. Of all the uses for Iberian ham that we tasted, croquettes are my favorite bite. There's a crunchy coating that opens to a velvety center dotted with the salty diced ham. If you are looking for a make-ahead appy, that freezes well, you have come to the right place! These creamy croquettes take a little bit of time to create, so make a big batch.

7 ounces dry cured smoked ham, such as jamon Iberico

1 cup unbleached all-purpose flour

1 teaspoon dried parsley

1 teaspoon ground cumin

½ teaspoon ground oregano

½ teaspoon garlic powder

½ teaspoon ground nutmeg

4 tablespoons butter

1 large shallot, peeled and chopped, about   cup

2 cups milk, room temperature

1 tablespoon dry sherry

8 ounces Manchego cheese, grated about 2 cups

2 eggs, beaten

2 to 3 cups breadcrumbs

Vegetable oil for frying

2 tablespoons chopped fresh parsley

Place the ham in the bowl of a food processor. Pulse to finely dice.

Whisk together the flour, parsley, cumin, oregano, garlic powder and nutmeg in a small bowl.

Heat the butter in a deep saucepan over medium-high heat. Add the shallot and cook until soft about 2 minutes. Whisk the seasoned flour into the butter and shallots and cook until the sauce bubbles and begins to pull away from the sides of the pan, about 2 to 3 minutes. Whisk in the milk and sherry. Reduce the heat to medium. Continue to whisk until the sauce thickens, about 5 minutes more. Remove the pan from the heat and whisk in the cheese until thoroughly melted. Stir in the diced ham. Pour this béchamel sauce into a baking dish and chill for at least four hours.

To form the croquettes, us a 1-inch ice cream scoop, to form a ball of béchamel. Form this ball into a small cylinder and place onto a parchment-line baking sheet. Continue until all the béchamel is used. Transfer the cylinders to the refrigerator. Make a dipping station by whisking together two large eggs in a shallow bowl. Pour bread crumbs into a second bowl. Use one hand to dredge one cylinder into the egg wash, tapping off any extra, and placing into the bowl with breadcrumbs. Then use your other hand to roll the cylinder in those breadcrumbs. Keep one had for wet and one hand for dry. It's less messy! Place the breaded croquettes back onto the baking sheet. Chill (or freeze) until you are ready to fry the croquettes.

Heat vegetable oil in a fryer, or a deep pot, to 375°degrees. Make sure that you use only enough oil to come one-third up the side of the pot as the oil will bubble up when you fry the croquettes. Place several croquettes into the hot oil. Use a slotted spoon to gently turn the croquettes in the oil. Cook until golden, about 3 to4 minutes. Transfer the croquettes to a paper towel lined baking dish to drain. Season with salt and place onto a serving platter. Serve with a sprinkle of fresh parsley.

Specialty of the Casa

BUTTERNUT SQUASH CHORIQUESO (SPICY CHEESE DIP)

serves a crowd

45 minute cuisine

Some of the best parts of traveling are the memories. Sue and I enjoy sitting on a back deck and partaking of a travel-inspired nibble. This one is a warm cheese dip, but we're not talking ordinary cheese dip here. This Spanish inspired, warm appy blends creamy, roasted butternut squash with chili-spiced sausage and mild, melting cheese in a dish designed to pair with your coldest margarita.

1 medium butternut squash, halved, seeds removed

1 tablespoon olive oil

1 teaspoon chili powder

1 teaspoon kosher salt

½ teaspoon coarse black pepper

1 tablespoon butter

1 small red onion, peeled and finely diced, about ½ cup

4 ounces fresh chorizo sausage

2 tablespoons unbleached all-purpose flour

1 cup homemade chicken broth, or prepared low sodium chicken broth

1 small chipotle chili in adobo sauce, minced, about 2 teaspoons

4 ounces fresh mozzarella cheese, about 1 cup

4 ounces Monterey Jack cheese, about 1 cup

Pickled jalapeno peppers

cilantro

tortilla chips

Preheat the oven to 375°. Drizzle the cut side of the butternut squash with olive oil and season with chili powder, salt and pepper. Place the squash cut-side-down into a rimmed baking sheet. Roast until the squash is soft, about 20 to 30 minutes. Scoop out the squash from the skin. Place the squash into the bowl of a food processor (or use an immersion blender) to puree.

Heat the butter in a cast iron skillet over medium-high heat. Add the onion and chorizo and cook for 4 to 5 minutes until the sausage is browned. Sprinkle the flour over the sausage and onion. Stir in the chicken broth and cook until the sauce starts to thicken, about 2 to 3 minutes more. Stir in the butternut squash puree and chipotle chili. Reduce the heat to medium and stir in the mozzarella cheese until melted. Stir in the Monterey Jack cheese. Top the choriqueso with slices of pickled jalapeno peppers and fresh cilantro. Serve with tortilla chips to dip.

BAKED BRIE WITH CHERRIES POACHED IN WINE

serves a crowd

30 minute cuisine

There are sweet cherries, and there are tart-sweet cherries. I like mine sweet. I like them so much that when I find them fresh and perfectly ripe, I buy a bunch of them. (I may have a problem.) What to do with all those leftover cherries after you eaten too many crumbles, pies and cakes? Well, let's soak them in some vino and spoon them over melting cheese. Uh-huh! That's good . . . Even better when you serve it with fresh apples and crackers for dipping!

1 (8-ounce) wheel brie cheese

8 ounces fresh sweet cherries, pitted, about 1 cup

½ cup red wine

1 teaspoon granulated sugar

1 teaspoon finely chopped fresh rosemary

¼ teaspoon kosher salt

¼ teaspoon coarse black pepper

Apples slices

Crackers

Preheat the oven to 350°. Place the cheese into a shallow baking dish, that is lined with parchment paper.

Place the cherries, wine, sugar, rosemary, salt and pepper into a saucepan over medium heat. Simmer the cherries until they are soft and beginning to burst, about 5 to 7 minutes. Remove from the heat.

Spoon the cherries and some of the juice over the top of the cheese. Place the baking dish into the oven and cook until the cheese begins to soften, about 5 to 8 minutes.

Serve the warm cheese and cherries with crackers and apple slices for dipping.

FISH AND FOWL

fish1

/fiSH/

noun

1. a limbless cold-blooded vertebrate animal with gills and fins and living wholly in water. "the sea is thick with fish"

/foul/

noun

1. a gallinaceous bird kept chiefly for its eggs and flesh; a domestic cock or hen.
2. any other domesticated bird kept for its eggs or flesh, e.g., the turkey, duck, goose, and guineafowl.
3. the flesh of birds, especially of the domestic cock or hen, as food; poultry.

Marche Couvert Beauvau

In so many of Sue's paintings, she captures the essence of the Paris fresh market. So why, when I look at her painting *Marche Couvert Beauvau,* do I also think about London? Probably, because my recent experience with Paris came by way of London. Our son attended the Chelsea College of Arts, as part of his educational career and we managed to fit in several visits. London is full of fresh markets. Our favorite was Borough's market, which offers all the beautiful produce and fresh meats, seafood and cheese one would expect to find in a major metropolitan city. However, because of its very nature, this market offers international wares from all over the world. It's a heady experience, one far different than the simple open-air markets found in the countryside.

Sampling London food is an event in itself. We tasted several versions of bangers and mash—roasted, grilled, or fried sausages over creamy mashed potatoes. We ate fish and chips, a pub favorite. The fish is light, delicate cod or other white fish, plucked fresh from the chilly ocean waters. It's fried in a vinegar-laced batter and served with crisp potatoes in newspaper cones. We sampled cockles, a close shellfish cousin to our clams, often served over pasta. We partook of afternoon tea, a traditional experience where one samples finger sandwiches alongside scones with thick cream and jam. We managed to share a glorious meal of salmon wellington that same trip. Only the royals dined better than us!

So how did I get to Paris? The bullet train! What a thrill to ride a train that travels so fast under the channel that fields and cities blur as you pass. It's a short couple of hours, and the change from London to Paris is just as swift. Where London is overcoats, leather cases, and newspapers, Paris is colorful scarves, wrapped shawls, and dogs on leashes. The food is as different as the people. London pub food is replaced with Parisian bistro fare. English dishes filled with root veggies contrast with French cuisine's small portions of fish or meat topped with rich, velvety sauces. English pies and puddings are replaced by delicate macarons and over-the-top flambés. Paris is a culture of finery in their dress, in their traditions and in their markets.

Which brings me back to Sue's paintings. In them you'll see tantalizing produce perfectly placed to draw you to it. Her paintings depict the fantasy food trip you take through stalls of ripe fruit vendors and pricey fishmongers. In the Paris market, you'll taste artisanal cheeses and smell freshly ground spices. French chefs stroll the markets alongside housewives and tourists. It's an amazing sight to behold.

Many years before we took that bullet train to from London to Paris, my husband and I visited there. We were young, raising a family on a shoestring. We used airline mileage and a gift certificate bought during a school auction to get ourselves to Europe for four whole days! Our first night, in a busy French bistro, saw us sipping too expensive wine, and ordering from a totally French menu . . . no English translation for us! Having had a year of French in grade school, I had no problems choosing from the menu. Or, so I thought! I ordered what I believed was a seafood appetizer. What we got was a seafood tower, three tiers high. Lobster, prawns, four types of oysters and clams, all served with lemon wedges and a vinegary mignonette sauce. Our next-door tablemates peered over at us in shock. I noted a bit of a sneer on the waiter's mustached smile. We had managed to order enough seafood to serve ten people! What was worse than my accidental over-ordering? It was over-ordering food my husband is allergic to—shellfish. We made the best of it, passing around the seafood to people sitting around us. They were nice enough to share their wine, and hubby made a meal out of the bread basket. It was a Parisienne experience to remember! Ahhhh, c'est la vie!

SEA BASS WITH PICKLED PANTRY SAUCE

serves 4

30 minute cuisine

When I travel from home to home, or Sue and I travel from place to place (a lucky and blessed problem to have), I perform a fridge clean out. You might think this is a dismal chore, but I view it as an opportunity to create a new dish. (I must have watched way too many episodes of Chopped!*) When I open the fridge door, I find jars and jars of half opened goodies. Because we all know that I can't throw anything away, I like to create a dish and use whatever I have on hand. The (jar) sauce in this recipe has just enough tang to brighten the most delicate piece of fish. Feel free to use your half-filled jars of pickled goodies as substitute for the ingredients listed here. Marinated artichoke hearts, pepperoncini peppers, banana peppers and capers are all great additions.*

4 (6-ounce) sea bass fillets, about 1 ½-inch thick

1 teaspoon kosher salt

½ teaspoon coarse black pepper

¼ cup unbleached all-purpose flour

2 tablespoons olive oil

4 tablespoons butter, divided

1 small onion, peeled and diced

6 garlic cloves, peeled and thinly sliced

1 cup julienned sun-dried tomatoes packed in oil

½ cup, pitted, sliced Kalamata olives

½ cup sliced hearts of palm, about half of a 15-ounce can

2 tablespoons pickled jalapeno peppers

½ cup dry white wine

Juice of 1 medium lemon, about 3 tablespoons

1 tablespoon chopped fresh cilantro

Season the sea bass with salt and pepper. Dust both sides with flour. You can do this by sifting the flour over the fish using a small colander, or by placing the flour into a resealable plastic bag, adding the fish and shaking to coat.

Heat olive oil and 2 tablespoons butter in a large skillet over medium-high heat. Place the fillets into the skillet and cook until golden on one side, about 3 to 4 minutes. Flip and cook on the second side for 3 to 4 minutes more. Transfer to a platter and tent with aluminum foil.

Place the onion and garlic into the skillet and cook until soft, about 2 to 3 minutes. Reduce the heat to medium. Add the sun-dried tomatoes (including up to 2 tablespoons of the oil from the jar) to the skillet. Stir in the olives, hearts of palm, and jalapeno peppers. Pour in the wine and cook until most of the liquid disappears. Stir in the lemon juice. Reduce the heat to low. Swirl in the remaining 2 tablespoons butter. Place the fish back into the skillet. Spoon the sauce over the fillets. Sprinkle fresh cilantro over the top.

COOK'S TIP

Cooking fish is really not hard to do once you figure it out. Here's the way I do the math: basically, fish cooks for about 8 minutes per 1-inch of thickness. And, more importantly, the fish will continue cooking after you remove it from the heat. Here's an example: for a 1 ½-inch-thick fish fillet you want to cook it for a total of less than 10 minutes. Even less, if you plan to finish the fish in a sauce. Undercooking is the way to go when you prepare any type of fish, which really makes it the home cook's fast food.

CAJUN-STYLE SHRIMP IN SPAGHETTI SQUASH BOATS

serves 4

30 minutes cuisine

I love the twang of the local cuisine found in Southern cities like Charleston. I love that chefs combine the freshest seafood ingredients with the bounty of the farms and then add Cajun spices to make the meal unique to the area. Charleston is a great walking city. I was pleased to find that shop owners are as welcoming to four-legged creatures as they are to us two-legged patrons. There are water bowls on the sidewalks and oodles of treats behind counters and in pockets. Not only did Sue and I love our visit to Charleston, but Maggie and Brownie were happy to be there, too! For this dish, delicate strands of spaghetti squash soak up spiced, lemony sauce. Scoop the squash strands onto a serving platter and ladle the shrimp and sauce over top . . . or take the squash boats to the table and invite everyone to dig in! Well, maybe not everyone . . . Arf, arf!!

FOR SQUASH:

2 medium spaghetti squash

1 tablespoon olive oil

1 teaspoon kosher salt

1 teaspoon coarse black pepper

FOR SAUCE:

½ cup butter, 4 tablespoons

½ cup olive oil

½ cup chili sauce

½ cup hot pepper sauce (I like Franks Hot Sauce)

Juice of 2 large lemons, about ¼ cup

2 tablespoons Worcestershire sauce

4 garlic cloves, peeled and minced, about 2 tablespoons

1 tablespoon Cajun seasoning

1 tablespoon chopped fresh parsley

½ teaspoon dried oregano

FOR SHRIMP:

1 tablespoon olive oil

1 teaspoon Cajun seasoning

2 pounds jumbo (21 to 25 count) frozen shrimp, peeled and deveined, thawed

Preheat the oven to 375°. Pierce the squashes with the tines of a fork. Microwave the squash on high for 2 to 3 minutes to soften (this will make it easier to cut). Cut the squash in half and remove the seeds and pulp. Place onto a baking sheet, cut-side facing up. Sprinkle the flesh of the squash with olive oil and season with some of the salt and pepper. Flip the squash and bake cut-side down until soft, about 30 to 40 minutes.

Combine the butter, ½ cup olive oil, chili sauce, hot sauce, lemon juice, Worcestershire sauce, garlic, 1 tablespoon Cajun seasoning, parsley and oregano in a pot over medium-low heat. Simmer on low heat for 10 minutes to blend all the flavors. Taste and season with salt and pepper.

Heat 1 tablespoon olive oil and 1 teaspoon Cajun spice in a large skillet over medium-high heat. Add the shrimp and cook, turning once, until the shrimp are pink, about five minutes. Reduce the heat to low. Pour the sauce into the skillet over the shrimp. Keep the warm while you move on to the squash.

Remove the squashes from the oven and flip over, flesh side up. Use a fork to pull spaghetti strands from the squashes. You can place the squash strands into a shallow bowl and ladle shrimp and sauce over top, or you can pour the shrimp and sauce into the squash boats so that each strand gets coated with the buttery, spicy goodness. Garnish with additional fresh parsley.

SHRIMP ÉTOUFFÉE WITH A SCOOPFUL OF CAULIFLOWER RICE

serves 4

40 minute cuisine

A trip to N'orleans is all about the food. Ragin' Cajun everything from cocktails to seafood. Étouffée is one of my favorite dishes. It begins with a slowly cooked roux that deepens the nutty, rich quality of the sauce. A simple spice mix creates the distinct flavor and a trinity of finely chopped onion, celery and pepper is the tradition. I like to chop the shrimp so that each piece swims in the sauce. Instead of a scoop of rice, I use my favorite "cauliflower rice" to further the veggie quotient in the dish. It all comes together in minutes, so it's perfect for a weekday meal. But, when company comes a callin', feel free to double the recipe and let it simmer until you're ready to serve. Just remember to add the shrimp at the last minute.

FOR CAULIFLOWER:

2 tablespoons butter

1 tablespoon olive oil

½ head cauliflower, trimmed and finely chopped into rice-size pieces (you can use a food processor for this)

1 teaspoon kosher salt

1 teaspoon coarse black pepper

1 to 2 cups homemade chicken stock or prepared low sodium broth

FOR ÉTOUFFÉE:

1 teaspoons paprika

1 teaspoons garlic powder

1 teaspoon dried thyme

1 teaspoon dried oregano

4 tablespoons butter

2 tablespoons all-purpose flour

1 medium red onion, finely diced

4 celery ribs, finely diced

½ green bell pepper, finely diced

2 large garlic cloves, peeled and minced

8 ounces diced tomatoes, about 1 cup

2 (8-ounce) bottles clam juice

1 teaspoon kosher salt

Juice of ½ lemon, about 1 tablespoon

4 to 6 drops hot pepper sauce

¾ pounds fresh jumbo (21–25 shrimp per pound) shrimp, previously frozen, thawed, tails removed, chopped into ½-inch pieces, about 1 ½ cups

3 green onions, finely sliced

Heat two tablespoons butter with 1 tablespoon olive oil in a skillet over medium-high heat. Add the cauliflower. Season with some of the salt and pepper. Cook for 2 minutes. Pour in 1 cup of the chicken broth. Reduce the heat to low and simmer the cauliflower until it is tender and most of the liquid has been absorbed, about 10 to 15 minutes. As the liquid disappears add more broth (a little bit at a time) until the cauliflower is as tender as rice.

Stir together the paprika, garlic powder, thyme, oregano, and 1 teaspoon black pepper in a small bowl to create a spice mix.

Heat 4 tablespoons butter in a large skillet over medium heat. Sprinkle the flour over the top and whisk into the butter. Cook until the roux becomes caramel colored, about 5 minutes. Add the onion, celery, bell pepper and garlic. Season with half of the spice mix. Cook until the veggies are soft, about 10 minutes more. Pour in the tomatoes and clam juice. Bring the sauce to a boil. Reduce the heat to low and simmer until the sauce is thick, about 5 to 8 minutes more. Add the lemon juice and as much hot pepper sauce as you like. Taste and season with salt.

Toss the chopped shrimp with the remaining spice mix. Add the shrimp to the sauce. Cook until the shrimp are opaque, about 5 minutes.

Serve shrimp Étouffée in a shallow bowl with a scoop of cauliflower rice in the center and garnish with green onion.

COCONUT CRUSTED TILAPIA WITH GRILLED PINEAPPLE AND BLACK BEAN SALSA

serves 4

30 minute cuisine

There is a very, very old house in Nassau that is home to one of the best restaurants I have ever visited. It's called Graycliff House. The maître d' checks your reservation and then shows you into the living room with other patrons. You are presented with a glass of champagne, while a piano player croons a couple of tunes. Waiters, clad in tuxes, greet each party, and group by group, guests are escorted to their table for the evening. The menu is French-inspired with a definite nod toward Caribbean flavor influences. The entire experience is delicious. You can bring home a taste of the Caribbean with ingredients that are all found in your local fresh market. Crunchy, coconutty crust surrounds flaky fish in this dish. Sweet pineapple takes on the spice of hot peppers in a savory salsa that is the perfect accompaniment. There might not be a piano player in the front room, but you can always ask your "Alexa" for some inspired island dinner music.

FOR SALSA:

½ small, pineapple, peeled, cored and cut into ½-inch thick slices

1 tablespoon olive oil

1 (15.5-ounce) can black beans, rinsed and drained

½ small red onion, peeled and finely diced, about ¼ cup

1 large jalapeno pepper, seeded, veins removed, diced, about 2 tablespoons

Juice of 1 large lime, about 2 tablespoons

1 teaspoon kosher salt

½ teaspoon coarse black pepper

2 tablespoons chopped fresh cilantro

FOR FISH:

4 (4 to 6-ounce) tilapia fillets

1 cup panko breadcrumbs

1 cup unsweetened coconut flakes

¼ cup almond flour

1 teaspoon curry powder

1 teaspoon garlic powder

1 teaspoon onion powder

2 egg whites

2 (or more) tablespoons olive oil

2 tablespoons sliced almonds, toasted

Heat a grill pan (or outdoor grill) to medium high. Brush the pineapple slices with olive oil. Grill the pineapple until just beginning to char, with grill marks showing, about 2 to 3 minutes per side. Remove the pineapple from the grill and cut into ¼-inch cubes. Place the pineapple, black beans, red onion, and jalapeno into a bowl. Squeeze lime juice over the top. Season with some of the salt and pepper and toss in fresh cilantro. Let the salsa sit on the counter for 15 minutes or more to let the flavors blend.

Season the fillets with salt and pepper. Whisk the bread crumbs, coconut and almond flour together in a shallow dish. Stir in the curry powder, garlic and onion powders. Whisk the egg whites with two tablespoons water in a separate shallow dish. Dip one fillet into the egg whites, coating both sides. Dredge the fish in the breadcrumb mixture, pressing down to coat well. Place the breaded fillets onto a parchment lined baking sheet. Continue until all the fish has been breaded.

Heat 2 tablespoons olive oil in a skillet over medium heat. Place the fillets into the pan (do this in batches adding additional oil as needed). Cook until golden on one side, about 2 to 4 minutes. Use a fish spatula to turn the fillets and continue cooking until the second side is golden, about 2 to 4 minutes more. Transfer the fillets to a platter. Garnish with toasted almonds and serve with a spoonful or two of pineapple and black bean salsa alongside.

Portofino Pineapple

FRESH FISH OF THE DAY IN PUTTANESCA SAUCE

serves 4

30 to 45 minute cuisine

Pasta Puttanesca is a traditional dish found on all the trattoria menus in Italy. The pasta dish has a fishy story that goes along with it . . . you can look it up to see what I mean! The sauce basically combines salty anchovies and capers with tomatoes and garlic. This spiced up tomato sauce is the perfect backdrop for flaky, fresh fish. When you scour the fish market, ask for the freshest variety of fish rather than one that has been previously frozen. I love this sauce with cod, but snapper and sea bass are great too! Puttanesca sauce is just the right background for whichever fish you choose.

2 tablespoons olive oil

1 medium red onion, peeled and finely diced (you can use a couple of pulses in the food processor for this step)

2 cloves garlic, peeled and minced

2 tablespoons tomato paste

2 tablespoons red wine

1 (15.5-ounce) can diced tomatoes

4 flat fillets of anchovies, packed in oil, drained

2 tablespoons capers, drained

1/3 cup Kalamata olives, pitted and chopped

1 (6-ounce) jar marinated artichoke hearts, about 4 to 5 medium size, chopped

½ teaspoon dried oregano

½ teaspoon kosher salt

¼ teaspoon crushed red pepper

4 (4 to 6-ounce) cod (or other mild fish) fillets

1 large lemon, cut into wedges

2 tablespoons chopped fresh basil

Heat the olive oil in a skillet (with a lid) over medium-high heat. Cook the onion in the oil until soft, about 4 to 5 minutes. Stir in the garlic, tomato paste and red wine vinegar. Pour in the diced tomatoes. Stir in the anchovies, capers, olives and artichoke hearts. Season with oregano, salt and pepper. Reduce the heat to low and simmer the sauce for 5 minutes.

Place the fish into the sauce. Cover the skillet with the lid and cook until a thermometer inserted into the middle of the fillet reads 145°, about 8 minutes per inch of thickness.

Serve the fish with the sauce, a garnish of lemon wedges and fresh basil.

Support Local Farmers

PAN-SEARED SNAPPER OVER RATATOUILLE WITH LEMON CAPER SAUCE

serves 4

45 minute cuisine

Ratatouille is a French casserole of stewed veggies, with fresh basil and a bit of Parmesan cheese. It stars eggplant, making it a hearty main dish often found on the menus in the most popular bistros. Also found on those menus is fresh fish, prepared meuniere, which is a preparation that uses capers, lemon and butter to make a delicate sauce. Pairing the two dishes allows you to savor the taste of your farmer's market veggies while enjoying fresh fish in a healthful, serve-it-to-company kinda way!

FOR VEGGIES:

2 tablespoons olive oil

1 medium onion, cut into 1-inch pieces, about 2 cups

1 green bell pepper, cut into 1-inch pieces

1 medium zucchini, cut into 1-inch pieces

1 yellow squash, cut into 1-inch pieces

1 small eggplant, peeled and cut into 1-inch pieces

1 teaspoon kosher salt

1 teaspoon coarse black pepper

3 garlic cloves, peeled and minced, about 1 tablespoon

1 (15.5-ounce) can crushed tomatoes

1 small bunch basil leaves, rolled and thinly sliced, about 2 tablespoons

FOR FISH:

2 tablespoons olive oil

2 whole (1 to 1 ½ -pounds) yellowtail snapper, skin and bones removed, 4 fillets

2 tablespoons unbleached all-purpose flour

1 lemon, thinly sliced

Juice of 1 lemon, about 2 tablespoons

¼ cup dry white wine

2 tablespoons capers, drained and rinsed

2 tablespoons butter

Heat 2 tablespoons olive oil in a skillet over medium-high heat. Add the onion, bell pepper, zucchini, yellow squash, and eggplant to the pan. Cook until the veggies are soft, about 8 to 10 minutes. Season with some of the salt and pepper. Stir in the garlic and pour in the tomatoes. Stir in the basil. Reduce the heat to low to keep the ratatouille warm.

Heat 1 tablespoon olive oil in a skillet over medium-high heat. Season the fish fillets with salt and pepper. Dust both sides of the fish with flour. Working two at a time, place the fillets into the pan. Cook until golden on one side, about 2 to 3 minutes. Use a fish spatula to gently turn the fillets and cook on the second side for 2 minutes more. The fish should be under-cooked in the center. Remove the fillets to a platter and cover with aluminum foil. Pour in one more tablespoon olive oil and repeat with the last two fillets. The fish will continue cooking while you prepare the sauce.

Add the lemon slices to the pan. Pour in the lemon juice, wine and capers. Stir, scraping all the brown bits from the bottom of the pan. Reduce the heat to medium-low. Swirl in the butter.

Place a spoonful of ratatouille onto a plate. Lay one fillet over the top of the veggies. Drizzle the sauce over the top of the fish.

COOK'S TIP

Sole is the fish that is most classically prepared with sauce meuniere. The word translates to miller's wife which is notably regarding the dredging of the fish in flour before it's added to the hot oil and butter. Lemon and capers are classic; however, do not let the French dictate your preference. I love to create a similar sauce using the oil from sun-dried tomatoes. I also like to add thin slices of garlic to the sauce. Any way you prepare your sauce, this dish really comes together quickly. In my kitchen, fish is our fast-food meal of choice!

Welcome Home

COD AND CHILI-INFUSED SWEET POTATO IN A COCONUT-LEEK MILK BROTH

serves 4

20 minute cuisine

When we visited Siem Reap in Cambodia, I was enthralled with the fresh seafood in the farmer's market. The fish are literally plucked from the sea and delivered to the fish monger's stall. There is very little (hardly any) refrigeration in the market, so that fish has to sell fast, fast! In the restaurants we visited, the dishes seemed to have a bit of French influence alongside their Asian roots. I remember one meal that featured fish served in a sweet and savory coconut milk broth. I used this inspiration as a twist on my poached fish dish. I bathe delicate cod fillets in a milk broth infused with the flavors of leeks and cilantro. The slightly sweet taste of sweet potatoes tossed with chili powder brings everything together in a bowl full of fun!

1 large sweet potato, peeled and cut into 1-inch cubes, about 2 cups

1 teaspoon chili powder

2 cups whole milk

1 cup coconut milk

2 whole leeks, white parts chopped, about 2 cups

2 tablespoons chopped fresh cilantro

4 garlic cloves, peeled and thinly sliced

4 (6-ounce) cod fillets

1 teaspoon kosher salt

½ teaspoon coarse black pepper

Olive oil

Steam, blanch, or boil the sweet potatoes until they are fork-tender. Transfer to a bowl and toss with chili powder.

In a large skillet with deep sides, bring the milk, coconut milk, leeks, cilantro and garlic to a simmer. Cook until the leeks are tender, about 6 to 8 minutes. Slide the cod pieces into the milk broth and simmer for 2 minutes. Add the sweet potato and continue simmering in the broth until the cod is cooked through and the flavors merge together, about 4 to 5 minutes more.

Use a slotted spoon to place the cod and veggies into shallow bowls. Pour a ladle full of the milk broth into the bowl. Drizzle a few drops of olive oil over the top and garnish with additional fresh cilantro.

COOK'S TIP

Here's a little truth about fresh fish. Unless you live near a lake or ocean, most of the fish you get in the market has been frozen. Fishermen keep the fish as cold as possible as soon as they catch it. So, when you see the words, "previously frozen" don't fret! Flash-freezing does not reduce the nutrients or the deliciousness of the fish. You want to choose fish that does have a strong, fishy smell and is moist to the touch. You might be concerned about fish that has been farm-raised. A smaller environment and controlled feed can sometimes reduce the quality of the fish that comes to market. The bottom line is that it pays to become friends with your local fishmonger and bow to his recommendations.

SWORDFISH KABOBS WITH KALE-MINT PESTO

serves 4 as a main or 8 as an appy

30 minute cuisine

You think pesto, and you automatically think Italian cuisine. But with today's blends of flavors and ethnicities, pesto has emerged as a condiment that adds rich, robust flavor to most every dish. I don't see a lot of swordfish on the menu when I travel, but I find it to be a great canvas for all different types of flavors. I also enjoy its meaty texture. This pesto, made mostly of kale leaves, is hearty enough to stand up to the fish.

FOR FISH:

1 ½ pounds swordfish steak, cut into 1-inch cubes

½ cup tomato juice

1 tablespoon Worcestershire sauce

Zest of 2 large limes, about 1 tablespoon

Juice of 2 large limes, about ¼ cup

FOR PESTO:

⅓ cup pine nuts, toasted

3 cups baby kale leaves

½ cup parsley leaves

½ cup mint leaves

4 garlic cloves, peeled

2 ounces Parmesan cheese, grated, about ½ cup

½ cup olive oil

1 teaspoon salt

½ teaspoon coarse black pepper

1 pint baby heirloom tomatoes

Soak 8 (8-inch) wooden skewers in a bowl of cold water for at least 30 minutes. Place the swordfish cubes into another bowl. Marinate in tomato juice, Worcestershire sauce, lime zest and lime juice while you prepare the pesto.

Place the pine nuts, kale, parsley, mint, garlic, and Parmesan into the bowl of a food processor. Pulse to combine. With the machine running, slowly pour the olive oil into the bowl. Season with salt and pepper and pulse again. The pesto should be the consistency of thick paste.

Heat a grill pan over medium-high heat. Season the swordfish with salt and pepper. Thread the fish cubes onto the skewers alternating the pieces with tomatoes. Grill, turning once until the fish is just cooked through, about 3 to 4 minutes total. While the fish is still warm, brush a spoonful or more of pesto sauce on all sides.

CHICKEN MILANESE
WITH ZUCCHINI, ARUGULA
AND FENNEL SALAD

serves 4

45 minute cuisine

Chicken is not as prevalent outside of the States as it is here. We are fortunate to have farmers dedicated to raising chickens. Remember the slogan "A chicken in every pot"? It kinda stuck. For this recipe, I use boneless breasts. The thinner the chicken the crunchier the end result will be. So, I butterfly and then pound on an ordinary chicken breast to form it into a tender, thin cutlet. The resulting portion is large enough to serve two normal people, but only just enough for one growing adolescent teen. So, plan accordingly.

FOR SALAD:

1 small shallot, peeled and diced, about 1 tablespoon

Juice of ½ medium lemon, about 1 tablespoon

1 teaspoon Dijon-style mustard

2 tablespoons olive oil

1 teaspoon kosher salt

½ teaspoon coarse ground pepper

3 cups baby arugula leaves

1 medium zucchini, shaved into long ribbons, about 2 cups

1 fennel bulb, tops trimmed, cored and very thinly sliced (using a mandoline slicer), about 1 cup

FOR CHICKEN:

2 large (6 to 8-ounce) boneless, skinless chicken breast halves

3 large eggs

6 (1-inch thick slices whole grain bread), toasted, crust removed, processed into coarse crumbs, about 3 cups

2 teaspoons dried basil

1 teaspoon dried thyme

1 cup unbleached all-purpose flour

Vegetable oil for frying

2 ounces Parmesan cheese, shaved

Whisk together the shallot, lemon juice, and mustard in a large bowl. Slowly whisk in the olive oil until the vinaigrette is pale and slightly thickened. Season some of the salt and pepper. Toss in the arugula, zucchini ribbons and fennel to just lightly coat the veggies with the vinaigrette. Set the bowl on your counter top while you prepare the chicken.

Place one chicken breast half on your work surface. Butterfly the breast by holding knife parallel to board and cutting through breast along the long side, stopping about ½ inch before you get all the way through. Open the breast up like a book, with the connected side acting as the spine. Place the now butterflied breast between 2 pieces of plastic wrap. Use a meat mallet to pound as thin as possible without tearing, about ¼-inch thick and about 8-inches in diameter. Repeat with remaining chicken breast.

Create a dredging station by first cracking and placing eggs into a shallow bowl (or pie pan) and stirring with a fork. Next place the breadcrumbs in a separate shallow bowl (or pie pan). Stir in the basil and thyme. Finally, place the flour into a third shallow bowl (or pie pan).

Season each chicken breast half with salt and pepper. Working with one at a time, dredge first in flour, shaking off excess. Next dip into the eggs, letting the excess drip back into bowl. Finally coat the chicken in breadcrumbs, pressing to make sure that the crumbs adhere, and the chicken is well coated. Place breaded chicken onto a baking sheet.

Pour vegetable oil one-third up the side of a large skillet over medium-high heat until very hot. The oil will look like it's rippling (about 350°to 400° if you are checking with a candy thermometer). Lower one chicken breast half into the oil. Carefully lift the pan from the flame and shake gently to make sure the chicken does not stick to the bottom. (This is a minimal gesture . . . not a show of strength!) Cook until golden on one side, about 1 to 2 minutes. Use tongs or a large spatula to carefully flip the chicken and cook on the second side, gently shaking the pan again, about 1 to 2 minutes more. Transfer the chicken to a platter. Repeat with the second chicken breast.

Serve the chicken breasts on a large platter. Mound the salad on top and shave parmesan cheese over all.

COOK'S TIP

Paper-thin veggies are perfect in this fresh salad. A mandoline slicer is the perfect tool to use to very thinly slice veggies. You can find a simple hand-held tool or a more intricate machine with various slicing blades. Whichever you use, be careful to use a towel or glove when slicing and leave a section of the veggie unsliced to prevent your fingers from getting too close to the blade.

Listen to the Beet

CHICKEN MARSALA BOWL WITH ORZO, SAUTÉED KALE, CURRIED EGGPLANT AND ROASTED CARROTS

serves 4

30 minute cuisine

Fusion cuisine is a mash-up of different flavors, ethnicities, and textures all crammed into one dish. I find the best way to present all these different tastes is to layer them in a bowl and drizzle with a sauce. This is a great recipe to serve when company comes a callin', and it's a great way to rally the troops to explore tasting veggies in a whole new way. Basically, it a whole lotta flavor poured into one big bowl full of insanity.

FOR CHICKEN:

4 large chicken thighs (or 8 smaller thighs)

1 teaspoon onion powder

1 teaspoon kosher salt

1 teaspoon coarse black pepper

3 tablespoons olive oil

½ large onion, thinly sliced

1 cup Marsala wine

1 cup homemade chicken stock, or prepared low sodium broth

1 tablespoon Dijon-style mustard

FOR VEGGIES:

8 whole carrots

6 tablespoons olive oil, divided

1 pound kale, about 4 cups, sliced

4 small Japanese eggplants, sliced into 1-inch rounds (substitute with 1 small eggplant)

2 tablespoon ground curry powder

2 cups orzo, cooked according to package directions

Season the chicken with onion powder and some of the salt, pepper. Heat 3 tablespoons olive oil in a deep sauté pan with lid, over medium-high heat. Place the chicken into the pan, skin side down. Cook until golden, about 4 to 5 minutes. Turn and cook on the second side until golden, about 5 minutes more. Transfer the chicken to a platter. Add the onion to the pan and cook until soft, about 3 to 5 minutes. Pour in the Marsala wine and simmer until most of the wine disappears. Pour in the chicken stock and stir in the mustard. Place the chicken back into the pan. Reduce the heat to medium, cover the pan and simmer until the chicken is cooked through, about 20 minutes more.

Preheat the oven to 400°. Place the carrots onto a baking sheet. Sprinkle with 1 tablespoon olive oil and season with salt and pepper. Roast the carrots, turning once until they are well browned, about 20 minutes.

Heat 3 tablespoons olive oil in a skillet over medium-high heat. Add the kale (in batches) and cook until wilted. Season with salt and pepper. Remove to a bowl and keep warm.

Heat 2 more tablespoons olive oil in the sauté pan over medium-high heat. Add the eggplant to the pan. Season with salt, pepper and 2 tablespoons curry powder. Cook until the eggplant is soft and golden, about 5 minutes. Keep warm.

To assemble the bowls, place the cooked orzo into the bottom of 4 pasta-size bowls. Top one side of the orzo with kale. Top the other side of the orzo with curried eggplant. Lay two roasted carrots atop the veggies. Place the chicken on top of the carrots and spoon the Marsala sauce over everything. I told you it was insanity.

LEMONY CHICKEN FINGERS WITH A SIDE OF SPAGHETTI SQUASH IN PEANUT SAUCE

serves 6 or more

45 minute cuisine

Lemon chicken is my go-to recipe. I serve it hot from the oven, room temperature on a buffet table, or chilled in lemon chicken salad, making it the perfect dish for entertaining. It's the dish I crave when I come home from traveling. For this fresh market twist, I add a side of delish Asian-inspired spaghetti squash that blends perfectly with the chicken bite for bite.

FOR SPAGHETTI SQUASH:

1 medium spaghetti squash

1 tablespoon olive oil

1 teaspoon kosher salt

1 teaspoon coarse black pepper

2 tablespoons peanut butter

1 tablespoon soy sauce

1 tablespoon rice wine vinegar

Juice of ½ large lime, about 1 tablespoon

1 (½-inch) piece ginger, peeled and grated, about 1 tablespoon

2 cloves garlic, peeled and minced, about 1 tablespoon

¼ teaspoon crushed red pepper

2 tablespoons salted peanuts, chopped

2 tablespoons chopped fresh mint

FOR CHICKEN:

Juice of 3 medium lemons, about ½ cup

3 tablespoons soy sauce

4 cloves garlic, peeled and minced, about 2 tablespoons

1 (1-inch) piece fresh ginger, peeled and minced, about 1 tablespoon

¼ cup olive oil

4 large chicken breast halves, cut into 1-inch wide "fingers"

1 cup unbleached all-purpose flour

1 teaspoon paprika

¼ cup butter, cut into small pieces, ½ stick

Preheat the oven to 375°. Pierce the squash with the tines of a fork. Microwave the squash on high for 2 to 3 minutes to soften (this will make it easier to cut). Cut the squash in half and remove the seeds and pulp. Place onto a baking sheet, cut-side facing up. Sprinkle the flesh of the squash with 1 tablespoon olive oil and season with some of the salt and pepper. Flip the squash and bake cut-side down until soft, about 30 to 40 minutes.

Place the peanut butter, 1 tablespoon soy sauce, rice wine vinegar, lime juice, 1 tablespoon ginger, 1 tablespoon garlic, and crushed red pepper into the bowl of a food processor. Pulse to form a paste. If the paste is too thick you can thin it with a bit of water.

While you are baking the squash, whisk together the lemon juice, 3 tablespoons soy sauce, 2 tablespoons garlic and 1 tablespoon ginger. Slowly whisk in ¼ cup olive oil. Place the chicken fingers into a resealable plastic bag. Add the flour and paprika to the bag. Season with salt and pepper. Seal the bag and shake to coat the chicken. Transfer the chicken fingers to a rimmed baking sheet. Top each with a bit of butter. Place into the oven and cook until the chicken begins to turn golden brown, about 15 minutes. Remove the pan from the oven. Pour the lemon sauce over the chicken fingers and place the baking sheet back into the oven. Continue baking until the chicken is cooked through, about 10 to 15 minutes more.

Use a fork to pull the strands from the squash into a serving bowl. Dollop the peanut paste onto the squash and toss to coat the strands. Garnish with chopped peanuts and mint.

Serve the chicken fingers on a platter with a drizzle of the lemon pan juices over the top. Serve with a mound of peanutty spaghetti squash.

Red, Yellow, Purple

CHICKEN AND MUSHROOM PAPRIKASH

serves 4

30 minute cuisine

Paprikash has its origins in Hungarian cooking where paprika is abundantly used. Sue and I didn't get to Hungary yet, but I see similar influences in Russian peasant food. For this dish, tender chicken simmers in a rich, creamy, tomatoey sauce that is packed with mushrooms. Yes, this could be a company's-comin'-to-dinner meal, but it's easy enough to make for the family on a busy weeknight.

4 large boneless, skinless chicken breasts halves

¼ cup unbleached all-purpose flour

2 tablespoons paprika

1 teaspoon ground red pepper

1 teaspoon kosher salt

2 tablespoons olive oil

2 tablespoons butter

2 pints button mushrooms, sliced

1 teaspoon black pepper

½ cup dry sherry

1 cup homemade chicken stock or prepared low sodium broth

2 tablespoons tomato paste

½ cup sour cream

2 tablespoons chopped fresh parsley

2 green onions, thinly sliced

Place the chicken breasts between two pieces of plastic wrap or waxed paper. Use a meat mallet (or rolling pin) to pound the chicken breasts to about ½-in thickness. Transfer the chicken breasts to a resealable plastic bag. Add in the flour, paprika, ground red pepper and salt. Seal the bag and shake it to coat all the chicken.

Heat olive oil in a large skillet over medium-high heat. Remove the chicken from the bag, shaking off the excess flour, and place into the skillet. Cook on one side until golden brown, about 5 to 6 minutes. Use tongs to flip and cook on the second side until golden, about 5 minutes more. Transfer the chicken to a platter.

Melt the butter in the same skillet. Add the mushrooms and walk away! Let the mushrooms turn a rich, golden color on one side before you flip them to cook the second side, about 5 minutes. Reduce the heat to medium. Season the mushrooms with salt and black pepper. Pour in the sherry and cook until most of the liquid has disappeared, about 3 to 4 minutes. Pour in the chicken broth and stir in the tomato paste. Place the chicken back into the skillet. Simmer the chicken in the sauce until it is cooked through, about 5 to 8 minutes.

Turn off the heat. Stir in the sour cream to create a velvety, rich, gravy-like sauce. Serve the chicken with a ladle full of sauce and garnish with fresh parsley and green onions.

FARMERS MARKET TIP

When you see a basket (or brown bag) full of mushrooms at the market don't hesitate to bring them home. The best way to clean them is with a dry (or slightly damp) paper towel. Gently rub the dirt away.

AFTER MARKET LEFTOVERS

If you have chicken paprikash leftovers, you can create a super panini. Thinly slice the chicken. Mix a tablespoon of creamy sauce with a tablespoon of mayonnaise. Spread the mayo over two pieces of thickly-sliced artisanal bread. Layer one side with chicken slices. Top with your favorite grated cheese (try Gruyere or fontina). Add a layer of arugula leaves and rings of thinly sliced red onion. Place the second piece of bread on top. Brush the outside of the sandwich with olive oil and place into a panini grill. Cook until the bread is golden and crisp, and the cheese is melted, about 4 to 6 minutes.

INDIAN BUTTER CHICKEN WITH GINGER-LEMON RICE

serves 4

45 minute cuisine, plus marinating

There is a small, authentic Indian restaurant on at least one street corner in every major city in the country. The food is spicy, flavorful, and FUN. To get the experience at home, you might have to enlarge your spice drawer, to make way for a few new jars. You'll find yourself coming back to them again and again, because you are expanding your palate. This dish is a riff on the Indian classic Chicken Makham. Marinate the chicken the night before or that morning (before you go to work) to make sure you get the full buttery bite experience.

FOR CHICKEN:

1 cup Greek yogurt

Juice of 1 medium lemon, about 3 tablespoons

2 tablespoons Garam masala (this is that spice I was telling you about)

8 bone-in chicken thighs with skin

½ cup butter, 1 stick

2 large yellow onions, peeled, and diced into ¼-inch pieces, about 2 cups

1 teaspoon kosher salt

1 teaspoon coarse black pepper

1 (15-ounce) can crushed tomatoes

1 cup homemade chicken stock or prepared low sodium broth

1 cup heavy cream

1 tablespoon chopped fresh basil

FOR RICE:

1 tablespoon butter

1 (1-inch) piece fresh ginger, peeled and grated, about 1 tablespoon

2 garlic cloves, peeled and minced, about 1 tablespoon

½ cup basmati rice

1 ½ cups homemade chicken stock or prepared low sodium broth

Zest of 1 medium lemon, about 2 teaspoons

6 ounces fresh spinach, chopped about 1 ½ cups

Juice of ½ medium lemon, about 2 tablespoons

Whisk together the yogurt, 3 tablespoons lemon juice and Garam masala in a large bowl. Trim the chicken thighs to remove any fatty parts or excess skin. Toss the chicken thighs in the yogurt sauce making sure each piece is covered in sauce. Cover the bowl with plastic wrap and refrigerate for at least 4 hours and as much as overnight.

Melt ½ cup butter in a large cast iron skillet (or Dutch oven) over medium heat. Cook the onions in the butter until soft, about 5 minutes. Season with salt and pepper. Add the chicken and yogurt sauce to the skillet. Stir in the tomatoes and 1 cup chicken broth. Bring the sauce to a simmer and cook for 20 minutes. Stir in the cream and cook until the chicken is cooked through, about 10 to 15 minutes more. Sprinkle basil into the sauce. Taste and season with salt and pepper.

Heat 1 tablespoon butter in a deep pot (with lid) over medium heat. Stir in the ginger and garlic and cook until fragrant, about 1 to 2 minutes. Stir in the rice and cook 1 minute more, stirring to prevent the rice from becoming brown. Pour in 1 ½ cups chicken stock and 2 teaspoons lemon zest. Cover the pot with the lid, reduce the heat to low, and simmer until all the liquid is absorbed by the rice, about 15 to 20 minutes. Uncover the rice and fluff with a fork. Stir in the spinach. Remove the pot from the heat and cover until the spinach is wilted, about 5 minutes. Remove the lid. Stir in 2 tablespoons lemon juice. Taste and season with salt and pepper.

Place a scoop of rice into a shallow bowl. Place a piece (or two) of chicken on top and ladle the sauce all around.

COOK'S TIP

Garam masala is a blend of spices that includes cumin, coriander, cardamom, pepper, cinnamon, cloves, and nutmeg. If you can't find the blend in your store, fool around with the listed spices to create your own.

STIR-FRY ORANGE CHICKEN AND CAULIFLOWER

serves 4 to 6

30 minute cuisine

In the market, at certain seasons, you can find cauliflower that comes in different colors. There's white, of course, but you can also find golden, purple, and even a combination of both. Using this fresh, colorful veggie in an Asian-inspired dish is a great way to satisfy that craving for quality Chinese take-out when you really have to have it. That said, learning to prepare take-out dishes at home is a great way to amp up the veggie quotient in the meal. In this dish, I give a nod to the traditional by teaming crisp-tender veggies with juicy, orange-tanged chicken.

6 boneless, skinless chicken thighs, cut into 1-inch pieces

1 teaspoon kosher salt

½ teaspoon coarse black pepper

2 tablespoons cornstarch

1 medium head cauliflower cut into florets, about 3 cups

Juice of 3 large orange, about 1 cup

¼ cup rice wine vinegar

¼ cup honey

¼ cup chili sauce

1 tablespoon sesame seed oil

3 tablespoons vegetable oil, divided

1 large yellow or orange bell pepper, seeded, veins removed, chopped into ½-inch pieces, about 1 cup

1 small red chili, seeded, veins removed, diced, about 1 teaspoon

3 cloves garlic, peeled and minced

1 (1-inch) piece fresh ginger, peeled and minced

3 to 4 green onions, thinly sliced, about 1 cup

1 tablespoon sesame seeds

Place the chicken pieces into a bowl. Season with some of the salt and pepper and toss with cornstarch. Set the bowl on the counter while you move on to the veg.

Blanch (or steam) the cauliflower florets until crisp tender. Cool in an ice water bath to stop the cooking process.

Whisk together the orange juice, rice wine vinegar, honey, chili sauce and sesame oil in a small bowl. Set this bowl next to the one holding the chicken pieces.

Heat 2 tablespoons vegetable oil in a large skillet (or wok) over medium-high heat. Cook the chicken in the oil until golden, about 3 to 5 minutes. Do this in batches depending on the size of your skillet. Do not crowd the pan so that each piece can crisp up in the hot oil. Use a slotted spoon or wire skimmer to transfer the chicken to a platter.

Add the remaining 1 tablespoon oil to the skillet. Reduce the heat to medium and add the peppers, garlic and ginger to the pan. Stir and cook until the veggies are soft, about 3 to 4 minutes. Add the cauliflower and cook for 2 minutes more. Pour in the orange sauce and cook until thickened, about 2 minutes. Stir in the chicken, coating the pieces with the sauce. Sprinkle the dish with green onions and sesame seeds.

COOK'S TIP

Our visit to China proved one thing: there are no Chinese take-out restaurants in China. Seriously, Chinese take-out is a totally American thing. Even the take-out boxes have their origins in Japanese origami. The dishes you enjoy here in the states, like General Tso's Chicken and Chow Mein, were created here. When you visit China, you'll have to look long and hard to get any of these American favorites. This does not mean that we don't love the combination of salt and sweet, soy and orange that you taste in Chinese take-out fare. It's something that you just have to have every once in a while. I like making this food at home, 'cause the leftovers don't come in a box!

Primary Colors

GRILLED LIME-CHILI CHICKEN OVER BLACK BEAN AND TOASTED CORN SALSA

serves 4

30 minute cuisine plus marinating

I've seen Sue pick up a blank canvas, set it on her easel, and begin to ponder. It doesn't take her long before the paint brush starts its bold path across the white space laying vivid colors and textures along the way. Chicken breasts are like an empty canvas. Brush them with the colors and flavors you choose, and they become a dish worth enjoying. This one has a little Tex-Mex inspiration.

FOR CHICKEN:

4 boneless, skinless chicken breast halves

Juice of 2 large limes, about 3 to 4 tablespoons

2 tablespoons chili powder

FOR SALSA:

2 tablespoons olive oil, plus 2 more for chicken

1 medium red onion, peeled and diced, about 1 cup

4 ears fresh corn, about 1 cup kernels

1 large jalapeno pepper, seeded, veins removed, diced, about 2 tablespoons

2 large garlic cloves, peeled and minced, about 1 teaspoon

2 (15.5-ounce) cans black beans, drained and rinsed

1 (14.5-ounce) diced tomatoes, drained

1 teaspoon ground cumin

½ teaspoon ground coriander

1 teaspoon kosher salt

½ teaspoon coarse black pepper

Place the chicken breasts between two pieces of plastic wrap. Use a meat mallet to pound the chicken to an even thickness, about ½-inch. Place the chicken breast into a resealable plastic bag. Squeeze the lime juice over the chicken and season with the chili powder. Seal the bag and massage the breasts to coat in the seasonings. Marinate the chicken in the fridge for at least 30 minutes and as much as overnight.

Heat 2 tablespoons olive oil in a large skillet over medium-high heat. Add the onion and cook until soft, about 3 to 5 minutes. Add the corn and cook until just beginning to brown, about 3 to 5 minutes more. Stir in the jalapeno pepper and garlic. Pour in the black beans and tomatoes. Stir in cumin and coriander. Taste and season with some of the salt and pepper. Reduce the heat to medium low and simmer to allow the flavors to blend, about 5 to 10 minutes.

Heat 2 tablespoons olive oil in a grill pan over medium-high heat. Remove the chicken breasts from the marinade and place onto the grill pan. Cook until the chicken begins to come away from the bottom of the pan, about 5 minutes. Flip the chicken and cook on the second side until cooked through, about 4 to 5 minutes more. Transfer the chicken to your work surface and tent with aluminum foil. Allow the chicken to rest for 5 minutes.
Spoon warm salsa onto the center of a dinner plate. Cut each chicken breast half into thin slices and fan out over the salsa.

FARMERS MARKET TIP

Speaking of blank canvases and bold colors, the coastal towns up and down the Amalfi coast boast not only food markets, but this area has also emerged as major center for ceramic production. Native red clay mixes with limestone for a perfect combination of material for pottery making. The colors are daring and bright and as vibrant as the sun and ocean. Ceramic production is a long tradition, having its roots in the Roman Empire. Today, artists are drawn to the area to learn techniques that have lived on for generations. We managed to come away with lovely items when we visited. I still serve my everyday chicken from the gorgeous bowls we purchased in Positano. It just makes everything taste better!

Lost In Translation

SAUTÉED CHICKEN BREASTS WITH VEGGIE BUTTER SAUCE

serves 4

45 minute cuisine

Sometimes when we go to the market, we overestimate the amount of veggies we can realistically eat in one week. Rather than waste these precious treasures, I like to collect all the strays, and blend them together into one dish. Veggie butter sauce is a perfect example. You can put whatever veggies you have into this sauce. Take this idea a bit further and you can make "pantry butter" sauce with your leftover sun-dried tomatoes, olives, and artichoke hearts. Serve this rich sauce over chicken, fish, or pork tenderloin. Plain old pasta will even benefit from a toss in veggie butter. Even better, this dish comes together in minutes, making it a showstopper and company worthy.

FOR CHICKEN:

2 tablespoons olive oil

4 large chicken breasts, butterflied and pounded to ½-inch thickness

1 teaspoon kosher salt

1 teaspoon coarse black pepper

1 cup breadcrumbs (make your own from toasted bread mixed with a bit of dried spice)

FOR VEGGIE BUTTER SAUCE:

2 tablespoons olive oil

1 medium onion, peeled and diced into ¼-inch pieces, about 1 cup

1 medium zucchini, diced into ¼-inch cubes, about 1 cup

1 red bell pepper, seeded and cut into ¼-inch cubes, about 1 cup

1 pint grape tomatoes, chopped, about 1 cup

2 medium jalapeno peppers, seeded and finely diced, about ½ cup

4 garlic cloves, peeled and diced, about 2 tablespoons

½ cup dry white wine

4 tablespoons butter, cubed, ½ stick

2 tablespoons chopped fresh basil

Heat 2 tablespoons olive oil in a large skillet over medium-high heat. Lay the chicken breasts onto you work surface and season both sides with salt and pepper. Dredge each one in bread crumbs, coating both sides. Sauté the chicken in olive oil until golden on one side, about 3 to 5 minutes. Turn and cook the other side until golden, about 3 minutes more. You can do this in batches depending on the size of your skillet. Transfer the chicken to a platter.

Heat 2 more tablespoons of olive oil in the same skillet. Add the veggies and garlic and cook until soft, about 5 minutes. Season with salt and pepper. When the veggies are soft and just beginning to turn brown, pour in the wine. Add the chicken back to the pan. Continue cooking until all the liquid disappears. Turn off the heat. Add the butter to the skillet and stir until the butter melts. Toss in the basil. Serve the chicken with spoons full of veggie butter sauce over top.

Farmers Market Tip

During the riverboat trip to Burgundy, Sue and I were fortunate to meet a lovely young winemaker, Susie Selby. Her vineyard, Selby Winery, is located in Healdsburg, CA. She spoke so lovingly about wine, and the production of wine, from growing the grape, to un-corking an aged bottle, that we were immediately captivated. Although I use wine in so many recipes, drinking wine with my meal is what I love the best. Susie, had these thoughts about wine and roses:

About Wine and Roses

"Throughout the world, one will frequently see roses planted at the end of each row of vines. This tradition started centuries ago because the roses would show signs of disease before the vines and would thus serve as an indicator of problems for winemakers. Legend also states that during the days of horse-drawn ploughs, the equine would make wide turns at the end of the rows to avoid the thorns, thus reducing the damage to the vines as well as the stakes and wires. Today the roses are a beautiful reminder of the wine industry's most recent history. Perhaps they also represent the vulnerability that the vineyards will always have to Mother Nature."

BREADS, PASTRIES AND SWEETS

/bred/

noun

1. food made of flour, water, and yeast or another leavening agent, mixed together and baked.
   "a loaf of bread"

pas·try

/pāstrē/

noun

1. a dough of flour, shortening, and water, used as a base and covering in baked dishes such as pies.
   synonyms: crust, piecrust, croute
   "two layers of pastry"
2. an item of food consisting of sweet pastry with a cream, jam or fruit filling.

/swēt/

noun

1. BRITISH a small shaped piece of confectionery made with sugar.
   synonyms: desserts, treats, cakes, cookies, pastries
   "a bag of sweets"

Positano Possibilities

Whether we travel to London, Lisbon, Barcelona, Madrid, Hoi An or Beijing, the one thing that Sue and I treasure the most is coming home to our friends and families here in the good ole' US of A. We are fortunate enough to live in two states that are perfect for growing fresh food. In North Carolina the summers yield seasonal produce that begins with spring onions and garlic scapes. Mid-summer brings ripe tomatoes and so many varieties of peppers that you might just have to pick a peck and pickle! Fall harvests produce squash, pumpkin and corn. As you can see in Sue's painting *Positano Possibilities*, every market is enticing to patrons young and old.

Florida produces a vast amount of citrus, with oranges and grapefruits at the top of the list. There's lots of sugarcane, too, as well as meat and milk from the cattle raised in the center of the state.

But, there is more than just the raw ingredients. There's the human factor. In Asheville, North Carolina, there's a mill that grinds artisanal grains from rye to graham, from pastry to bread flours. You can have the flours delivered to your front door; thus, conveniently beginning my love affair with baking.

In Boone, there is a farmer who raises bees in hives and produces honey for your tea as well as scented soaps and lotions for your bath.

Lee, a farmer in Watauga county, grows the gorgeous flowers used in so many of the outdoor weddings held there. She also grows edible flowers to decorate your favorite cakes and pastries.

Miss Joan makes the best sourdough bread you'll ever taste. Her cinnamon loaf is slathered with vanilla glaze. My grandson, Sam, loves it so much that when we visit the market he runs to her stall, to grab her "Sammy Loaf" that he is convinced, she bakes just for him,

A older woman at the Naples, Florida, Sunday market grows fresh turmeric and ginger that she claims has medicinal as well as flavor value. A grating of fresh ginger and turmeric adds just a little bit of uh huh to your favorite ginger cookie.

On Main Street in Blowing Rock, a simple gourmet shop grinds a special blend of their favorite sugar with spices and offers it in small packets, perfect for sprinkling on the simplest sugar cookie.

The point is that all we have to do is look around us to take advantage of the freshest foods that our farmers offer, and then make them our own.

This is what *Canvas and Cuisine* is all about. The foodie consumes, the artist memorializes. Your kitchen is your canvas, the food around you is your palette and the two together are your masterpiece. It's time to dig in and enjoy!

A TALE OF TWO LOAVES

makes 2 yummy loaves
20 minute cuisine plus 2 hours to rise and 30 minutes to bake

Whaaaat? Who wants to bake bread? We've all heard the excuses: It takes too long. I can buy it at the bakery. I'm not Martha Stewart. But . . . what if it's the easiest thing in the world? What if you can make it your own by using artisanal flours and home mixed seasonings? What if there is nothing better than a warm slice of bread, slathered with farm fresh butter? Here's a recipe that is so easy, you'll be embarrassed if you don't try it. Don't forget to check out my artisanal baking tips at the very end.

1 large egg, beaten
2 cups milk, warmed on the stove top
1 tablespoon brown sugar
1 tablespoon natural cane sugar
2 ¼ teaspoons active dry yeast, 1 package
2 tablespoons unsalted butter, melted
2 teaspoons kosher salt
2 ½ cups white or whole-wheat bread flour
2 ½ to 3 cups unbleached all-purpose flour

Stir the beaten egg into the warm milk. Stir in the sugars. Sprinkle the yeast over the top and stir. Let sit for 5 minutes.

Place the melted butter, salt and whole-wheat flour into the bowl of an electric mixer fitted with a dough hook. Pour in the wet ingredients. Stir on low to medium speed, until the flour and milk are combined. Add the all-purpose flour, about ½ cup at a time, gradually increasing the speed of the mixer to form a soft, wet dough. This process will take you about 5 minutes. Once the dough wraps around the hook, continue mixing until you have a smooth, shiny ball of dough wrapped around the dough hook, about another 6 to 8 minutes. Transfer the dough to a large bowl that has been coated with vegetable oil spray. Cover the bowl with plastic wrap and place in a warm place for 1 ½ hours to rise. I use my warming drawer on the proof setting for this.

Coat 2 (8 ½ x 4 ½ x 2 ½-inch) loaf pans with vegetable oil spray. THIS IS IMPORTANT! If the pans are larger than this, your dough may not rise. If your pans are smaller, the dough may not cook properly.

Turn the dough out onto a floured board. Punch the dough down and shape into two round loaves. Place each loaf into a pan. Cover and let rise in a warm place until doubled in volume, about 30 to 45 minutes. If you are adding mix-ins into your loaf, now is the time. Roll out the dough on a lightly floured board. Fold in your favorite items. (Mine is a brushing of melted butter with cinnamon and brown sugar.) Shape the dough into a loaf and continue with the recipe.

Preheat the oven to 375°. Bake the bread until the tops are golden and the bread sounds hollow when you tap it, about 30 to 40 minutes. Remove from the oven and cool on wire racks.

COOK'S TIP

Up your loaf by trying some of these experiments:

Add a tablespoon of your favorite spice mix to the flour like apple pie spice, gingerbread spice, pumpkin pie spice, chili blend, Indian spice blend. Be creative.

Add mix-ins like raisins, nuts, cheese, and olives.

Experiment with artisanal flours like rye, graham, spelt, or brown rice.

Batter your bread and fry it in oil for French Toast.

Accompany your loaf with flavored butters and homemade jams.

Turn your leftover loaf into breadcrumbs.

SEEDED WHOLE GRAIN BREAD

Makes 1 Loaf

30 minutes prep, several hours to rise, 30 minutes to bake

Traveling among different cultures, you see some things that are foreign and some that are incredibly familiar. Bread is one of those things that is common to all cultures. Maybe the breads are more fanciful in Paris, more artisanal in Rome, more dark and dense in Moscow or unleavened in Asia, but bread is bread. It is the staff of life (who said that?). This recipe is for you bread lovers and health nuts. It is a loaf made with whole grains, seeds and nuts; not only delish, but full of good carbs that your body needs to fuel its engine. It has a crispy crust and a moist center. It's perfect for toast in the morning or for your tomato sandwich for lunch!

2 ¼ teaspoons yeast

2 tablespoons sorghum syrup (substitute with maple syrup or honey)

2 teaspoons salt

2 cups whole wheat pastry flour

1 ¾ cups unbleached all-purpose flour

2 tablespoons roasted sunflower seeds

2 tablespoons pepita seeds

2 tablespoons old fashioned rolled oats

1 tablespoon flaxseed

Pour 1 ½ cups warm water into the bowl of an electric mixer. Add the yeast, sorghum and salt. Add both flours. Use a dough hook to mix the ingredients to form a smooth dough that pulls away from the side of the bowl. Start on medium speed and then increase the speed to medium-high as the dough comes together. This should take about 5 to 6 minutes. The dough will be smooth and elastic. Transfer the dough to a bowl that has been lightly coated with vegetable oil spray. Cover with plastic wrap and let rise at room temperature for 2 hours. Transfer the bowl to the refrigerator and let rise for 2 hours or as much as overnight.

Use your fingers to make a hole in the center of the dough. Pour the seeds and oats into the hole. Transfer the dough to a lightly floured board. Knead the seeds into the dough, turning about 2 dozen times. Form the dough into a loaf and place into an 8½ x 4½ x 2¾-inch pan coated with vegetable oil spray. Dust the top of the loaf with flour to keep the dough moist. Cover with plastic wrap and let rise at room temperature for another hour.

Preheat the oven to 425°. Place a baking sheet onto the bottom shelf of the oven. When the oven is ready, and the dough has risen for the last time, cut ½-inch deep slits into the top of the bread. Pour 1 cup hot water into a pitcher. Place the loaf pan into the oven on the center shelf. Carefully pour the hot water into the hot baking sheet. The water will bubble! This will create steam for a crunchy crust. Bake until the top is golden brown, about 30 minutes. When you tap the top of the bread it will sound hollow. Remove the loaf from the pan and transfer to a rack. Cool completely before slicing.

FOCACCIA BREAD

serves 6 to 8

20 minute cuisine, plus a couple of hours for bread to rise

With six kids, Sue had a bunch of hungry mouths to feed. She baked a fresh loaf of bread every day, and by the time the day was gone, so was the bread. There's something to be said for the aroma of baking bread, warming your kitchen on a crisp fall day. When you add local ingredients to the mix, it soothes the soul! I love to source local artisan millers to find exotic bread and pastry flours to experiment with. My favorite is Carolina Ground in Asheville, North Carolina. I used a crema bread flour for this recipe, but it will work just fine with good old unbleached all-purpose flour from the grocery store.

2 ¼ teaspoons active dry yeast

1 tablespoon natural cane sugar

5 cups bread flour (preferably crema bread flour)

1 tablespoon kosher salt

½ cup olive oil, plus ½ cup more for topping

2 tablespoons Parmesan cheese

2 teaspoons sea salt

1 teaspoon dried thyme

1 teaspoon dried rosemary

Place the yeast and sugar into a small bowl. Stir in 1 ¾ cups warm water. Place the bowl in a warm place until the yeast is bubbling and fragrant, about 15 minutes. I use the proof setting on my warming drawer for this.

Use an electric mixer fitted with a dough hook to combine the flour, kosher salt, ½ cup of olive oil and the yeast mixture to form a dough. Once the dough comes together, continue to knead the dough in the machine until smooth. Stop the machine and check the dough every couple of minutes. The dough should be smooth and elastic, hold its shape around the dough hook and spring back when you indent it with your finger. This takes anywhere from 5 to 8 minutes using the mixer. If you are kneading by hand, knead until you can't knead anymore!

Transfer the dough to a lightly floured surface. Knead it by hand for an additional 30 seconds. If the dough is too sticky, you can sprinkle with additional flour. Form the dough into a ball and transfer to a bowl that has been lightly coated with olive oil. Cover and place in a warm place to rise until doubled in size, about 1 hour. I use my warming drawer for this step, too.

Pour the remaining cup of olive oil into the bottom of a 12 ½ x 17 ½ x 1-inch jelly roll pan. Transfer the dough to the pan, stretching it out to the edge. Turn and coat with oil on both sides. Use your finger to poke indentations into the dough. These will be the "nooks and crannies" that will hold the seasonings in the next step. Place the dough in a warm place to rise again, for 1 hour. Yep, the warming drawer is still the best place!

Preheat the oven to 400°. After an hour, transfer the pan from its warm place. Sprinkle with Parmesan cheese, sea salt, thyme and rosemary. Drizzle with a bit more olive oil. Bake until the top of the bread is golden brown, about 15 to 20 minutes. Cool the bread in the pan before cutting into squares.

COOK'S TIP

You can really get creative with your focaccia toppings. In addition to the ones in the recipe try a combination of roasted tomatoes, caramelized onions, pitted olives and roasted garlic. You can also make a sweet/tart version by adding prunes or dates to the mix. It's not a far stretch to turn your focaccia bread into pizza with a topping of pepperoni, red sauce and mozzarella cheese. If there are (and there probably won't be) any leftovers, simply process them into bread crumbs for use in all sorts of recipes.

REALLY CHEESY GARLIC BREAD

serves 10

20 minute cuisine

There's bread and then there's bread. There's the basket of slices that the waiter brings to the table, and then there's that artisanal loaf that arrives with compound butter. There's garlic bread that you purchase from a frozen package and then there is really cheesy garlic bread that you can make at home and you will just devour! Just bite into this cheesy, gooey, garlicky bread and relive a childhood memory or two. It's just that good!

12 ounces cheddar cheese, grated, about 3 cups

4 ounces Monterey Jack cheese, grated, about 1 cup

2 ounces Parmesan Cheese, grated, about 1 cup

½ cup mayonnaise

1 bunch green onions, thinly sliced, about 1 cup

¼ teaspoon kosher salt

1 loaf crusty French bread

½ cup butter, 1 stick

4 cloves garlic, peeled and minced

Preheat the oven to 425°. Stir together the cheeses, mayo, green onions and salt in a bowl.

Cut the loaf of bread in half horizontally, and place onto a baking sheet lined with aluminum foil. Melt the butter in a skillet over medium heat. Add the garlic and cook until soft and fragrant, about 1 to 2 minutes being careful that the garlic does not burn. Brush the garlic butter over the cut side of the bread. Place the bread into the oven and toast until just golden, about 3 to 4 minutes. Remove the bread from the oven.

Spread cheese mixture on warm loaves and place back into the oven until the cheeses melt and begin to bubble, about 8 to 10 minutes. Slice the bread into wedges and serve warm. To prepare garlic bread in advance, simply tent the bread with aluminum foil and keep warm.

Belles Maison de Familles

BREAKFAST FLATBREADS

serves 4

20 minute cuisine

Want to know a secret? The real reason that so many hungry shoppers get out of bed early on Saturday morning to visit their local farmer's market, is not just to get the best parking space, but rather to sample the yummy breakfast they find there. You'll see everything from uber-large frosted muffins, to tub-size cinnamon rolls, to piled high ham and biscuit sammies and then there's the breakfast pizza. Everything breakfast—eggs, bacon, sausage, and then a hint of sweetness with a drizzle of maple syrup. Here's a recipe that will allow you to stay in bed just a bit longer and still get the same great meal. But, do this during the week. You don't want to miss the weekend market!

1 tablespoon olive oil

2 green onions, thinly sliced, about 2 tablespoons

½ red bell pepper, diced, about 2 tablespoons

4 ounces pork sausage

4 slices bacon

4 large eggs

½ teaspoon kosher salt

½ teaspoon coarse black pepper

2 prepared flatbreads

4 ounces shredded Monterey jack cheese, about ½ cup

2 tablespoons pure maple syrup

Preheat the oven to 400°. If you have a pizza stone, you can heat the stone in the oven. Heat the olive oil in a skillet over medium heat. Add the onions, pepper and sausage. Cook until the sausage is browned and crumbled, about 3 to 5 minutes. Remove the sausage to a bowl. When the skillet is cool enough to handle, use paper towels to wipe it out.

Place the bacon in the skillet and cook over medium heat until browned and crisp, about 5 minutes. Remove the bacon to paper toweling to drain. Cool the skillet, pour off the excess fat and use paper towels to wipe out the pan.

Whisk together the eggs in a small bowl. Pour the eggs into the skillet and cook over low heat until the eggs begin to form curds. You want to undercook the eggs rather than firmly scramble them. Season with salt and pepper.

Lay the flatbreads onto a baking sheet layered with parchment paper. If you are using a stone, you can lay the flatbreads onto your pizza peel dusted with flour. Top each flatbread with the cheese. Layer the sausage on top. Spoon the eggs over the sausage and cheese. Crumble the bacon on top of the eggs.

Bake the flatbreads until the eggs cook through and the cheese melts, about 5 to 8 minutes. Remove from the oven and drizzle the top of the flatbreads with maple syrup. Cut each one into four slices and dig in!

FARMERS MARKET TIP

Yes, breakfast pizza is delish. Mallory loves it the most. And Sammy loves the cinnamon rolls and Ben loves the giant muffins. But I love, love, love the breakfast burrito. It's gigantically sinful. Take a large flour tortilla. Layer cheese down the center. Top with hash brown potatoes. Top potatoes with the cooked sausage mixture created above. Top this with eggs, more cheese and a big splash of hot sauce. Wrap it up (if you can) and dig in.

BLUEBERRY-LIME BREAKFAST ROLLS

makes 12 rolls

20 minute prep, plus a couple hours using a bread maker, then another 15 to 20 minutes to bake

Some of the best mornings spent touristing around new cities are the ones when you find yourself in a quaint coffee shop that serves not only your favorite variety of brewed bev, but also serves fresh (not pre-packaged) pastries baked right in the back of the shop. It's a whole different experience biting into fresh-baked pastry. One that you shouldn't need to travel across the pond to find! Sweet and tart (some say just like Sue and I), these sticky spirals are just the perfect treat to start your morning adventures. You can substitute lemons for limes and raspberries for blueberries because it's really all about the pull apart, flaky dough and luscious glaze.

FOR DOUGH:

1 cup whole milk, room temperature

½ cup unsalted butter, room temperature, 1 stick

3 large eggs

½ cup natural cane sugar

3 ½ cups unbleached all-purpose flour

1 cup pastry flour

½ teaspoon kosher salt

2 ½ teaspoons dry active yeast

FOR FILLING:

1 pint fresh blueberries, about 2 cups

½ cup natural cane sugar

3 large limes, zested, about 6 tablespoons

1 tablespoon cornstarch

½ cup unsalted butter, melted, 1 stick

2 tablespoons half-and-half

FOR GLAZE:

1 cup confectioners' sugar

Juice of 1 large lime, about 1 to 2 tablespoons

1 tablespoon heavy cream

Place the milk, butter and eggs into the pan of a bread maker. Add ⅓ cup can sugar, flour and salt. Place the yeast into the yeast compartment (or follow the specific directions for your machine). Start the machine on the dough cycle.

Coat a 13 x 9 x 2-inch baking dish with vegetable oil spray. (You can also choose to place the rolls into two small pans. Bake one and freeze one!) When the dough is ready, turn it out of the pan onto a lightly floured work surface. Use a rolling pin to roll the dough out to a large rectangle, about 12 x 14-inches with the longest end horizontally across your board. Use extra flour so that the dough does not stick to the board or to the rolling pin.

Toss the blueberries with ½ cup cane sugar, lime zest, and cornstarch. Use a brush to spread the melted butter over the dough. Spread the blueberry filling over the dough. From the side nearest you, roll the dough up and over the filling to form a 14-inch log. Cut the log in half, and then in half again. Cut each piece into 3 (about 2-inch) slices. This will give you 12 rolls. Place each roll, cut side down into the baking dish. Cover the rolls with a towel and let them rise until they are puffy, about 2 hours. (Or, you can cover the rolls with plastic wrap and put in the refrigerator overnight.)

Preheat the oven to 375°. Brush the rolls with half-and-half, and place into the oven. Bake until they are golden, about 15 to 20 minutes. Remove the dish from the oven.

Whisk together the confectioners' sugar, lime juice and cream until the glaze is pourable. Drizzle the glaze over the warm rolls.

COOK'S TIP

Of course, you do not need a bread maker to make the dough for this recipe. I just like using all the time-saving appliances I can find! You can do it yourself. Mix the dough together using a dough hook attachment for your electric mixer (I know . . . another appliance . . .) You want to have the dough come together on the hook. After it does come together keep the machine running for about 5 minutes. This gets those glutens working! Place the dough onto your lightly floured surface and knead until you have a smooth ball. Place the dough into a lightly oil bowl and cover with plastic wrap. Let the dough rise in a warm place until doubled in size, about 1 hour. I use the proof setting in my warming drawer for this. Continue with the recipe.

Farm Fresh

ORANGE-POPPY SEED SCONES

makes 8 scones

40 minute cuisine

You can't travel anywhere these days without waking up to a breakfast buffet that includes a wide array of baked goods. So many that it is hard to resist. It's even harder not to gorge! But, one thing we agree on is that traveling is hard work! Well, not really, but you do spend a lot of energy walking the city, taking routes down cobbled paths and for just this reason, you need to keep up your strength with a hearty breakfast. At least that's my excuse!! These citrus-laced bakery gems are inspired by the ones we had on the trip to France and are just light enough that you might even delight in more than one.

FOR SCONES:

1 ¼ cups unbleached all-purpose flour

1 cup pastry flour

¼ cup natural cane sugar

1 tablespoon baking powder

Zest of 1 medium orange, about 2 teaspoons

1 teaspoon kosher salt

2 teaspoons poppy seeds

½ cup unsalted butter, chilled, cut into small pieces, 1 stick

1 cup half-and-half, plus more for the tops

FOR GLAZE:

1 cup confectioners' sugar

Juice of 1 medium orange, about ¼ cup

1 teaspoon poppy seeds

Preheat the oven to 375°. Place the flours into the bowl of a food processor. Add the cane sugar, baking powder, orange zest, salt and 2 teaspoons poppy seeds. Pulse to combine. Add the butter to the bowl and pulse several times to form coarse crumbs. Add the half-and-half and pulse until the dough comes together. Transfer the dough onto a floured board. Knead the dough a couple of times until it just comes together. It will be sticky! Flour a rolling pin and your work surface. Roll the dough into a 9 x 6-inch rectangle. Cut the dough into 8 scones. Use a spatula to transfer the scones to a parchment lined baking sheet. Brush the tops with additional half and half. Bake until the tops are golden, about 20 to 25 minutes. Transfer the scones to a rack to cool.

Whisk together the confectioners' sugar with orange juice. Brush the scones with this glaze. Sprinkle with poppy seeds.

MAPLE FROSTED HAZELNUT SCONES

makes 12 scones

30 minute cuisine

One of the most "bestest" things at the farmers market is the wide assortment of home baked pastries and breads. Stroll through the aisles and see everything from hand-hold-able fried pies (don't judge) to oversized cinnamon rolls that can feed a family of four! I love the 3-inch high biscuits and salty Virginia ham sammies. But my absolute favorites are the scones. Not those dense things you get wrapped in cellophane, but a light-as-air, biscuit-like pastry with a sugary frosting and just a hint of nut. This is my home cook version. It's a hit with my clan. I bet yours will jump on the scone bandwagon too!

FOR SCONES:

½ cup old-fashioned oats

½ cup hazelnuts

2 ¾ cups pastry flour

1/3 cup natural cane sugar

2 tablespoons baking powder

½ teaspoon kosher salt

1 cup unsalted butter, cut into pieces

¾ cups heavy cream

1 large egg

FOR FROSTING:

4 cups confectioners' sugar

¼ cup milk

2 tablespoons butter, melted

2 tablespoons maple extract

1 tablespoon brewed coffee

Preheat the oven to 350°. Place the oats and hazelnuts into the bowl of a food processor. Pulse to finely chop. Add the flour, cane sugar, baking powder and salt into the bowl. Pulse to combine. Add 1 cup butter pieces to the bowl. Pulse to form coarse crumbs. Whisk together the cream and egg. With the machine running, pour the liquid through the feed tube. The dough will come together around the blade.

Transfer the dough onto a floured board. The dough will be sticky and that's okay! You can add a bit more flour to make the dough easier to handle while you use your hands to form it into a rectangle about ¾-inch thick and about 8 x 9 inches. Use a knife to cut the dough into 6 rectangles. Cut each rectangle into 2 triangles. Use a spatula to transfer each triangle onto 1 large or 2 smaller parchment lined baking sheets. Bake until the scones puff up and just begin to turn golden, about 20 to 25 minutes. Cool scones on the baking sheet.

For the frosting, whisk together confectioners' sugar, milk, melted butter, maple extract and brewed coffee. You want the frosting to be thick, but pourable. Drizzle the frosting on the scones. Store scones in an airtight container for up to 4 days.

STRAWBERRY-RICOTTA TOPPED FRENCH TOASTS

serves 4

30 minute cuisine

My first taste of Italy took place on an Air Italia flight over the ocean. One of the many courses of really fun fare we were served, included fresh strawberries dipped in black pepper. It was really, really good. Since then, I dabble with pepper and fruit a lot in my recipes. This one is perfect for a Sunday brunch but comes together quick enough so that you can make it for a dash-and-go weekday breakfast. Give it a try!

FOR TOPPING:

6 ounces fresh strawberries, stems removed, chopped, about 1 cup

1 teaspoon balsamic vinegar

½ teaspoon coarse black pepper

1 cup ricotta cheese

2 tablespoons maple syrup

1 tablespoon chopped fresh mint

FOR TOASTS:

Vegetable oil for frying

2 eggs, beaten

½ cup heavy cream

1 teaspoon ground cinnamon

½ teaspoon ground nutmeg

½ teaspoon ground ginger

1 small (hoagie-size) artisanal whole grain loaf, sliced into 1-inch slices

Toss the strawberries with balsamic vinegar and pepper in a small bowl.

Stir together the ricotta cheese, maple syrup and mint in another small bowl until smooth.

Heat vegetable oil in a large skillet about 1-inch deep, over medium-high heat. Remember the oil will bubble up, so don't over-fill the pan. Whisk together the eggs, cream, cinnamon, nutmeg and ginger in a shallow bowl or pie pan. Submerge a bread slice into the egg until well coated. Shake off any excess. Place the soaked bread into the hot oil. Cook the toast in the oil until golden on one side, about 2 to 3 minutes. Flip and fry until the second side is golden, about 2 to 3 minutes more. Transfer to a paper towel lined baking sheet. Repeat with remaining bread slices, frying just a few at a time.

Top each toast with a slather of ricotta cheese and a dollop of strawberries.

Fruit Fresh

COBBLER BARS WITH JAM FILLING

makes about 2 dozen (2-inch) bars
45 minute cuisine

Sue loves to hike. She's gone on hiking trips on several continents. I love to picnic. You might say these two activities have nothing in common, but I say, "Oh yes they do—the power bar!" Power bars come in all shapes and varieties, but one thing this recipe will teach you is that the best power bars do not come in paper wrappers. For this recipe, I use the taste of warm fruit cobbler, but these bars are screaming for your own special touch! That's quite some power!

1 cup butter, cut into pieces, 2 sticks
2 cups unbleached all-purpose flour
2 cups old-fashioned rolled oats
1 cup brown sugar
1 teaspoon baking powder
½ teaspoon salt
1 ½ cups your favorite jam

Preheat the oven to 350°. Spray a 9 x 13-inch baking pan with vegetable oil spray and line with parchment paper.

Place the butter, flour, oats, sugar, baking powder and salt into the bowl of a food processor. Pulse until coarse crumbs form and the dough begins to clump together, about 3 to 4 minutes of pulsing.

Spread half of the dough into the bottom of the pan pressing down to form a layer. Spread the jam over the top. Sprinkle the rest of the dough onto the top of the jam. Press down lightly.

Bake until the bars are golden brown on the top, about 30 to 40 minutes. Remove from the oven, cool to room temperature and cut into squares.

Pears Palette

CHOCOLATE SWIRL SOUR CREAM BANANA BREAD

serves a crowd

60 minute cuisine

To tell you the truth, I really don't have a handle on "Tea" in London. I'm not sure if it is a meal, or an excuse to wear a hat. In the British novels that I read, tea can be the evening meal. When I go to the fancy hotels, tea is a treat served in the late afternoon where everyone dresses and sips. Either way, I like teatime treats like sweetbreads. This recipe is one of my favorites. A wonderful twirl of chocolate in a moist spiced-banana bread. Perfect with a cup of tea!

1 ½ cup all-purpose flour

1 teaspoon baking soda

½ teaspoon kosher salt

½ teaspoon ground cinnamon

¼ teaspoon ground nutmeg

½ cup butter, room temperature, 1 stick

1 cup natural cane sugar

2 large eggs

½ cup sour cream

1 teaspoon vanilla extract

3 very ripe bananas, mashed

¼ cup cocoa powder

Preheat the oven to 350°. Whisk together the flour, baking soda, salt, cinnamon and nutmeg in a small bowl. In a speerate bowl, combine the butter and sugar. Stir in the eggs. Stir in the sour cream, vanilla, and bananas. Pour the flour on the top. Use a spoon or large whisk to combine all the batter ingredients. Pour half of the batter into a 9 x 9 x 2-inch baking dish that has been coated with vegetable oil spray and dusted with flour. Stir the cocoa powder into the remaining batter. Spoon the chocolate batter on top of the vanilla batter. Use a knife to cut through the batter, swirling the chocolate into the vanilla. Bake until a tester inserted into the bread comes out clean, 35 to 40 minutes. Cool in the pan and cut into wedges.

Susu's Garden

RICOTTA-ALMOND PANCAKES WITH BERRY-MAPLE SYRUP

serves 4

30 minute cuisine

These pancakes are fluffy and springy, thanks to the cheese and whipped egg whites. Then to make things even better, we drown these little sponges in a fruit-infused maple syrup and top them with crunchy nuts; this means you'd better be prepared to make a BIG batch.

FOR SYRUP:

1 pint fresh berries, about 2 cups

Zest of ½ medium lemon, about 1 teaspoon

½ teaspoon ground cinnamon

½ teaspoon ground ginger

1 cup pure maple syrup

FOR PANCAKES:

¾ cup unbleached all-purpose flour

¼ cup almond flour

1 teaspoon baking powder

½ teaspoon kosher salt

1 cup ricotta cheese

½ cup milk

2 tablespoons natural cane sugar

2 tablespoons butter, melted plus more for the griddle

2 eggs, separated into yolks and whites

1 teaspoon vanilla extract

Zest of ½ medium lemon, about 1 teaspoon

1 tablespoon sliced almonds, toasted

Place the berries, lemon zest, cinnamon, ginger and syrup into a small pot over low heat. Simmer the syrup until the berries begin to break down, about 5 to 7 minutes. Watch carefully so that the syrup does not bubble up over the pot. Reduce the heat and keep the syrup warm while you prepare the pancakes.

Whisk together the flours, baking powder and salt in a large bowl. Whisk together ricotta cheese, milk, sugar, melted butter, egg yolks, vanilla, and the remaining lemon zest in a smaller bowl. Stir the wet ingredients into the dry ingredients. Whisk egg whites until foamy in a third bowl. Fold the egg whites into the batter.

Heat a non-stick griddle over medium heat. Coat the griddle with melted butter. Ladle ¼ cup batter onto the griddle. Cook on one side until you see bubbles on the surface of the pancake, about 1 to 2 minutes. The pancakes will brown quickly, so watch carefully. Flip and cook on the second side about 3 to 4 minutes more. The pancakes will have a slightly crunchy surface and a spongy center. Serve with warm syrup and a sprinkling of toasted almonds.

PEANUT BUTTER AND MOCHA CAKE IN MINI-MASON JARS

makes about 12 individual desserts or enough for a crowd

60 to 90 minute cuisine

The fresh marketplace is not all about veggies. Artisanal farmers raise animals that produce rich eggs, milk, and cream that leads to delicious baked goods. Take advantage of these products and incorporate them into your favorite baked goods. I like to make individual desserts when I'm entertaining. Reason number one is that I can make most of the components days in advance and then assemble the desserts before the guests arrive. Secondly, a grouping of various individual desserts makes for a great dessert table. I use small juice glasses and layer the desserts as you would a trifle. Save leftover cake in the freezer for up to several months and simply defrost when you need more desserts.

FOR CAKE:

1 ½ cups unbleached all-purpose flour

½ cup whole wheat flour

⅔ cup unsweetened cocoa powder

1 tablespoon baking soda

1 teaspoon kosher salt

1 cup buttermilk

1 cup brewed coffee, cooled

1 teaspoon pure vanilla extract

1 ½ cups natural cane sugar

¾ cup vegetable oil

1 large egg

FOR CREAM:

2 cups heavy cream

1 ½ cups peanut butter

½ cup confectioners' sugar

½ cup peanuts, chopped

Preheat the oven to 350°. Spray an 11 x 7 x 2-inch baking pan with vegetable oil spray. Line with parchment paper leaving several inches overlapping the top of the pan. Spray the paper with vegetable oil spray. Whisk together the flours, cocoa powder, baking soda and salt in a large bowl. Whisk together the buttermilk, coffee and vanilla in a separate bowl.

Use an electric mixer to combine the cane sugar and vegetable oil until smooth. Mix in the egg. Mix in one third of the dry ingredients followed by one third of the liquid ingredients until smooth. Continue alternating dry with wet until you have a smooth batter. Spread the batter into the baking pan. Lick the beaters . . . just kidding! Bake until a toothpick inserted into the center of the cake comes out clean, about 25 to 30 minutes. Cool the cake in the pan for 5 minutes. Pull up the sides of the parchment paper and remove the cake from the pan. Cool on a rack.

Use an electric mixer to whip together the cream, peanut butter and confectioners' sugar until fluffy.

Assemble the desserts in small 3 to 4-ounce mini-mason jars, shot or juice glasses. Start with a dollop of peanut cream. Drizzle a few chopped peanuts and then crumbled up pieces of cake. Continue layering, finishing with cream and chopped peanuts. You can refrigerate the desserts for up to 24 hours. Bring to room temperature before serving.

Alternatively, you can cut the cake into squares. Top each with a dollop of peanut butter cream and a scattering of chopped peanuts.

After Market Leftovers

You probably will only use half of the cake for 12 individual desserts. But this is great news. You can store the extra cake in an airtight resealable bag and freeze it for up to 1 month. The next time you want to make this or any other individual dessert, your cake is ready to go!

BLUEBERRY CRUMBLE PARFAITS

makes about 12 individual desserts or enough for a crowd
60 minute cuisine

Triple the berries and triple the FUN! Here, I use dried blueberries to make a deliciously fruity, crispy-crumbly, nutty-rich granola. Creamy, blueberry yogurt is all in for blueberry component number two. Berry number three are the sun-kissed sweet berries found in the farmers market—especially in spring. This desert is berry, berry delicious!

FOR BLUEBERRIES:

1 pint fresh blueberries, about 2 cups
Zest of ½ medium lemon, about 1 teaspoon
1 teaspoon natural cane sugar

FOR GRANOLA:

¼ cup brown sugar
½ cup white grape juice
¼ cup maple syrup
1 teaspoon ground cinnamon
½ teaspoon ground nutmeg
2 cups old-fashioned rolled oats
½ cup sliced almonds
¼ cup roasted pumpkin seeds
¼ cup roasted sunflower seeds
¼ teaspoon kosher salt
1 cup dried blueberries

FOR PARFAITS:

1 pint fresh blueberries
2 cups blueberry yogurt
1 teaspoon chopped fresh mint

Place the fresh blueberries into a bowl. Stir in lemon zest and cane sugar. Place the bowl onto the counter to allow the berries to absorb the flavors.

Preheat the oven to 325°. Line a rimmed baking sheet with parchment paper.

Whisk together brown sugar, vegetable oil, maple syrup, cinnamon and nutmeg in a saucepan over medium-low heat. Cook until the sugar is dissolved and syrupy, about 3 to 5 minutes.

Place the oats, almonds, pumpkin seeds, sunflower seeds, and salt into a bowl. Pour the warm syrup over the oats and seeds. Toss and then spread into the baking sheet. Bake for 20 minutes. Remove the baking pan from the oven. Stir in the dried blueberries. Bake until the oats are golden, about 10 to 15 minutes more. Remove the baking sheet from the oven and cool. The granola will crisp up as it cools to room temperature.

Assemble the desserts in small (3 to 4-ounce) mini-mason jars, shot or juice glasses. Start with a layer of granola. Dollop blueberry yogurt over top. Top with the fresh berries. Continue layering, ending with yogurt and fresh berries. Top with a bit of fresh mint. You can refrigerate the desserts for up to 24 hours. Bring to room temperature before serving.

Alternatively, you can layer the dessert in a clear bowl or trifle dish.

COOK'S TIP

You can find seeds and nuts already roasted and salted or you can purchase them raw and toast them yourself. Spread seeds and nuts on a baking sheet. Sprinkle with just a bit of fine salt. Bake at 325°until just beginning to turn golden and smell fragrant, checking every several minutes. Seeds and especially nuts can go from richly golden to desperately dark in just a few moments, so don't Facebook your friends while your toasting your nuts!

We Can't Elope

SOUTHERN-STYLE STRAWBERRY SHORTCAKE

makes about 12 individual desserts or enough for a crowd

60 minute cuisine

I have a favorite springtime ritual . . . picking strawberries from the local strawberry patch with my kiddos. I'm not sure how the farmer makes his profit, because I see countless kids with little faces that are stained rosy red from tasting, before they turn in their baskets to be weighed. What to do with the strawberries that have escaped those little tummies? Why, strawberry shortcake of course. This twist is just the right combination of delish and portion control!

FOR BERRIES:

1 pint strawberries, hulled and chopped, about 2 cups

1 tablespoon balsamic vinegar

Juice of ½-medium lemon, about 1 tablespoon

FOR SHORTCAKES:

¾ cup buttermilk

1 large egg

2 ¼ cups pastry flour, plus more for dusting

2 teaspoons baking powder

¼ teaspoon baking soda

1 teaspoon kosher salt

½ cup natural cane sugar

⅓ cup shortening, chilled

FOR WHIPPED CREAM:

1 cup whipping cream

½ cup confectioners' sugar

2 teaspoons pure vanilla extract

Place one half cup of chopped berries aside on your work surface. You will fold these into the shortcake dough later on.

Combine the remaining chopped berries with balsamic vinegar and lemon juice in a small bowl. Place the bowl onto the countertop to allow the flavors to blend.

Preheat the oven to 400°. Line a baking sheet with parchment paper. Whisk together the buttermilk and egg in a small bowl. Pour the flour, baking powder, baking soda, salt and cane sugar into the bowl of a food processor and pulse to combine. Open the top and pinch off pieces of the shortening over the flour. Pulse until the flour begins to climb up the sides of the bowl, forming coarse crumbs. With the machine running, slowly pour the buttermilk into the flour. The dough will clump together quickly. Stop the machine and dump the wet dough onto a well-floured board.

Sprinkle a little additional flour over the dough. Place the half cup chopped strawberries on top of the dough. Sprinkle the berries with a little more flour. Use your hands to gently fold the berries into the dough trying to evenly distribute them. You can add more flour if the dough is too sticky to work with, but it is meant to be a sticky dough. Pat the dough into a rectangle about 4-inches wide, 8-inches long and about ½-inch thick. Cut the dough into 8 (2-inch) squares. Lift the shortcakes onto the baking sheet and place into the oven. Bake until the tops are golden, about 10 to 12 minutes. Transfer to a rack to cool.

Chill the bowl and whipping attachment of an electric mixer. Pour the whipping cream, confectioners' sugar and vanilla into the bowl. Whip the cream on high speed until stiff peaks form, about 3 to 5 minutes.

Assemble the desserts in small 3 to 4-ounce mini-mason jars, shot or juice glasses. Start with a layer of whipped cream. Top with a layer of crumbled shortcake followed by a spoonful of balsamic-laced berries. Continue layering ending with a dollop of cream topped with a bit of strawberry. You can refrigerate the desserts for up to 24 hours. Bring to room temperature before serving.

Alternatively, you can cut each biscuit in half. Scoop some ice cream onto the bottom layer. Top the ice cream with berries. Place the top half of the biscuit on the berries and spoon whipped cream all over. That's the way we do it in the South!

After Market Leftovers

You will have more shortcake than you need for 12 individual desserts. You can freeze the extras in an airtight container. Or serve them for breakfast in the morning. Preheat the oven to 300°. Brush the tops of the shortcakes with melted butter and sprinkle with sugar. Bake for 5 to 10 minutes. Serve the biscuits right out of the oven with a dollop of butter and a drizzle of honey. Yumm!

LAYERED BANANA SPLIT BROWNIES

makes about 12 individual desserts

60 minute cuisine

I've talked a lot about Sue and I bonding over foie gras and a lot more about our love of fresh veggies and fruit, but I may have left out our other most bonding of all experiences . . . chocolate. I'm not talking about a bite of chocolate cake. I'm talking about that chunk of rich, dark cocoa-laden sweet, eaten late at night (often alone in a closet) kinda chocolate. Let's face it. We may have an issue. This recipe just may fill that craving. These darkly rich, deeply chocolatey brownies are just really good on their own. But why not add bananas, whipped cream, and even a cherry on top to make this dessert a real show stopper! Now this is an All-American dessert!

FOR BROWNIES:

10 tablespoons unsalted butter

6 ounces dark chocolate, about 1 ¼ cups (preferably 70% cacao)

¾ cup natural cane sugar

¾ cup brown sugar

3 large eggs

½ cup unsweetened cocoa powder

1 teaspoon espresso powder

¼ teaspoon kosher salt

½ teaspoon pure vanilla extract

½ cup pastry flour

FOR HOT FUDGE:

1 (14-ounce) can sweetened condensed milk

1 ½ cups semi-sweet chocolate chips

FOR WHIPPED CREAM:

1 cup whipping cream

½ cup confectioners' sugar

Long and Lonely

2 teaspoons pure vanilla extract

4 bananas, diced, about 2 cups

1 pint vanilla ice cream

12 fresh cherries, pitted

Preheat the oven to 325°. Coat an 8 x 8 x 2-inch baking pan with vegetable oil spray. Line with parchment paper leaving several inches overlapping the top of the pan. Coat the paper with vegetable oil spray. Place the butter and dark chocolate into a large, microwave safe bowl. If you have a "melt" setting on your microwave—use it! If not, microwave on medium power for 30 second intervals. Remove the bowl and stir. Repeat this process until the butter and chocolate are melted. Stir until smooth. Stir in cane and brown sugars. Stir in the eggs, one at a time. Use a wooden spoon to vigorously stir the batter for at least one minute. This will give the brownies a shiny, crackling top and help with your daily strength training. Stir in the cocoa powdered, espresso powder, salt and vanilla. Stir in the flour until just combined. Spread the batter into the pan. Bake until the top is glossy and beginning to crack about 30 to 35 minutes. The brownies will be fudgy in the center. Cool the brownies in the pan for 5 minutes and then use the parchment paper to lift the brownies out of the pan. Cool on a rack. These brownies will be sticky and fudge-like. This is what we want!

Place sweetened condensed milk into a microwave safe bowl. Add in the chocolate chips. Place the bowl into the microwave oven and cook on high for 30 seconds. Remove the bowl and stir. Continue this process until the chocolate is melted into a smooth sauce.

Chill the bowl and whipping attachment of an electric mixer. Pour the whipping cream, confectioners' sugar and vanilla into the bowl. Whip the cream on high speed until stiff peaks form, about 3 to 5 minutes.

Assemble the desserts in bowls, 3 to 4-ounce mini-mason jars, shot or juice glasses. Start with a layer of diced bananas. Top with crumbled brownie. Top the brownie with ice cream. Continue layering brownie, banana and ice cream. The final layering ends with brownie, banana, ice cream, fudge sauce, whipped cream, and a cherry on top.

Alternatively, cut the brownie into 16 pieces. Top each piece with a scoop of ice cream, diced bananas, hot fudge sauce, whipped cream and one or two of those cherries!

COOK'S TIP

If you would like to make this dessert in advance, substitute banana pudding for ice cream. It's really, really good.

CARAMEL APPLE CAKE DESSERTS

makes about 12 individual desserts, or enough for a crowd
90 minute cuisine

Early fall is the time when apple pickin' is a common weekend pastime. There are so many varieties to choose from. Gala, Jonagold, Red Delicious, Honey Crisp just to name a few. At my farmer's market in the Carolinas, one farm stand offered over thirty varieties on one Saturday alone. This recipe takes advantage of your apple pickin' efforts. It is a caramel apple in a dessert cup! This sweet treat comes together even faster when you prep in advance. You can bake the cake, days ahead—just try not to eat it first. You can sauté the apples hours before, then simply assemble the desserts and serve to your delighted friends and family! Yumm!!

FOR CAKE:

1 ½ cups pastry flour
1 teaspoon baking powder
¼ teaspoon kosher salt
¼ cup milk
¼ cup buttermilk
1 teaspoon pure vanilla extract
½ cup unsalted butter, room temperature, 1 stick
¼ cup vegetable shortening
1 ½ cups natural cane sugar
3 large eggs
1 cup natural cane sugar

FOR APPLES:

3 tablespoons unsalted butter
3 tablespoons dark brown sugar
½ teaspoon ground cinnamon
2 medium apples, peeled, cored and diced, about 2 cups
Vanilla ice cream
Whipped cream

Preheat the oven to 350°. Coat a 9 x 9 x 2-inch baking pan with vegetable oil spray. Line with parchment paper, leaving several inches overlapping the top of the pan. Coat the paper with vegetable oil spray. Whisk together the flour, baking powder and salt in a bowl. Whisk together the milk, buttermilk and vanilla in a separate bowl. Use an electric mixer to mix together the butter and shortening until smooth and fluffy. Add the sugar, ½ cup at a time. Mix in the eggs. Stir in a third of the flour followed by a third of the liquid ingredients. Continue until all the flour and liquids are mixed in, and the batter is smooth. Pour the batter into the prepared pan. Bake until a tester inserted into the middle of the cake comes out clean, about 30 to 35 minutes. Cool the cake in the pan for 5 minutes. Use the parchment paper to lift the cake out of the pan and onto a rack to cool completely.

Melt 3 tablespoons butter with 3 tablespoons brown sugar in a skillet. Stir in cinnamon. Add the apples and cook until they are softened and sugary. Cool to room temperature.

Assemble the desserts in small 3 to 4-ounce mini-mason jars, shot or juice glasses. Start with chunks of cake. Top with diced apples and a spoonful of vanilla ice cream, ending with whipped cream topped with a few sautéed apples.

Alternatively, you can serve this dish in a large, clear bowl or trifle dish. Pass out the spoons and dig in!

AFTER MARKET LEFTOVERS

If you have cake pieces leftover, do not fear! I like to cut the cake into cubes, toss in melted butter and sugar and bake in a 350°oven until golden. Poof . . . now you have cake croutons to serve with a scoop of your favorite ice cream.

COOK'S TIP

If you want to make this dessert in advance, substitute pudding for the ice cream.

APPLE BUTTER CAKE WITH CREAM CHEESE FROSTING

serves a crowd

60 minute cuisine

In a little town called Valle Crusis, there's a county fair held every October, high up in the mountains of North Carolina. Featured is their home churned apple butter. You MUST arrive early, stand in line, and ask politely if you want more than one jar per customer. It's so good . . . the smell of spiced, simmering apples wafts for counties! I was indeed the early bird this year, and managed to grab an extra jar before the crowds drifted in. This cake is my ode to apple butter. It's really, really good!! If you can't make it to the fair (and it's is worth your effort to get there), you can find apple butter in your local grocery store.

FOR CAKE:

1 ½ cups pastry flour

1 ½ cups unbleached all-purpose flour

2 teaspoon ground cinnamon

1 ½ teaspoon baking soda

¼ teaspoon kosher salt

1 cup unsalted butter, room temperature, 2 sticks

1 cup brown sugar

¾ cup natural cane sugar

3 large eggs

1 ½ cups apple butter

FOR FROSTING:

2 cup confectioners sugar

2 cups cream cheese, room temperature, 2 (8-ounce) packages

½ cup unsalted butter, room temperature, 1 stick

1 teaspoon vanilla extract

1 to 2 tablespoons milk (as needed to thin frosting)

1 cup walnuts, chopped

Preheat the oven to 350°. Coat two 9 x 9-inch (you can certainly change the size of the pan if you choose) cake pans with vegetable oil spray. Place a layer of parchment paper in the bottom of each pan and coat the paper.

Whisk together the flours, cinnamon, baking soda and salt in a small bowl.

Use an electric mixer to combine 1 cup butter with brown and cane sugars until fluffy. Mix in the eggs. Pour in ⅓ of the flour mixture followed by ½ cup of the apple butter. Mix well and continue alternating ingredients until all the flour and apple butter are mixed into the batter. Spread the batter into the two pans. Bake until a tester inserted into the cake comes out clean, about 30 minutes. Cool the cakes in the pan for 10 minutes. Carefully invert the cakes onto a rack. Remove the parchment paper and cool the cakes completely.

Use an electric mixer to combine confectioners' sugar with the cream cheese, ½ cup butter and the vanilla until smooth and creamy. You can mix in a teaspoon or two of milk to get the consistency that you prefer for frosting. Place one cake onto your serving platter. Slather the cake with frosting. Top with the remaining cake. Cover the sides and top of the cake with the remaining frosting. Sprinkle the top of the cake with chopped walnuts.

COOK'S TIP

Making apple butter is not hard (unless you're making enough for the crowds at the fair). You simply cook down the apples and push them through a sieve to create a really smooth puree. Mix in some sugar, spices, and perhaps some lemon zest. Then cook for a couple hours over a low flame, until the sauce is thick and slightly syrupy. If you are making a big batch, you might want to take up canning, in order to store your apple butter for months and months. My Grammy used to call this "puttin' up the apples." But, since making apple butter is just not that difficult, you might find that keeping a jar or two in the fridge will satisfy your craving.

FAVORITE FRUIT CRUMBLE

serves a crowd

60 minute cuisine

I usually make crumbles when I have a bowl of over ripe fruit. You can use absolutely any combination of fruit on hand to enjoy this dish! If you don't have apples, use pears. No peaches, how about plums or apricots? Not feelin' the cherries, no worries as you're sure to have berries, somewhere, that make for a sweet filling.

FOR FILLING:

4 Granny Smith apples, cored and thinly sliced

4 peaches, pitted and thinly sliced

1 pound fresh sweet cherries, pitted, about 2 1/2 cups, pitted and halved

¼ cup natural cane sugar

¼ cup orange juice

1 teaspoon pure vanilla extract

1 teaspoon, finely chopped fresh sage

FOR CRUMBLE:

1 cup old-fashioned rolled oats

¾ cup unbleached all-purpose flour

¼ cup dark brown sugar

1 teaspoon ground cinnamon

½ teaspoon ground nutmeg

¼ teaspoon kosher salt

6 tablespoons unsalted butter, chilled and cut into small pieces

Preheat the oven to 350°. Place the fruit into a shallow baking dish, coated with vegetable oil spray. Add sugar, juice, vanilla, and sage. Toss to combine.

Place the oats, flour, brown sugar, cinnamon, nutmeg and salt into a bowl. Add the butter pieces. Use your hands to smush the butter into the dry ingredients to form the crumble. Crumble the crumble on top of the fruit. Bake until the top is golden, and the fruit juices begin to bubble up, about 40 to 50 minutes.

Serve the warm crumble with a garnish of ice cream or chilled whipped cream.

MEYER LEMON OLIVE OIL CAKE WITH THYME

serves a crowd

60 minute cuisine

I guess when I look back at all the travels we've traveled, my happy place remains that orchard in Sorrento. Sitting with a glass of wine, watching the sun dip in the blue sky, and breathing the air scented with fresh lemons. This is where my mind wanders in my happiest of memories. Meyer lemons are the closest ones I've found to remind me of the rich, fragrant lemons grown there. This cake makes for a simple and perfect dessert, especially when served with fresh sorbet or a robust cuppa first thing in the morning. It's perfect for visiting your happy place.

FOR CAKE:

1 cup all-purpose flour

½ cup pastry flour

1 teaspoon baking powder

½ teaspoon kosher salt

1 cup natural cane sugar

½ cup olive oil

2 large eggs

Juice of 2 Meyer lemons, about ¼ cup

Zest of 2 Meyer lemons, about 1 tablespoon

2 teaspoons chopped, fresh thyme, plus sprigs for garnish

1 teaspoon pure vanilla extract

½ cup whole milk

FOR THE GLAZE:

¾ cup confectioners' sugar

Juice of 1 medium Meyer lemon, about 2 tablespoons

Preheat the oven to 350°. Coat a 9 x 5 x 3-inch loaf pan with vegetable oil spray. Line the pan with parchment paper and spray again. Whisk together the flours, baking powder and salt in a small bowl.

Use an electric mixer to combine the cane sugar, olive oil, eggs, lemon juice, lemon zest, thyme and vanilla until creamy. Mix in ⅓ of the flour, followed by ⅓ of the milk. Continue until all the flour and milk is incorporated into the batter. Pour the batter into the loaf pan. Bake until a tester comes out clean, about 40 to 50 minutes. Remove the cake from the oven and cool completely. Remove the cake from the pan and place onto a serving platter

Place the confectioners' sugar into a small bowl. Whisk in 2 tablespoons lemon juice until smooth. Pour the glaze over the cake. Garnish the platter with fresh lemon slices and thyme sprigs.

Citrus Celebration

ICED THYME-LEMON PECAN SANDIES

makes about 3 dozen cookies

45 minute cuisine

The flavors of the farmers markets found on the Italian coast, like thyme and lemon come together in these tender, crumbly refrigerator cookies. These do perfectly with an afternoon cup of espresso, or as a special after-dinner treat with a chilled glass of limoncello to wash it down.

FOR COOKIES:

1 (2-ounce) package pecan pieces, about 1/3 cup

1 ½ cups all-purpose flour

½ cup almond flour

½ teaspoon kosher salt

½ cup natural cane sugar

2 tablespoons finely chopped fresh thyme

Zest of 1 medium lemon, about 2 teaspoons

¾ cups coconut oil

FOR ICING:

2 ½ cups confectioners' sugar

Zest of 1 medium lemon, about 2 teaspoons

Juice of 1 medium lemon, about 3 tablespoons

1 tablespoon heavy cream

1 teaspoon finely chopped fresh thyme

Place the pecans into the bowl of a food processor. Pulse until finely ground. Add all-purpose flour, almond flour and salt and pulse to combine.

Use your fingers to combine cane sugar, 2 tablespoons thyme and 2 teaspoons lemon zest together in a bowl to form moist clumps. Use an electric mixer to combine the thyme-sugar with the coconut oil until smooth. Add the dry ingredients to the wet ingredients until the dough just comes together. Pour the dough onto a piece of plastic wrap and form into a 12-inch log. Roll the log in the plastic wrap twisting the ends to tighten. Chill in the freezer for at least 4 hours or overnight.

Preheat the oven to 350°. Remove the cookie log from the freezer and take off the plastic wrap. Slice the log into ½-inch rounds placing each one onto a parchment lined baking sheet. Bake until the cookies are just beginning to turn golden, about 10 to 15 minutes. Cool for 5 minutes on the baking sheet and then transfer to wire racks to cool completely.

Whisk confectioners' sugar, 2 teaspoons lemon zest, lemon juice, cream, 1 teaspoon thyme and just a smidge of salt together in a small bowl until smooth. Just a bit of salt will actually highlight the sweetness of the sugar. The frosting should be spreadable and not too runny. If it is too thick add a touch more cream. If it is too thin, add a bit more confectioners' sugar. Spread about 1 tablespoon frosting over each cookie. Let the cookie sit on the rack until the frosting firms up, about 30 minutes. Store the cookies in a single layer in an airtight container. That is if there are any left to store!

COOK'S TIP

It wasn't until I visited Italy that I discovered limoncello. It's a sweet-tart, lemony drink often served after our meal. Certainly, you can buy a bottle at your local liquor store, but it's even more FUN to make your own. First, choose wonderful lemons. I use Meyer lemons for my limoncello. These are the closest I find to the ones grown in the orchards I visited in Positano. Next, choose a vodka; almost anyone will do. Then infuse those lemons into the vodka and put your patience cap on. The longer you infuse the flavors, the better will be your limoncello. After (at least 4 days—and I waited 3 weeks), you add a simple syrup to give the drink it's sweet component. You can bottle it up at this point. Drink limoncello chilled and straight up, on the rocks, or mix into your favorite cocktail. It's delish!

CHOCOLATE CHUNK, CRANBERRY AND PISTACHIO COOKIES

makes about 3 dozen (3-inch) cookies

30 minute cuisine

The all-American favorite dessert? My vote is the chocolate chip cookie. Every home cook bakes a batch at least several times a year. I bake them and add everything I can find in the pantry. This recipe is my favorite twist on the standard chocolate chip cookie. It's a chunky, nutty, fruity, chocolatey version. Use any nut, any chocolate, raisins instead of cranberries, a sprinkle of sea salt or sugar on the top; it's all good.

2 ½ cups all-purpose flour

1 teaspoon baking soda

½ teaspoon kosher salt

¾ cup shortening (don't judge . . . this combination of shortening and butter makes better cookies)

¼ cup unsalted butter, room temperature, ½ stick

¾ cup brown sugar

¾ cup natural cane sugar

2 large eggs

1 teaspoon vanilla extract

1 cup old-fashioned rolled oats

6 ounces dark chocolate, about 1 cup, chopped

1 cup dried cranberries

1 cup shelled pistachio nuts, chopped

Preheat the oven to 375°. Line two baking sheets with parchment paper. Whisk together the flour, baking soda and salt in a bowl.

Use an electric mixer to combine the shortening and butter until fluffy. Mix in sugars until combined. Stir in the eggs and vanilla. Mix in the flour a little at a time. Stir in the oats followed by the chocolate, cranberries and nuts.

Use a medium-size ice cream scoop to drop the batter onto the parchment-lined baking sheets about 3-inches apart. Bake until the cookies are golden and spring back when lightly touched, about 10 to 12 minutes. Cook on the baking sheet for several minutes. Transfer to a rack to cool completely. DO not hesitate to eat these while they are still warm. Melting chocolate cookies are just the best!

COOK'S TIP

There is a science to baking and it involves the chemical reaction of one ingredient with another. In this case, the combination of shortening and butter produces a crisp outside and a chewy, cakey inside which I think is just perfect for a chunky cookie. Of course, you can substitute shortening with butter and that's fine. The results will be flatter, crispier cookies . . . but the melting chocolate will be just the same!

ROASTED PEACH AND CARAMEL ICE CREAM

serves a crowd

30 minute cuisine, plus cooling and chilling

There's just nothing better than a fresh picked peach, one that is ripe and sweet and soft. I can't wait until they come in season. It's not a long one, so we have everything peach for several weeks mid-summer. Roasting fresh-picked peaches intensifies the flavor and gives them a hint of smokiness. Caramelizing the sugar in this recipe intensifies the burnt-tinged sweetness. Seems to me it's a match made in ice cream heaven!

6 to 8 medium peaches, peeled and thinly sliced

3 tablespoons brown sugar

3 cups half-and-half

2 teaspoons pure vanilla extract

1 cup natural cane sugar

6 large egg yolks

Preheat the oven to 425°. Place the slice peaches onto a rimmed baking sheet. Sprinkle the brown sugar over the peaches and gently toss. Roast the peaches until they begin to break down and turn golden, about 10 to 15 minutes. Cool slightly and then transfer the peaches to a blender and puree. You will get about 2 cups of really yummy peach puree.

Heat the half-and-half and vanilla in a saucepan over medium heat until little bubbles begin to form on the sides of the pan, about 5 to 6 minutes. Remove the pan from the heat.

Heat the sugar in a separate saucepan pan with ¼ cup water over medium heat until the sugar dissolves, about 2 minutes. Increase the heat and bring the sugar to a boil. Continue boiling until the sugar begins to turn caramel in color, about 8 minutes. Gently swirl the pan to make sure that the sugar colors evenly. Now, here is the tricky part. SLOWLY pour the warm half-and-half into the caramel. As it first blends, the hot caramel will bubble up and expand up the sides of the pan. Stop pouring until the bubbles settle down and then pour in the rest of the half and half.

Whisk the egg yolks in a small bowl. Carefully pour about ¼ cup of the caramel/half and half into the eggs, whisking constantly. This will temper the egg yolks and help to prevent them from scrambling. Pour the tempered egg yolks into the pan. Reduce the heat to medium and stir until the caramel custard thickens enough to coat the back of a spoon, about 5 minutes. Pour the custard through a fine sieve or colander into a clean bowl. Stir in the peach puree. Place that bowl into a larger bowl filled with ice cubes. Chill the peach custard, stirring occasionally, until it comes to room temperature, about 20 minutes. Cover the custard with plastic wrap and chill in the refrigerator for at least 4 hours. Process according to the directions of your ice cream maker.

Lavender Relaxed

FROZEN STRAWBERRY AND AVOCADO CREAM WITH COCONUT

makes about 2 quarts

45 minute cuisine

I got the idea for this treat from a booth I saw at the local farmer's market. Two young ladies were selling popsicles with flavors like blueberry/lavender, peppered strawberry/basil, and orange/chocolate. The pops were frozen, creamy, and colorful. I knew they were a hit when the queue was not only long but held everyone from toddlers to grey hairs. I got home and looked around. I had one lonely avocado sitting in the bowl and a bag of fresh strawberries from the market. What came next was divine (farmer) intervention. With a few quick churns of the ice cream machine, my solitary avocado was transformed into a luscious bowl of cool creaminess. It's really yummy!

1 (14-ounce) can sweetened condensed milk

1 medium avocado, halved, pitted and peeled, about 1 cup

Juice of 1 medium lemon, about 2 tablespoons

¼ teaspoon kosher salt

2 cups half-and-half

10 medium fresh strawberries, stems removed and mashed, about ½ cup

½ cup shredded sweetened coconut

Pour condensed milk into a bowl. Add the avocado, lemon juice, salt and half-and-half. Use an electric mixer or emulsion blender to puree the ingredients into a thick cream. Pour the cream into the bowl of a chilled ice cream maker. Follow the directions for your machine. Add the strawberries during the last several minutes of churning. Scoop the ice cream into a resealable plastic container. Chill in the freezer for several hours. Scoop the ice cream into bowls. Garnish with shredded coconut.

FARMERS MARKET TIP

Just because the outside of that desolate avocado is shriveled up doesn't mean that the inside isn't bursting with rich, creaminess. You needn't discard the overripe avocado. Its thick peel will maintain the natural velvety texture for many of your favorite recipes.

HANDY FRIED PEACH PIES

serves 8

30 minute cuisine

Fried hand pies are a Southern favorite. You can't go to a fresh market without finding at least one stall that has a table full of white packages, each one holding a palm-size, super flaky pie. You'll see lots of patrons walking around eating from that bag. Don't look too close at those pie-eaters, unless you're looking for me! Using prepared dough helps jump start the process and makes this dish as easy as . . . well, as easy as pie!

5 to 6 ripe, fresh peach, peeled and diced, about 5 cups

⅔ cup natural cane sugar

½ teaspoon ground cinnamon

Juice of ½ small lemon, about 1 tablespoon

⅓ cup unbleached all-purpose flour

2 (13.2 ounce) packages refrigerated puff pastry dough

Vegetable oil for frying

Confectioners' sugar for dusting

Place the diced peaches into a bowl. Add the cane sugar, cinnamon, lemon juice and flour. Stir and let sit while you prepare the dough.

Cut 4-inch rounds from the pastry dough. Cut as many as you can, about 8 per sheet.

Heat vegetable oil to 375°. If you are using a large pot, pour the oil one third up the side of the pot and use a candy thermometer to gauge the temperature. Remember the oil will bubble up the sides of the pot when you add the pies.

Place one round of pastry dough onto your work surface. Use a slotted spoon to place 1 to 2 spoonfuls of peach filling into the center of the dough. Leave a border around the edge. (You want the peaches, not much of the liquid.) Take another round of dough and place it on the top of the filling. Use a fork to crimp the edges together. Repeat with the remaining rounds.

Gently place the pies into the hot oil. Cook until golden on one side. Use a slotted spoon or wire basket to carefully flip the pies to cook until golden on the second side. This whole process will only take a couple of minutes. Transfer the pies to a baking sheet lined with paper towels. Sprinkle with confectioners' sugar and a bit more cinnamon.

CHURROS WITH CINNAMON SUGAR AND CHOCOLATE DIPPING SAUCE

serves a crowd

30 minute cuisine

You cannot eat your way through Spain without finding your way into a Churro shop. I know this to be true. Kinda like the round donuts on the conveyor belt at a Krispy Crème shop, these crinkly, thick strings of donuts are served warm, right out of the fryer. They differ in that instead of a rich sugar bath, these are doused in cinnamon sugar and served with a pot of warm chocolate for dipping. It's pretty darn delicious.

FOR CHURROS:

3 tablespoons unsalted butter

2 tablespoons natural cane sugar

1 teaspoon vanilla extract

½ teaspoon kosher salt

2 cups unbleached all-purpose flour

2 large eggs, beaten

Vegetable oil for frying

FOR COATING:

½ cup natural cane sugar

2 teaspoons ground cinnamon

FOR CHOCOLATE SAUCE:

½ cup heavy cream

12-ounces semi-sweet chocolate chips

Heat 2 cups water, butter, 2 tablespoons sugar, vanilla and salt in a deep sauce pot over medium-high heat until the butter is melted, about 3 to 4 minutes. Remove the pot from the heat and add the flour. Use a wooden spoon to mix the flour into the wet ingredients until it forms a dough ball. You want everything mixed together well. Let the dough cool to room temperature, about 5 to 10 minutes. Use an electric mixer to combine the dough with the eggs. Transfer the dough (in batches) to a pastry bag fitted with a large star tip. Pipe the dough onto parchment lined baking sheets. Chill until you are ready to fry.

Mix together ½ cup sugar with ground cinnamon in a bowl. Transfer this mixture to a sugar shaker. Heat heavy cream with chocolate chips in a bowl in the microwave, cooking 1 minute at a time. Stir in between cooking, until all the chocolate is melted.

Heat the oil in a fryer or deep pot to 375°. Remember to make sure that the oil only comes one third up the side of the pot. The oil will bubble up when you add the churros. Cut the piped dough into 4 to 6-inch long pieces. (Basically, churros can be as long as you like as long as they fit into your fryer). Place the dough into the hot oil. Use a slotted spoon to gently move the churros in the oil. Cook until just golden brown. Transfer the churros to a paper towel lined baking sheet. Generously sprinkle the hot churros with cinnamon sugar. Serve with hot chocolate for dipping.

APPLE CIDER DONUT HOLES WITH CINNAMON SUGAR AND CARAMEL SAUCE

serves a crowd

30 minute cuisine plus chillin' the dough

Remember that apple butter fair I told you about? Well, in addition to apple butter, the church supporters brew their own spiced apple cider. If it's a chilly day in fall, it's served piping hot. If is a sun-kissed Indian summer fall day, you'll have yours over a couple of ice cubes. If you have enough arms to hold your jars of apple butter and a jug of apple cider, you'll arrive home with apple gold! I use that apple cider to create the dough for these donut holes—individual puddles of soft dough are fried to a crispy outside and a pillowy inside. Oh, sure you can have a donut with your coffee in the morning. But, how many donut holes can you eat for dessert? The answer is a whole bunch!

FOR LIQUID INGREDIENTS:

3 cups apple cider

2 tablespoons ground cinnamon

½ cup apple butter

½ cup buttermilk

2 teaspoon vanilla extract

FOR DRY INGREDIENTS:

3 cups unbleached all-purpose flour

2 teaspoons ground cinnamon

½ teaspoon baking soda

½ teaspoon kosher salt

¼ teaspoon ground nutmeg

FOR DOUGH:

6 tablespoons butter, room temperature (¾ stick)

1 cup natural cane sugar

½ cup brown sugar

2 large eggs

Vegetable oil for Frying

FOR CINNAMON SUGAR:

¼ cup natural cane sugar

1 tablespoon ground cinnamon

FOR CARAMEL SAUCE:

1 cup brown sugar

½ cup heavy cream

4 tablespoons butter

1 teaspoon pure vanilla extract

To make the dough, pour the apple cider and 2 tablespoons cinnamon into a deep saucepan, over medium-high heat. Bring to a boil and continue to cook until the liquid reduces to about ½ cup, about 20 minutes. Cool to room temperature and then whisk in the apple butter, buttermilk and vanilla. Whisk together the flour, 2 teaspoons ground cinnamon, baking soda, salt and nutmeg in a bowl. Use an electric mixer to combine 6 tablespoons butter, 1 cup cane sugar and ½ cup brown sugar together until pale in color and fluffy, about 5 minutes. Mix in the eggs, one at a time. Add the dry ingredients in three additions alternating with the wet ingredients. The dough will be sticky!

Spread some flour onto your work surface. Pour out the dough. Use your hands to mix some of the extra flour into the dough until it comes together into a loose ball. Place the dough onto a parchment-lined baking sheet and pat out to about ½-inch thickness. Refrigerate the dough for at least 3 hours. (You can also chill the dough for up to two days.)

Whisk together ¼ cup cane sugar and 1 tablespoon cinnamon in a small bowl to make the cinnamon sugar.

For the caramel sauce, place the brown sugar, cream, and 4 tablespoons butter into a deep pot over medium-low heat. Add a pinch of salt. Whisk and cook until the sauce begins to thicken, about 5 to 7 minutes. Stir in the vanilla and cook another minute or so until the sauce is thick and creamy.

Heat vegetable oil in a large pot or fryer. Remember to add only enough oil to come up one third of the side of your pot as it will bubble up when you add the donut holes. Use a small biscuit cutter (about 2-inches in diameter) to cut holes out of the dough. Fry the holes in batches until golden brown. Transfer the fried holes to a baking sheet lined with paper towels. Immediately sprinkle with cinnamon sugar. Serve with caramel sauce for dunking.

Spice of Life

BAKLAVAH!

makes about 2 dozen (2-inch) pieces
30 minute prep, 40 minute baking, at least 2 hours to cool

It's summer. It's hot. You're sitting on the front porch fanning yourself with an old magazine. The ice melts in your glass as the lemonade quenches your thirst. You reach for that little sumthin' sweet and here it is, a sticky, buttery, rich bite of nuttiness. It may have its origins in the Lebanese kitchen, but this baklava has a lot of Southern soul. I use pecans (the national nut of Southern cooks) in the nut mix and sorghum to create the syrup. This gives this sticky-sweet dessert a bit of a bourbonish hint. It's not authentic . . . but it sure is good.

For baklava:

½ pound frozen phyllo dough, thawed

2 cups walnuts

2 cups pecans

1 teaspoon ground cinnamon

½ teaspoon ground nutmeg

½ to 1 cup butter, 1 to 2 sticks

For syrup:

½ cup butter, 1 stick

2 cups sorghum syrup (substitute with maple syrup)

½ cup natural cane sugar

1 tablespoon pure vanilla extract

Thaw the phyllo dough in the fridge overnight or by leaving the package (rolled up) on the countertop for about 2 hours. Do not unroll it until you are ready to rock and roll!

Place the nuts into the bowl of a food processor. Pulse to form course crumb size pieces. Add the cinnamon and nutmeg and pulse one to two times more.

Preheat the oven to 350°. Melt 1 stick of butter using a saucepan over low heat or a microwave oven. You may need more butter depending on how heavy-handed your butter-brushing is. More is better! Use a pastry brush to butter the bottom and sides of an 11 x 7 x 2-inch baking pan.

Dampen a clean dish towel. Roll out the phyllo dough on your work surface and cover with the damp towel. (Phyllo dough is a bit tricky. If you leave it out, it can dry up and become very difficult to work with. Keeping a damp towel on top of the sheets will prevent this.)

Brush the top sheet of phyllo with butter. Use the sheet below it to help you lift both sheets into the pan, butter side down. Repeat this process so that you have a total of 6 phyllo sheets in the bottom of the pan. Now, cover the remaining phyllo sheets with your damp towel.

Cover the phyllo sheets in the pan with a layer of chopped nuts. Remove the towel from the unused sheets and brush the top sheet of phyllo with butter. Again, use the sheet below it to lift two sheets of phyllo on top of the nuts, butter side down. Do this again, so that you have four sheets of phyllo on top of the nuts. Cover the remaining phyllo dough with your damp towel.

Keep layering buttered phyllo sheets and nuts until all the nuts are gone and you have 4 sheets of phyllo left. Brush the top sheet of phyllo with butter and use the sheet below it to lift the two sheets into the pan, butter side down. Repeat with the final two sheets, but this last time leave the buttered side up.

Use a sharp knife to carefully cut the baklava into pieces. Start in one corner and cut to the opposite corner. Repeat the process to create an "X." Continue to cut diagonally creating 2-inch diamond shape pieces. Bake until the baklava is golden brown, about 35 to 40 minutes.

Make the syrup by placing 1 stick of butter, sorghum syrup, sugar, vanilla and ½ cup water into a saucepan over medium heat. Cook until the butter melts and the sauce begins to boil. Reduce the heat to very low and simmer for 5 minutes. The syrup will turn a caramel color and thicken slightly. Keep the sauce warm until the pastry comes out of the oven.

Remove the baking pan from the oven. Pour half of the syrup over the entire pan of baklava. Wait a minute or two while the pastry sucks up the syrup. Pour the rest of the syrup over the pastry. Let the baklava cool in the pan, uncovered for several hours (at least 2). Slice the pieces again, using the same cuts you made earlier. Carefully remove the pieces to a serving platter. Try not to lick your fingers until after all the slices have been removed!

ACKNOWLEDGEMENTS

Most importantly, Sue and I want to thank Tom Fazio and George Morgan. If it was not for their undying love and devotion to us, who would we be? We love you guys to death!!!

To our kids and grandkids, thank you for giving us the opportunity to be the parents and grandparents that we always dreamed about. We love you all (and I do mean ALL) forever and ever.

To the recipe testers that helped to make Jorj's recipes as cravable as Sue's paintings, thank you for coming along on yet another foodie journey with me. Thank you to Adrienne Lee, Barbara Pagano, Brenda Erp, Chris Petti, Diana Shelton, Donna Fox, Joyce Shields, Kimber Morgan, Lucy Weber, Pam Morgan, P.J. Forbes, and Sharon Murrah. You guys really are the best!

A special shout out to Susie Selby of Selby Winery in Healdsburg, CA. You enticed us with your love of wine and made our trip to Burgundy ever more memorable.

To Jen, my English-major teacher-friend and assistant for the last umpteen years. Thanks for helping the words come outta my mouth and onto the page . . . with some sense. And, to Julia Laroche-Morgan, thanks for making sure that those words are spelled correctly with proper comma placement! A special thank you to Chris Morgan who photographed all of Sue's paintings and provided the artwork for the jacket cover.

To the professional team at Dorrance, we thank you for putting our passions into a beautiful and most delectable book. It's yummy to work with you.

And finally, to you, the readers of this book. Thank you for helping to make a difference in someone's life. After all, isn't that why we all do what we can do?

Thank you,

Jorj and Sue

INDEX OF CANVASES
BY SUSAN FAZIO

INDEX OF RECIPIES

ROOTS AND SEEDS

STEMS AND TUBERS